Praise for *Kubeflow Operations Guide*

"This book is the go-to resource for enterprise deployment of Kubeflow from on-premise to the cloud. It will take you through how to think about Kubeflow on an operational level and then through the ways a team needs to think about integrating with their infrastructure for resources such as GPUs and Identity management."

—*Jeremy Lewi, Cofounder of Kubeflow,*
Principal Software Engineer, Primer

"Patterson, Katzenellenbogen, and Harris have pulled together a terrific book that describes not just the components of setting up a production-ready Kubeflow deployment, but the tactical steps necessary to do so on-premises or on any of the hyperscale clouds. This is an essential book for understanding how to bring Kubeflow from experimentation to enterprise-ready."

—*David Aronchick, Cofounder of Kubeflow*

"A concise guide that covers planning, installing, and managing ML infrastructure across on-premises and cloud. This book provides a sorely needed step-by-step tutorial for using Kubeflow to support notebooks and autoscaled ML pipelines across hybrid cloud setups."

—*Lak Lakshmanan, Director of Analytics*
and AI Solutions, Google Cloud

"Kubeflow Operations is a great resource that dives deep into the operational aspects of running real-world Kubeflow and Kubernetes clusters. This book also includes best practices for managing Kubernetes security, multitenancy, traffic routing, service mesh, GPUs, autoscaling, and capacity planning."

—*Chris Fregly, Developer Advocate, AI and*
Machine Learning at AWS

T0256861

"Kubeflow is a favored development platform to simplify building and deploying AI capabilities into modern applications that utilize Kubernetes to scale and evolve efficiently. The Kubeflow Operations Guide provides valuable insights for planning, implementing, and operating Kubeflow."

—*Zeki Yasar, Principal Solutions Architect,*
ePlus Technology, Inc.

"This book provides an exceptional deep dive into the operation of Kubeflow on-premise or via cloud providers. Kubeflow is a vital project in the machine learning engineering ecosystem and this publication provides a missing puzzle piece in the ecosystem: an excellent guide on how to set up and operate your machine learning engineering stack with Kubeflow or how to deploy machine learning models with KFServing effectively. I see this book as the go-to reference for machine learning or DevOps engineers wanting to understand a production Kubeflow setup. I wish the book would have been around when I set up my first clusters running Kubeflow; it would have saved me hours."

—*Hannes Hapke, Senior Machine Learning Engineer*
at SAP Concur

"This book helped me to fully get my head around all the different parts of the Kubeflow system and understand what role Kubeflow plays in helping build a more reliable and reproducible data science deployment pipeline. From security to Jupyter implementation and on to deployment, this book was the guide that helped me see how the pieces fit together."

—*JD Long, RenaissanceRe*

"This book is a must-read guide for any DevOps team considering standardizing model deployments. Learn from the best and understand how machine learning works."

—*Axel Damian Sirota, Machine Learning Research Engineer*

Kubeflow Operations Guide
Managing Cloud and On-Premise Deployment

Josh Patterson, Michael Katzenellenbogen,
and Austin Harris

Beijing · Boston · Farnham · Sebastopol · Tokyo

Kubeflow Operations Guide

by Josh Patterson, Michael Katzenellenbogen, and Austin Harris

Copyright © 2021 Josh Patterson, Michael Katzenellenbogen, and Austin Harris. All rights reserved.

Published by O'Reilly Media, Inc., 1005 Gravenstein Highway North, Sebastopol, CA 95472.

O'Reilly books may be purchased for educational, business, or sales promotional use. Online editions are also available for most titles (*http://oreilly.com*). For more information, contact our corporate/institutional sales department: 800-998-9938 or *corporate@oreilly.com*.

Acquisitions Editor: Jonathan Hassell
Development Editor: Michele Cronin
Production Editor: Deborah Baker
Copyeditor: Piper Editorial, LLC
Proofreader: Sonia Saruba

Indexer: Potomac Indexing, LLC
Interior Designer: David Futato
Cover Designer: Karen Montgomery
Illustrator: Kate Dullea

December 2020:   First Edition

Revision History for the First Edition
2020-12-04:   First Release

See *http://oreilly.com/catalog/errata.csp?isbn=9781492053279* for release details.

978-1-492-05327-9

[LSI]

For my sons Ethan, Griffin, and Dane: Go forth, be bold, be persistent.

—J. Patterson

Table of Contents

Preface. xv

1. Introduction to Kubeflow. 1
   Machine Learning on Kubernetes   1
      The Evolution of Machine Learning in Enterprise   2
      It's Harder Than Ever to Run Enterprise Infrastructure   4
      Identifying Next-Generation Infrastructure (NGI) Core Principles   6
      Kubernetes for Production Application Deployment   8
      Enter: Kubeflow   12
      What Problems Does Kubeflow Solve?   14
      Origin of Kubeflow   16
      Who Uses Kubeflow?   17
   Common Kubeflow Use Cases   18
      Running Notebooks on GPUs   18
      Shared Multitenant Machine Learning Environment   21
      Building a Transfer Learning Pipeline   21
      Deploying Models to Production for Application Integration   23
   Components of Kubeflow   24
      Machine Learning Tools   26
      Applications and Scaffolding   28
      Machine Learning Model Inference Serving with KFServing   35
      Platforms and Clouds   37
   Summary   39

2. Kubeflow Architecture and Best Practices. 41
   Kubeflow Architecture Overview   41
      Kubeflow and Kubernetes   43
      Ways to Run a Job on Kubeflow   44

Machine Learning Metadata Service   44
Artifact Storage   45
Istio Operations in Kubeflow   45
Kubeflow Multitenancy Architecture   48
Multitenancy and Isolation   48
Multiuser Architecture   49
Multiuser Authorization Flow   49
Kubeflow Profiles   50
Multiuser Isolation   52
Notebook Architecture   53
Notebook Server Launcher UI   53
Notebook Controller   55
Pipelines Architecture   56
Kubeflow Best Practices   57
Managing Job Dependencies   57
Using GPUs   60
Experiment Management   62
Summary   63

3. Planning a Kubeflow Installation. 65
Security Planning   65
Components That Extend the Kubernetes API   66
Components Running Atop Kubernetes   66
Background and Motivation   67
Kubeflow and Deployed Applications   68
Integration   69
Users   70
Profiling Users   70
Varying Skillsets   72
Workloads   73
Cluster Utilization   73
Data Patterns   75
GPU Planning   75
Planning for GPUs   76
Models that Benefit from GPUs   77
Infrastructure Planning   79
Kubernetes Considerations   79
On-Premise   80
Cloud   81
Placement   82
Container Management   83
Serverless Container Operations with Knative   83

Sizing and Growing   84
    Forecasting   84
    Storage   85
    Scaling   86
    Summary   87

4. Installing Kubeflow On-Premise. 89
Kubernetes Operations from the Command Line   89
    Installing kubectl   90
    Using kubectl   93
    Using Docker   95
Basic Install Process   97
    Installing On-Premise   97
        Considerations for Building Kubernetes Clusters   97
        Gateway Host Access to Kubernetes Cluster   99
        Active Directory Integration and User Management   99
        Kerberos Integration   100
        Storage Integration   100
        Container Management and Artifact Repositories   103
Accessing and Interacting with Kubeflow   104
    Common Command-Line Operations   104
    Accessible Web UIs   104
Installing Kubeflow   105
    System Requirements   105
    Set Up and Deploy   105
Summary   107

5. Running Kubeflow on Google Cloud. 109
Overview of the Google Cloud Platform   110
    Storage   111
    Google Cloud Identity-Aware Proxy   112
    Google Cloud Security and the Cloud Identity-Aware Proxy   114
    GCP Projects for Application Deployments   118
    GCP Service Accounts   119
    Signing Up for Google Cloud Platform   120
Installing the Google Cloud SDK   120
    Update Python   121
    Download and Install Google Cloud SDK   121
Installing Kubeflow on Google Cloud Platform   121
    Create a Project in the GCP Console   122
    Enabling APIs for a Project   123
    Set Up OAuth for GCP Cloud IAP   125

  Deploy Kubeflow Using the Command-Line Interface 131
  Accessing the Kubeflow UI Post-Installation 141
 Summary 142

6. Running Kubeflow on Amazon Web Services................................. **143**
 Overview of Amazon Web Services 143
  Storage 144
  Amazon Storage Pricing 145
  Amazon Cloud Security 145
  AWS Compute Services 145
  Managed Kubernetes on EKS 146
 Signing Up for Amazon Web Services 146
 Installing the AWS CLI 147
  Update Python 147
  Install the AWS CLI 147
 Kubeflow on Amazon Web Services 150
  Installing kubectl 151
  Install the eksctl CLI for Amazon EKS 151
  Install AWS IAM Authenticator 151
  Install jq 151
 Using Managed Kubernetes on Amazon EKS 152
  Create an EKS Service Role 152
  Create an AWS VPC 154
  Creating EKS Clusters 157
  Deploying an EKS Cluster with eksctl 158
 Understanding the Deployment Process 158
  Kubeflow Configuration and Deployment 159
  Customize the Kubeflow Deployment 161
  Customize Authentication 161
  Resizing EKS Clusters 161
  Deleting EKS Clusters 162
  Adding Logging 163
  Troubleshooting Deployments 164
 Summary 165

7. Running Kubeflow on Azure.. **167**
 Overview of the Azure Cloud Platform 167
  Key Azure Components 168
  Storage on Azure 169
  The Azure Security Model 172
  Service Accounts 174
  Resources and Resource Groups 174

	Azure Virtual Machines	175
	Containers and Managed Azure Kubernetes Services	176
	The Azure CLI	177
	Installing the Azure CLI	177
	Installing Kubeflow on Azure Kubernetes	177
	Azure Login and Configuration	178
	Create an AKS Cluster for Kubeflow	179
	Kubeflow Installation	182
	Authorizing Network Access to Deployment	189
	Summary	189

8.	Model Serving and Integration.	191
	Basic Concepts of Model Management	191
	Understanding Training Models Versus Model Inference	192
	Building an Intuition for Model Integration	194
	Scaling Model Inference Throughput	197
	Model Management	200
	Introduction to KFServing	201
	Advantages of Using KFServing	203
	Core Concepts in KFServing	204
	Supported Pre-Built Model Servers	212
	KFServing Security Model	216
	Managing Models with KFServing	217
	Installing KFServing on a Kubernetes Cluster	217
	Deploying a Model on KFServing	220
	Managing Model Traffic with Canarying	226
	Deploying a Custom Transformer	228
	Roll Back a Deployed Model	230
	Removing a Deployed Model	231
	Summary	231

| A. | Infrastructure Concepts. | 233 |

| B. | An Overview of Kubernetes. | 247 |

| C. | Istio Operations and Kubeflow. | 255 |

| | Index. | 269 |

Preface

What Is in This Book?

This book focuses on the DevOps and MLOps sides of deploying and operating Kubeflow. The authors feel that this is compelling and relevant content for today's practicing DevOps/MLOps teams as this sector is still changing. Many machine learning platforms today take different approaches to the architecture and solution space of managing machine learning workflows. The difficulty of considering all aspects of operating a machine learning platform is where this story kicks off in Chapter 1. "Where are we today and what do we need to be thinking about from ground zero for machine learning platforms?"

This book starts by taking you through today's machine learning infrastructure landscape and explaining the challenges and trade-offs faced by many enterprise teams today. We then go on to outline the core principles needed to support the full life cycle of machine learning operations and explain how Kubernetes solves some of the issues that arise. We'll further show the remaining functional gaps in how Kubernetes fits into the MLOps picture, and how Kubeflow functions to complete the picture.

This book has three major parts. The first section (Chapters 1, 2, and 3) focuses on understanding the core concepts of Kubeflow and its architecture.

Chapter 1 covers machine learning architecture concerns, such as "Why is Kubernetes compelling here?" and "What does Kubeflow add beyond Kubernetes?" It includes a discussion of understanding today's machine learning platforms. Chapter 2 moves oon to the architecture of Kubeflow. Chapter 3 walks you through ways to plan a Kubeflow deployment.

The second part (Chapters 4, 5, 6, and 7) covers how to install Kubeflow 1.0.2 on-premise and on the three major cloud vendors: Google Cloud Platform, Amazon Web Services, and Microsoft Azure. These chapters are intended to walk engineers through the steps required to deploy Kubeflow both on-premise, and on each of the major cloud platforms. Some readers may skip some of this material depending on how they are deploying Kubeflow.

Chapter 8 closes the book by focusing on deploying models into production for inference with KFServing. This chapter is compelling in that it starts by defining model inference and then outlining considerations you need to take into account when wiring the output of a saved model into a production application. Chapter 8 closes out with a deep dive into KFServing, the model deployment framework included with Kubeflow.

Finally, the appendixes give background information on infrastructure core concepts, Istio and the control plane, and also core Kubernetes concepts.

This book does not cover specific use case examples in machine learning, as there are many existing books that already cover that topic.

Who Is This Book For?

DevOps and MLOps teams will benefit from this book the most as the book focuses on both the architecture of Kubeflow and also its operational side. There are many infrastructure debates to be had in every organization and this book should help arm a DevOps team with at least a grounding in the trade-offs to look for in a machine learning platform architecture.

Data scientists may find its material good background information from the user perspective but they may get bored with so much discussion around topics such as Kubernetes and identity management. However, with some patience, a data scientist may find value in the book as they can better understand what is happening behind the scenes, allowing them to be better-informed users of Kubeflow.

This book assumes you are familiar with basic Kubernetes concepts and can already build machine learning code.

Conventions Used in This Book

The following typographical conventions are used in this book:

Italic
Indicates new terms, URLs, email addresses, filenames, and file extensions.

`Constant width`
Used for program listings, as well as within paragraphs to refer to program elements such as variable or function names, databases, data types, environment variables, statements, and keywords.

Constant width bold

Shows commands or other text that should be typed literally by the user.

Constant width italic

Shows text that should be replaced with user-supplied values or by values determined by context.

 This element signifies a tip or suggestion.

 This element signifies a general note.

 This element indicates a warning or caution.

Using Code Examples

Supplemental material (code examples, etc.) is available for download at *https://github.com/jpatanooga/kubeflow_ops_book_dev*.

If you have a technical question or a problem using the code examples, please email *bookquestions@oreilly.com*.

This book is here to help you get your job done. In general, if example code is offered with this book, you may use it in your programs and documentation. You do not need to contact us for permission unless you're reproducing a significant portion of the code. For example, writing a program that uses several chunks of code from this book does not require permission. Selling or distributing examples from O'Reilly books does require permission. Answering a question by citing this book and quoting example code does not require permission. Incorporating a significant amount of example code from this book into your product's documentation does require permission.

We appreciate, but generally do not require, attribution. An attribution usually includes the title, author, publisher, and ISBN. For example: "*Kubeflow Operations Guide* by Josh Patterson, Michael Katzenellenbogen, and Austin Harris (O'Reilly).

If you feel your use of code examples falls outside fair use or the permission given above, feel free to contact us at *permissions@oreilly.com*.

O'Reilly Online Learning

 For more than 40 years, *O'Reilly Media* has provided technology and business training, knowledge, and insight to help companies succeed.

Our unique network of experts and innovators share their knowledge and expertise through books, articles, and our online learning platform. O'Reilly's online learning platform gives you on-demand access to live training courses, in-depth learning paths, interactive coding environments, and a vast collection of text and video from O'Reilly and 200+ other publishers. For more information, visit *http://oreilly.com*.

How to Contact Us

Please address comments and questions concerning this book to the publisher:

O'Reilly Media, Inc.
1005 Gravenstein Highway North
Sebastopol, CA 95472
800-998-9938 (in the United States or Canada)
707-829-0515 (international or local)
707-829-0104 (fax)

We have a web page for this book, where we list errata, examples, and any additional information. You can access this page at *https://oreil.ly/Kubeflow_Operations_Guide*.

Email *bookquestions@oreilly.com* to comment or ask technical questions about this book.

For news and information about our books and courses, visit http://oreilly.com.

Find us on Facebook: *http://facebook.com/oreilly*

Follow us on Twitter: *http://twitter.com/oreillymedia*

Watch us on YouTube: *http://www.youtube.com/oreillymedia*

Acknowledgments

Josh

I'd like to start out by thanking my wife Leslie and my sons Ethan, Griffin, and Dane for their patience while I worked late, often, and sometimes (many times) while on vacation.

I'd like to thank my coauthors (Michael and Austin) for their efforts in putting together this book. I'd also like to thank my editor, Michele Cronin, who was wonderful to work with during the course of the writing process. We had to finish a book during a pandemic, and we made it work.

I want to give a measure of appreciation to Jeremy Lewi for all of his help and discussion around what should be in the book and how it should approach the reader.

I'd like to thank James Long for being my "shadow editor" and "voice of the reader." It's a challenge to know which critiques to digest in order to make a better book, but when James makes a point, I generally make the change.

I'd further like to thank Zeki Yasar and Richard Dibasio for their feedback on versions of the book. Hamel Husain and Hannes Hapke also gave valued feedback on many of the topics in the book.

I'd like to mention a measure of appreciation for the work Adam Gibson did in our previous book together for O'Reilly. Writing that book, the content and the process, helped set up and make this book better than it would have been alone.

Following are some other folks I'd like to recognize who had an impact on my career leading up to this book: my parents (Lewis and Connie), Dr. Andy Novobiliski (grad school), Dr. Mina Sartipi (thesis advisor), Dr. Billy Harris (graduate algorithms), Dr. Joe Dumas (grad school), Ritchie Carroll (creator of the openPDC), Paul Trachian, Christophe Bisciglia and Mike Olson (for recruiting me to Cloudera), Malcom Ramey (for my first real programming job), the University of Tennessee at Chattanooga, and Lupi's Pizza (for feeding me through grad school).

Michael

Writing a book was never really one of the items on my bucket list. Yet, after this endeavor, I found that writing can be an enjoyable, relaxing, and most importantly ever-educating experience. Working with Josh and Austin on this book provided me with an opportunity to stop and reflect on what I thought I knew, and challenged me to become more articulate and purposeful in how I convey information, both in speech and writing.

There are many folks who can be thanked for their support and encouragement throughout the process, but I think the largest kudos go to Josh for the initial idea and execution of this project. Whether it was brainstorming sessions or the relentless reminders about deadlines (and I really do thank you for them!), it was he who provided the encouragement and devotion to bring this book to fruition.

I would really like to thank the entire free and open source community, the contributors and those that make code available for all to read, use, and share. The amount of knowledge, and information available is truly unbelievable. Open source software has truly allowed me to gain the knowledge needed to navigate the complex technical world we live in.

There are many other folks who can and should receive acknowledgments, but I'll err on the side of naming none rather than forgetting some.

Austin

First, I want to thank my friend and colleague, Josh Patterson, for the opportunity to join him on this journey and for providing direction every step of the way throughout the writing process. Josh has also been a great mentor throughout my career and I cannot thank him enough. Secondly, I want to say a huge thank you to Mina Sartipi for her continued support and guidance throughout graduate school and my career. Mina introduced me to Josh, which kicked off our relationship and led to this opportunity.

Next, I want to thank my amazing wife, Victoria Harris, for supporting me through the late nights working and her continuous love and encouragement throughout my career. Lastly, I want to thank my mother, Marlyce Harris, and my father, Steve Harris, for their love and support throughout my life.

Introduction to Kubeflow

Kubeflow (*https://github.com/kubeflow*) is an open source Kubernetes-native platform for developing, orchestrating, deploying, and running scalable and portable machine learning (ML) workloads. It is a cloud native platform based on Google's internal ML pipelines. The project is dedicated to making deployments of ML workflows on Kubernetes simple, portable, and scalable.

In this book we take a look at the evolution of machine learning in enterprise, how infrastructure has changed, and then how Kubeflow meets the needs of the modern enterprise.

Operating Kubeflow in an increasingly multicloud and hybrid-cloud world will be a key topic as the market grows and as Kubernetes adoption grows (*https://oreil.ly/eNVNA*). A single workflow may have a life cycle that starts on-premise but quickly requires resources that are only available in the cloud. Building out machine learning tooling on the emergent platform Kubernetes is where life began for Kubeflow, so let's start there.

Machine Learning on Kubernetes

Kubeflow began life as a basic way to get rudimentary machine learning infrastructure running on Kubernetes. The two driving forces in its development and adoption are the evolution of machine learning in enterprise and the emergence of Kubernetes as the de facto infrastructure management layer.

Let's take a quick tour of the recent history of machine learning in enterprise to better understand how we got here.

The Evolution of Machine Learning in Enterprise

The past decade has seen the popularity and interest in machine learning rise considerably. This can be attributed to developments in the computer industry such as:

- Advances in self-driving cars
- Widespread adoption of computer vision (CV) applications
- Integration of tools such as Amazon Echo into daily life

Deep learning tends to get a lot of the credit for many tools these days, but fundamentally applied machine learning is foundational to all of the developments. Machine learning can be defined as:

> In everyday parlance, when we say learning, we mean something like "gaining knowledge by studying, experience, or being taught." Sharpening our focus a bit, we can think of machine learning as using algorithms for acquiring structural descriptions from data examples. A computer learns something about the structures that represent the information in the raw data.
>
> —*Deep Learning* by Josh Patterson and Adam Gibson (O'Reilly)

Some examples of machine learning algorithms are linear regression, decision trees, and neural networks. You should consider machine learning to be a subset of the broader domain of artificial intelligence (AI).

Defining Machine Learning, Deep Learning, and Artificial Intelligence

Deep learning is a subset of machine learning (as illustrated in Figure 1-1) where neural networks use their specialized architecture to perform automated feature learning. Typically we see deep learning applied in areas such as computer vision, time series modeling, and audio classification; and the training of these advanced neural networks is often done best with GPUs.

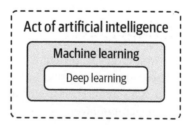

Figure 1-1. Thinking about the relationship between artificial intelligence, machine learning, and deep learning

Artificial intelligence is difficult to define as it tends to get used as a label for things ranging from basic optimization to "something the public considers magic."

Let's start with *what AI is not*. AI is not alive, self-aware, nor near any level of media hype that results in inflated expectations and disappointment in the technologies within the market. We've seen these cycles before (*https://oreil.ly/nHtEz*) (two times, previously), where AI gets overmarketed and then crashes. The progress and results of each cycle, while impressive and driving new industry sectors, always fall short of "magical."

Why do we keep doing this to ourselves?

AI has long held a place in society's collective imagination because it poses an existential threat (*https://oreil.ly/qufww*) to our fundamental role in society. People's place and identity in society are strongly related to their working roles. People fear being rendered irrelevant by AI.

Artificial intelligence really means "applied machine learning" (with deep learning included). This definition can be expanded further, from the automation viewpoint, to "artificial intelligence is a term for algorithms that increase user productivity." We can make this designation because some techniques, such as game-state search, are not defined as machine learning yet fall under the historical banner of AI. For more on what AI is, check out Appendix A of *Deep Learning* (O'Reilly).

The mid-2000s saw the rise of deep learning research fueled by the availability of GPUs, better labeled datasets, and better tooling. This rise reignited interest in applied machine learning across all enterprises in the early 2010s, in their quest to leverage data and machine intelligence to be "more like Google and Amazon."

Many early efforts in applied machine learning focused on the Apache Hadoop platform, as it had seen a meteoric rise in enterprise adoption in the first half of the 2010s. However, where Apache Hadoop was focused on leveraging commodity hardware with CPUs and distributed processing, deep learning practitioners were focused on single machines with one or more GPUs and the Python programming environment. Apache Spark on Apache Hadoop gave robust options for applied machine learning on the JVM, yet the graduate-level practitioner tended to be trained with the Python programming language.

Enterprises began hiring more graduate program–educated machine learning practitioners, which created a large influx of users demanding support for Python for their applied machine learning workflows.

In earlier years, Spark had been a key technology for running machine learning jobs, but in more recent years we see enterprises shifting toward GPU-based training in containers that may not live on a Hadoop cluster. The DevOps, IT, and platform teams working with these data scientists wanted to make sure they were setting the teams up for success, while also having a manageable infrastructure strategy.

The folks in charge of these platforms wanted to use the cloud in a way that did not cost too much, and took advantage of the transient nature of cloud-based workloads.

There is a growing need to make these worlds work together on data lakes—whether on-premise, in the cloud, or somewhere in between. Today, a few of the major challenges in the enterprise machine learning practitioner space are:

- Data scientists tend to prefer their own unique cluster of libraries and tools.
- These kinds of tools are generally heterogeneous, both inside teams and across organizations.
- Data scientists needs to interoperate with the rest of the enterprise for resources, data, and model deployment.
- Many of their tools are Python-based, where Python environments prove difficult to manage across a large organization.
- Many times, data scientists want to build containers and then just "move them around" to take advantage of more powerful resources beyond their laptop, either in the on-premise datacenter or in the cloud.

This makes operating a platform to support the different constituents using the system harder than ever.

What Is a Data Lake?

We'll use the definition provided on the Amazon Web Services (AWS) website (*https://oreil.ly/yU9_L*):

> A data lake is a centralized repository that allows you to store all your structured and unstructured data at any scale. You can store your data as is, without having to first structure the data, and run different types of analytics—from dashboards and visualizations to big data processing, real-time analytics, and machine learning to guide better decisions.

It's Harder Than Ever to Run Enterprise Infrastructure

We progressively live in an age where developers and data scientists feel empowered to spin up their own infrastructure in the cloud, so it has become antithetical for many organizations to enforce strict infrastructure rules for machine learning practitioners. We've seen this in the space where customers end up with three or four different machine learning pipeline systems because groups cannot agree (and simply run off to AWS or GCP to get what they want when they get told "no").

Hadoop and Spark are still key tools for data storage and processing, but increasingly Kubernetes has come into the picture (*https://oreil.ly/Jhhyp*) to manage the on-premise, cloud, and hybrid workloads. In the past two years we've seen Kubernetes adoption increase rapidly. Many enterprises have made infrastructure investments in previous technology cycles such as:

- RDBMs
- Parallel RDBMs
- Hadoop
- Key-value stores
- Spark

Just like the systems before them, these systems have a certain level of legacy inertia in their adoptive organizations. Therefore, it's easy to predict that integration between Hadoop workloads and specialized Kubernetes-based machine learning workloads are on the horizon—as we see Cloudera using Kubernetes (*https://oreil.ly/NyzoX*) for their new data science tools as opposed to YARN (*https://oreil.ly/X5dCl*), and Google changing out YARN for Kubernetes for Spark (*https://oreil.ly/xFDu_*).

Other factors that make running infrastructure more complex than ever include how the evolution of open source acceptance in enterprise is using both on-premise and cloud infrastructure. On top of this, the security requirements are necessary to support the complexity of multiple platforms and multitenancy. Finally, we're also seeing demands for specialized hardware such as GPUs and TPUs.

Some overall infrastructure trends we note as of interest as we go forward:

- Mixtures of on-premise, cloud, and hybrid deployments (*https://oreil.ly/0YLO2*) are becoming more popular with enterprises.
- The three major "big cloud" vendors continue to capture a number of workloads that move to the cloud; some of these workloads oscillate between cloud and on-premise.
- Docker (*https://www.docker.com*) is synonymous with the term *container*.
- Many enterprises are either using Kubernetes or strongly considering it as their container orchestration platform (*https://oreil.ly/uCXyT*).

Beyond an on-premise cluster, Kubernetes clusters can be joined together with cluster federation within Kubernetes. In a truly hybrid world, we can potentially have a job scheduling policy that places certain workloads on the cloud because the on-premise resources are oversubscribed, or, conversely, restrain certain workloads to be executed on-premise only and never get executed in the cloud. Kubernetes also makes workloads more platform-agnostic, because it abstracts away the underlying platform specifics, making Kubernetes the key abstraction.

There are many factors to consider when dealing with cloud infrastructure, or a hybrid federated cluster infrastructure, including:

- Active Directory (AD) integration
- Security considerations
- Cost considerations for cloud instances
- Which users should have access to the cloud instances

We look at all of these topics in more depth in Chapter 2 and in the rest of this book.

Identifying Next-Generation Infrastructure (NGI) Core Principles

In the age of cloud infrastructure, what "big cloud" (AWS, Azure, Google Cloud Platform [GCP]) does tends to significantly impact how enterprises build their own infrastructure today. In 2018 we saw all three major cloud vendors offer managed Kubernetes as part of their infrastructure:

- Google Kubernetes Engine (GKE) (*https://oreil.ly/YUqzY*)
- Amazon Elastic Kubernetes Service (EKS) (*https://aws.amazon.com/eks*)
- Azure Kubernetes Services (AKS) (*https://oreil.ly/LnGce*)

In late 2017, after intially offering their own container service (*https://oreil.ly/f2bwQ*), Amazon joined the other two members of big cloud and offered Amazon EKS (*https://oreil.ly/8albq*) as a first-class supported citizen on AWS.

All three major cloud vendors are pushing Kubernetes, and these tailwinds should accelerate interest in Kubernetes and Kubeflow. Beyond that, we've seen how containers are a key part of how data scientists want to operate in managing containers from local execution, to on-premise infrastructure, to running on the cloud (easily and cleanly).

Teams need to balance multitenancy with access to storage and compute options (NAS, HDFS, FlashBlade) and high-end GPUs (Nvidia DGX-1, etc.). Teams also need a flexible way to customize their applied machine learning full applications, from ETL, to modeling, to model deployment; yet in a manner that stays within the above tenants.

We see that cloud vendors have an increasing influence on how enterprises build their infrastructure, where the managed services they tend to advocate for are likely to get accelerated adoption. However, most organizations are separated from getting results from data science efforts in their organization by obstacles listed in the last section. We can break these obstacles down into the following key components:

Composability

This component involves breaking down machine learning workflows into a number of components (or stages) in a sequence, and allowing us to put them together in different formations. Many times, these stages are each their own systems and we need to move the output of one system to another system as input.

Portability

This component involves having a consistent way to run and test code:

- Development

- Staging

- Production

When we have deltas between those environments, we introduce opportunities to have outages in production. Having a machine learning stack that can run on your laptop, the same way it runs on a multi-GPU DGX-1 and then on a public cloud, would be considered desirable by most practitioners today.

Scalability

Most organizations also desire scalability, and are constrained by:

- Access to machine-specific hardware (e.g., GPUs, TPUs)

- Limited compute

- Network

- Storage

- Heterogeneous hardware

Unfortunately scale is not about "adding more hardware," in many cases it's about the underlying distributed systems architecture. Kubernetes helps us with these constraints.

GPUs, TPUs, and FPGAs

We want to take a second to mention some compute hardware that some readers may not be familiar with. Users will initially experiment on their local machines with ML workflows, but over time, their workflows tend to demand more compute and begin to take longer to complete.

This tends to cause users to seek out more performance hardware for machine learning, and the hardware market has responded in kind with specialized components such as GPUs, TPUs, and FPGAs.

A *graphics processing unit* (GPU) is designed to process the type of math (linear algebra) that we typically see in the 3D rendering pipelines of video games (where they originate from). As machine learning became more popular, users discovered that GPUs were naturally good at linear algebra, and that ML algorithms could similarly be accelerated on the same GPUs as video games (with some software tricks). Today, speeding up linear algebra processing in machine learning is most commonly associated with GPUs.

Tensor processing units (TPUs) are accelerator application-specific integrated circuits (ASICs) (*https://oreil.ly/QqfcB*) developed by Google specifically to accelerate the training of neural network machine learning training and inference.

Finally, a *field-programmable gate array* (FPGA) is an integrated circuit that can be configured by the customer with a hardware description language (HDL). Today FPGAs are not as widely used for accelerating ML workloads as GPUs and TPUs.

Kubernetes for Production Application Deployment

Kubernetes is an orchestration system for containers that is meant to coordinate clusters of nodes at scale, in production, in an efficient manner. Kubernetes works around the idea of pods (*https://oreil.ly/2bwp0*) which are scheduling units (each pod containing one or more containers) in the Kubernetes ecosystem. These pods are distributed across hosts in a cluster to provide high availability. Kubernetes itself is not a complete solution and is intended to integrate with other tools such as Docker, a popular container technology.

A container image (*https://oreil.ly/tY89A*) is a lightweight, standalone, executable package of a piece of software that includes everything needed to run it (code, runtime, system tools, system libraries, settings). Colloquially, containers are referred to as "Docker," but what the speaker typically means are containers in the general sense. Docker containers make it significantly easier for developers to enjoy parity between their local, testing, staging, and production environments. Containers allow teams to run the same artifact or image across all of those environments, including a developer's laptop and on the cloud. This property of containers, especially when combined with container orchestration with a system like Kubernetes, is driving the concept of hybrid cloud in practice.

A major reason we see widespread container (e.g., Docker) and Kubernetes adoption today is because together they are an exceptional infrastructure solution for the issues inherent in composability, portability, and scalability. Kubernetes shines when we have a lot of containers that need to be managed across a lot of machines (on-premise, in the cloud, or a mixture of both).

What Are Containers?

A container image is a lightweight, standalone, executable software package that includes the code, runtime, system tools and libraries, and settings needed to run it. Containers and container platforms provide more advantages than traditional virtualization because:

- Isolation is done on the kernel level without the need for a guest operating system.
- Containers are much more efficient, fast, and lightweight.

This allows applications to become encapsulated in self-contained environments. Other advantages include quicker deployments, scalability, and closer parity between development environments.

Docker and Kubernetes are not direct competitors but complementing technologies. One way to think of it is Docker is for managing images and individual containers, while Kubernetes is for managing pods of containers. Docker provided an open standard for packaging, and distributing containerized applications, but it did not solve the container orchestration (inter-communication, scaling, etc.) issue. Competitors to Kubernetes in this space are Mesos and Docker Swarm, but we're seeing the industry converge on Kubernetes as the standard for container orchestration.

With Kubernetes we also have the ability to dynamically scale applications on a cluster. With installable options such as Kubernetes Horizontal Pod Autoscaler, we also have the ability to scale clusters themselves.

Not Every Application Can Be Dynamically Scaled

Some types of applications are not candidates for dynamic scaling. There are multiple potential reasons for this, such as an application that is dependent on data-locality where its data needs to be on the local instance's drives for effective operations. Other examples may include (legacy) applications that are monolithic by design, whch, due to their architecture constraints, require them to be "scaled up" as opposed to being "scaled out."

Kubernetes allows applications to scale horizontally in the node and container (pod) scope, while providing fault tolerance and self-healing infrastructure improving reliability. Kubernetes also provides efficient use of resources for applications deployed on-premise or in the cloud. It also strives to make every deployed application available 24/7 while allowing developers to deploy applications or updates multiple times per day with no downtime.

Kubernetes is, further, a great fit for machine learning workloads because it already has support for GPUs (*https://oreil.ly/N01yj*) and TPUs (*https://oreil.ly/DOzcj*) as resources, with FPGAs (*https://oreil.ly/FkJ0g*) in development. In Figure 1-2 we can see how having key abstractions with containers and other layers is significant for running a machine learning training job on GPUs in a similar fashion to how you might run the same job on FPGAs.

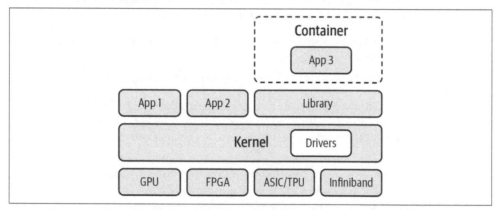

Figure 1-2. Containers and abstraction from hardware

We highlight the abstractions in Figure 1-2 because they are all components in the challenges involved with workflow portability. An example of this is how our code may work locally on our own laptop yet fail to run remotely on a Google Cloud virtual machine with GPUs.

Why Don't We Just Plug All Needed Drivers into Our Containers?

Hardware drivers are designed for controlling the underlying hardware they are intended to support. In the same way that a specialized Ethernet driver, or a specialized disk driver, control a network card or a disk, respectively, the GPU drivers control (and drive) the GPUs in a machine. Drivers typically operate at or near the kernel level.

Considering that containers are a namespaced process (that is, a process that has been isolated from many or all other processes in a system), installing the driver in the container would require that process be allowed to inject and remove elements from the running kernel, in effect, providing exclusive control of the hardware to that container. The container would need to run with elevated privileges, removing a chunk of security semantics containers provide.

In other words, giving a container exclusive control of underlying hardware sort of defeats the notion of the "containerized process." It binds it to a highly specific hardware set—thus making it less portable (consider what happens if the container attempts to load the driver, but the hardware is different on another machine the container runs on). It also requires the container to have elevated system privileges.

In a containerized environment, the underlying host is typically best suited to control its own hardware, and to expose the availability of that hardware to containers.

Kubernetes also already has controllers for tasks such as batch jobs and deployment of long-lived services for model hosting, giving us many foundational components for our machine learning infrastructure. Further, as a resource manager, Kubernetes provides three primary benefits:

- Unified management
- Job isolation
- Resilient infrastructure

Unified management allows us to use a single-cluster management interface for multiple Kubernetes clusters. Job isolation in Kubernetes gives us the ability to move models and extract, transform, and load (ETL) pipelines from development to production with less dependency issues. Resilient infrastructure implies how Kubernetes manages the nodes in the cluster for us, and makes sure we have enough machines and resources to accomplish our tasks.

Kubernetes as a platform has been scaled in practice (*https://oreil.ly/m4Rzn*) up into the thousands of nodes. While many organizations will not hit that order of magnitude of nodes, it highlights the fact that Kubernetes (the platform itself) will not have scale issues from a distributed system aspect as a platform.

 Kubernetes Is Not Magic

Every distributed systems application requires thoughtful design. Don't fall prey to the notion that Kubernetes will magically scale any application just because someone threw the application in a container and sent it to a cluster.

Although we can solve issues around moving containers and machine learning work-flow stacks around, we're not entirely home free. We still have other considerations such as:

- The cost of using the cloud versus the on-premises cost
- Organizational rules around where data can live
- Security considerations such as Active Directory and Kerberos integration

These are just to name a few. Modern datacenter infrastructure has a lot of variables in play, and it can make life hard for an IT or DevOps team. In this book we seek to at least arm you with a plan of attack on how to best plan and meet the needs of your data science constituents, all while keeping in line with organizational policies.

Kubernetes solves a lot of infrastructure problems in a progressively complex infrastructure world, but it wasn't designed specifically for machine learning workflows.

 For a Deeper Dive on Kubernetes

Check out Appendix B of this book, or one of the other O'Reilly books on Kubernetes such as *Kubernetes: Up and Running*, by Brendan Burns et al.

Let's now take a look at how Kubeflow enters the picture to help enable machine learning workflows.

Enter: Kubeflow

Kubeflow was conceived of as a way to run machine learning workflows on Kubernetes and is typically used for the following reasons:

- You want to train/serve machine learning models in different environments (e.g., local, on-premise, and cloud).
- You want to use Jupyter Notebooks (*https://oreil.ly/QwPDB*) to manage machine learning training jobs (not just TensorFlow jobs).
- You want to launch training jobs that use resources (such as additional CPUs or GPUs, which aren't available on your personal computer).
- You want to combine machine learning code from different libraries.

Sometimes, as the last example describes, we want to combine our TensorFlow code with other processes. In this example, we might want to use TensorFlow/agents to run simulations to generate data for training reinforcement-learning (RL) models. With Kubeflow Pipelines we could chain together these two distinct parts of a machine learning workflow.

With our machine learning platform, typically, we'd like an operational pattern similar to the "lab and the factory" pattern. In this way, we want our data scientists to be able to explore new data ideas in "the lab," and once they find a setup they like, move it to "the factory" so that the modeling workflow can be run consistently and in a reproducible manner. In Figure 1-3 we can see a generalized representation of a common machine learning workflow.

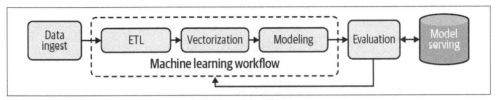

Figure 1-3. The generalized machine learning workflow

Kubeflow was designed to operate machine learning workflows, such as the one represented in Figure 1-3, across the many different constraints we've called out so far in this chapter. Two key systems (covered in architectural detail in Chapter 2) that are great examples of the value Kubeflow provides beyond Kubernetes are the notebook system in Kubeflow, and Kubeflow Pipelines. We'll refer back to this diagram several times in the book to contextualize how the parts of Kubeflow interact as a whole to achieve the goals of the DevOps and data science teams.

Kubeflow is a great option for Fortune 500 infrastructure, because it allows a notebook-based modeling system to easily integrate with the data lake ETL operations on a local data lake or in the cloud in a similar way. It also supports multitenancy across different hardware by managing the container orchestration aspect of the infrastructure. Kubeflow gives us great options for a multitenant "lab" environment while also providing infrastructure to schedule and maintain consistent machine learning production workflows in "the factory."

While teams today can potentially share a server, when we attempt to manage 5 or 10 servers, each with multiple GPUs, we quickly create a situation where multitenancy can become messy. Users end up having to wait for resources, and may also be fighting dependencies or libraries that other users left behind from previous jobs. There is also the difficulty of isolating users from one another so users cannot see each other's data.

Hidden Technical Debt in Machine Learning Systems

Most of the time, the applications that grab headlines are wonderful (visual) applications of deep learning models. However, for the majority of machine learning pipelines, there is a lot more that goes into building a model than just running a training loop and making a pretty render in a Jupyter Notebook. Figure 1-4, from the paper by D. Sculley et al., "Hidden Technical Debt in Machine Learning" (*https://oreil.ly/2CsNW*), gives a better overall representation of proportionally what goes into building a machine learning pipeline.

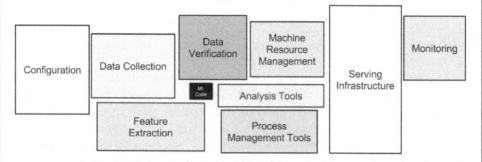

Figure 1-4. Only a small fraction of a real-world ML system is composed of the ML code, as shown by the small black box in the middle; the required surrounding infrastructure is vast and complex

This diagram is a great visual metaphor for why platforms such as Kubeflow are critical for (and popular with) enterprise practitioners today.

If we have any hope of sustaining a robust data science practice across a cluster of heterogeneous hardware, we will need to use a system like Kubeflow and Kubernetes. Beyond just the obstacles we mention here, machine learning workflows tend to have much technical debt right under the visible surface.

What Problems Does Kubeflow Solve?

The goal of Kubeflow is to simplify the deployment of machine learning workflows to Kubernetes. The issue with using the Kubernetes API directly is that it is too low-level for most data scientists. A data scientist already has to know a number of techniques and technologies without the necessity of adding the complexities of the Kubernetes API to the list.

Wrapping Python machine learning models in containers is how many people start putting initial models into production. From that point, deploying the container on a pod on Kubernetes is a natural next step (as we can see from the market trends). As more machine learning applications are deployed on Kubernetes, this gravity effect tends to pull more of the machine learning work in as well. However, from a DevOps viewpoint, soon you're implementing a full multitenant data science platform on Kubernetes from scratch.

There are many extra details to worry about, with all of the "glue" code involved in making things like notebook servers and pipelines work consistently and securely as a distributed system. Many times, data science work consists largely of scripts, as opposed to full-fledged applications, and this makes deploying them as a production workflow from scratch that much harder. Beyond just the Kubernetes API, you'd have to also write custom code to integrate different running components and also orchestrate the components for things like workflow orchestration.

Just adding nodes on Kubernetes and expecting them to operate as a cohesive platform doesn't always go that easily. It is common for organizations to put together automation scripts that will quickly set up a user on a cloud environment, run the set of job or jobs, and then tear down the environment. However, this becomes cumbersome as there can be nontrivial integration issues around Active Directory (user management) or Kerberos, for example.

You want a data scientist to focus on the work of developing, training, testing, and deploying models and less on how to get the Kubernetes API to work in such a way that makes their primary work possible. The issues Kubeflow solves beyond just the core Kubernetes API are:

- Faster and more consistent deployment
- Better control over ports and component access for tighter security
- Protection against over-provisioning resources, saving costs
- Protection against tasks not being deallocated once complete, saving costs
- Workflow orchestration and metadata collection
- Centralized monitoring and logging
- Infrastructure to move models to production, securely and at scale

The name Kubeflow is a portmanteau of Kubernetes and TensorFlow. All three projects originated from teams at Google as open source projects. However, even though Kubeflow started as a way to put TensorFlow workflows and models into production, it has evolved beyond the initial state.

Kubeflow Doesn't Lock You Into TensorFlow

Your users can choose the machine learning framework for their notebooks or workflows as they see fit.

Today, Kubeflow can orchestrate workflows for containers running many different types of machine learning frameworks (XGBoost, PyTorch, etc.). In some cases, a team may want to use Kubeflow to manage notebook servers for a multitenant environment that may not even focus on machine learning.

A job in Kubeflow can be a Jupyter Notebook or it can be a Python script in a series of pipeline-connected jobs. A job in Kubeflow can also be as simple as running a Python script in a container on a pod in Kubernetes via kubectl. We use notebooks, the CLI, or pipelines to set up machine learning workflows that run a job or a series of jobs to build machine learning models.

For any of these workflows, we use Kubeflow as the infrastructure beyond the low-level Kubernetes API to securely orchestrate heterogeneous machine learning workflows over heterogeneous hardware as managed and scheduled by Kubernetes. Kubeflow is the layer between the user and the Kubernetes API that makes it possible to operate this consistently as a scalable multitenant machine learning platform.

In Chapter 2 we'll look more closely at the architecture of Kubeflow and its subsystems. We'll see how the architecture solves specific problems in this space, and how the components fit together to form the machine learning platform solution that is Kubeflow.

Origin of Kubeflow

At Google Next in 2016, Google announced (*https://oreil.ly/_iAL2*) Cloud Machine Learning (Cloud ML) on the Google Cloud Platform (GCP). Cloud ML uses GKE, a precursor to what we know as Kubeflow today. In December 2017 at KubeCon, the initial version of Kubeflow was announced (*https://oreil.ly/rU9G4*) and demoed by David Aronchick and Jeremy Lewi. This version included:

- JupyterHub
- TFJob v1alpha1
- TFServing
- GPUs working on Kubernetes

In January 2018, the Kubeflow Governance Proposal (*https://oreil.ly/fiG4m*) was published to help direct how the community around the project would work. In June 2018, the 0.1 version of Kubeflow was introduced (*https://oreil.ly/tTe_W*), containing an expanded set of components, including:

- JupyterHub
- TFJob with distributed training support
- TFServing
- Argo
- Seldon Core
- Ambassador
- Better Kubernetes support

Kubeflow version 0.2 was announced (*https://oreil.ly/GHrJE*) only two months later in August 2018, with such advancements as:

- TFJob v1alpha2
- PyTorch and Caffe operators
- Central UI

The project is still (as of the writing of this book) growing, and Kubeflow continues to evolve. Today the project has expanded such that over 100 engineers are working on it (compared to the 3 at the beginning), with 22 member organizations (*https://oreil.ly/hO1yf*) participating.

Who Uses Kubeflow?

Some of the key enterprise personnel that have the most interest in Kubeflow include:

- DevOps engineers
- Platform architects
- Data scientists
- Data engineers

DevOps and platform architects need to support everyone with the right infrastructure in the right places, cloud or on-premise, supporting the ingest, ETL, data warehouse, and modeling efforts of other teams. Data engineers use this infrastructure to set up data scientists with the best denormalized datasets for vectorization and machine learning modeling. All of these teams need to work together to operate in the modern data warehouse, and Kubernetes gives them a lot of flexibility in how that happens.

Team alignment for the line of business, DevOps, data engineering, and data science

Another challenge for organizations in the space of machine learning infrastructure is how multifaceted the efforts are to build and support these pipelines. As we saw in Figure 1-4, there is a lot of "hidden technical debt" in most machine learning workflows, and the components in these workflows are owned by multiple teams. These teams include:

Line of business
> The part of the company that intends to use the results of the machine learning model to produce revenue for the organization

DevOps
> The group responsible for making sure the platform is operational and secure

Data engineering
> The group responsible for getting data from the system of record (or data warehouse) and converting it into a form for the data science team to use

Data science
> The team responsible for building and testing the machine learning model

Each of these teams has to work in concert or the business will likely find no value from their individual efforts. Let's now take a look at some specific scenarios where we might see Kubeflow used for the above teams.

Common Kubeflow Use Cases

Specific scenarios for how we'd use a technology are always critical because otherwise it's just "more infrastructure to manage." In this section we'll look at some specific use cases for how Kubeflow can be used, and how each of the teams from the previous section might be involved.

Running Notebooks on GPUs

Users commonly start out on local platforms such as Anaconda and design initial use cases. As their use cases need more data, more powerful processing, or data that cannot be copied onto their local laptop, they tend to hit roadblocks in terms of advancing their model activities.

We also note that running Jupyter locally gives the user the same experience of running it remotely on Kubeflow, because a local install is a server install just running on the desktop. From that perspective, users enjoy the same user experience from Jupyter Notebooks on their desktop as they do on the Kubeflow notebook platform.

Common Usage Patterns of Notebooks for New Users

The Jupyter Notebook App is a client-server application that supports running notebooks locally. It allows us to look at a web browser and interact with the current running notebook.

For the desktop user, we typically see Jupyter Notebook App installed via a Python distribution. This is easier for most users because of the dependency complexity involved with all of the needed Python packages out of the box. The most popular distribution is the Anaconda Distribution (*https://orcil.ly/r7GiD*).

Notebooks are popular because they provide compelling flexibility in how data scientists can use the library (language independent as well) of their choice in a notebook, or outside of a notebook on Kubeflow. It becomes a compelling offering, as now a data scientist can quickly move a workload built in the language of their choice from their laptop to an on-premise enterprise cloud, or to a public cloud, and leverage more hardware. This fits in with the pattern where machine learning jobs typically are prototyped on a user laptop and then once validated are moved to a more powerful system for training and then model deployment.

Advantages of notebooks on GPUs

Given that many notebook users start locally on their laptop, this naturally leads us to the question: "why use Kubeflow for hosted notebook infrastructure?" Machine learning, and especially deep learning training algorithms, are notoriously hungry for processing power for their linear algebra routines. GPUs have become the industry standard for speeding up linear algebra processing in machine learning. Most laptops do not have GPUs onboard, so users go looking for places to eventually run their modeling code. A common platform stack on which users have converged is this:

- Jupyter Notebook
- Python code
- Dependency management with containers, typically Docker

These developers are good at getting this stack just how they want it on their laptop. However, operating like this in a Fortune 500 company has side effects such as:

- Security
- Data access
- Driver management
- Model integration

The IT organizations in most Fortune 500 companies take security and data access seriously. The idea of PhDs experimenting with sensitive corporate data on their local laptops conflicts directly with most IT information-security policies, and this creates natural contention in an organization. This contention revolves around the line of business's need for more value from its data, versus the IT information security's mandate in keeping key information safe.

Given that companies will not give up their security requirements, we need to find ways to better serve data scientists and how they want to operate, while keeping security policies intact. Kubeflow is a great option for this scenario because it allows a data scientist to keep their preferred working environment, built in a container, to execute in an environment blessed by IT corporate security.

This internal infrastructure can be secured with Active Directory and Kerberos, while providing GPUs (e.g., Nvidia's DGX-1) and large storage arrays with object stores, proprietary storage (e.g., Pure's FlashBlade, NetApp's storage), or HDFS.

GPUs and Model Accuracy

We want to make a clear distinction around what we gain from GPUs, as many times this seems to be conflated in machine learning marketing. We define "predictive accuracy of model" as how accurate the model's predictions are with respect to the task at hand (and there are multiple ways to rate models).

Another facet of model training is "training speed," which is how long it takes us to train for a number of epochs (passes over an entire input training dataset) or to a specific accuracy/metric. We call out these two specific definitions because we want to make sure you understand:

1. GPUs will not make your model more accurate.
2. However, GPUs will allow us to train a model faster and find better models (which may be more accurate) faster.

So GPUs can indirectly help model accuracy, but we still want to set expectations here.

Team alignment for notebooks on GPUs

In this scenario, the DevOps team can enable the data scientists to build models faster with Kubeflow. This allows the data scientists to explore more concepts for the line of business faster, and this lets them eliminate poor candidate use cases faster.

If the line of business can validate use cases faster with the data science team, they can find the best fits for the business to make the most money from its data.

Shared Multitenant Machine Learning Environment

Many times, an organization will have either multiple data scientists who need to share a cluster of high-value resources (e.g., GPUs) or they will have multiple teams of data scientists who need the same access to shared resources. In this case, an organization needs to build a multitenant machine learning platform, and Kubeflow is a solid candidate for this scenario.

Often we'll see organizations buy machines with one or more GPUs attached to specialized hardware such as an Nvidia DGX-1 or DGX-2 (e.g., eight GPUs per machine). This hardware is considerably more costly than a traditional server, so we want as many data scientists leveraging it for model training as possible.

Advantages of on-premise multitenant environment

Each data scientist will have their own model workflow and code dependencies, as described earlier in this chapter. We need a system such as Kubeflow that can execute each user's workflow while keeping the workflow dependencies and data separate from other user's work on the same set of resources (e.g., isolation).

Kubeflow and Kubernetes handle these requirements for us with their scheduling and container management functionality. A great example is how we may have three different data scientists all needing to each run their own notebook on a single GPU. Kubernetes with Kubeflow handles keeping track of who is running what code on what machine and which GPUs are currently in use. Kubernetes also keeps track of which jobs are waiting in the job queue, and will schedule the waiting jobs once an in-process job finishes.

Team alignment

Multitenant systems make DevOps teams' lives far simpler, because they handle a lot of infrastructure complexity for us. DevOps can focus on keeping the Kubernetes cluster and the Kubeflow application operational, which lets us leverage all the benefits of scheduling, container scheduling, and resource management in Kubernetes.

When data scientists have more flexible access to the resources they need (e.g., GPUs), they can build models faster. This in turn allows the line of business to evaluate a data product faster to see if it can be effective enough to be viable for the organization.

Building a Transfer Learning Pipeline

Let's use a computer vision scenario to better understand how Kubeflow might be deployed to solve a real problem. A realistic example would be a team wanting to get a computer vision transfer learning pipeline working for their team so they can build a custom computer vision model for detecting specific items in a retail store.

The team's basic plan consists of:

- Getting a basic computer vision model working from the TensorFlow model zoo (*https://oreil.ly/cVaxC*)
- Updating the model with an example dataset to understand transfer learning
- Moving the model training code to Kubeflow to take advantage of on-premise GPUs

The team starts off by experimenting with the object detection example notebook (*https://oreil.ly/iRKJE*) provided in the TensorFlow object detection tutorial. Once they have this notebook running locally, they know they can produce inferences for objects in an image with a pre-built TensorFlow computer vision model.

Next, the team wants to customize a computer vision model from the model zoo with their own dataset, but first they need to get a feel for how transfer learning works in practice. The team checks out the TensorFlow documentation on transfer learning (*https://oreil.ly/ysR4T*) to learn more about building a custom computer vision model.

Once they get the transfer learning example running with the custom dataset, it should not be hard to label some of their own product data to build the annotations needed to further train their own custom computer vision model.

The original flower example shows how to use the notebook on Google Cloud as a Google Colab notebook, but the team wants to leverage a cluster of GPUs they have in their own datacenter. At this point, the team sets up Kubeflow on their internal on-premise Kubernetes cluster and runs the transfer learning notebook as a Jupyter Notebook on Kubeflow. The team had previously built their own custom annotated dataset that they can now use for building models on their own internal Kubeflow cluster.

Advantages of running computer vision pipeline on Kubeflow

The major reasons the team moves their pipeline to Kubeflow are:

- Secure access to sensitive data for multiple users (data that may not be allowed to live on users' laptops)
- Cost savings by using on-premise GPUs
- Ability for multiple users to share the same cluster of GPUs

The team reasons that in some training scenarios, Kubeflow on-premise can be more cost-effective per GPU-hour than cloud GPUs. They also want to securely control where the core training dataset lives, and they want the ability to allow multiple data scientists to share the same consistent training dataset while trying different variations of models.

Team alignment for computer vision pipeline

This transfer learning scenario on Kubeflow allows the DevOps team to more tightly control who has a copy of the sensitive training data. The line of business has tasked the data science team with building a model that has a mAP score of a minimal level to be economically viable to the business unit.

To accomplish this modeling goal, the data science team needs to try many variations of hyperparameters and feature selection passes (in concert with the data engineering team) to drive up their model's effectiveness. The faster the data science team can train models, the more variations of training runs the team can try. In the case of deep learning and computer vision, GPUs make training runs take significantly less time, so these are a key resource for the data science team.

The business unit wants to hit their target minimum model effectiveness goal but they have to do so within a budget. Using Kubeflow on-premise with GPUs is a cheaper way to build models for the data science team, so costs end up being lower. The cost is forecasted as cheaper by the business unit because the data science team forecasts that they will need to model many times a week for a long period of time.

GPUs in the Cloud

GPUs in the cloud give us more flexibility than GPUs on-premise because we can spin them up ad hoc, on demand, making it more convenient to try new ideas.

However, this convenience may cost more than if we bought a GPU and used it locally all of the time.

The cost versus flexibility trade-off is something we should always keep in mind when deciding where to run our jobs.

Using Kubeflow on-premise with GPUs also allows the data science team to model faster, while running multiple computer vision jobs on the cluster at the same time, under the multitenant nature of the system.

Deploying Models to Production for Application Integration

Once a model is trained, it typically exists as a single file on a laptop or server host. We then need to do one of the following:

- Copy the file to the machine with the application for integration.
- Load the model into a server process that can accept network requests for model inference.

If we choose to copy the model file around to a single application host, then this is manageable. However, when we have many applications seeking to get model inference output from a model this becomes more complex.

One major issue involves updating the model once it has been deployed to production. This becomes more work as we need to track the model version on more machines and remember which ones need to be updated.

Another issue is rolling back a model once deployed. If we have deployed a model and then realize that we need to roll the version back to the previous model version, this is a lot of work when we have a lot of copies of the model floating around out there on different hosts. Let's now take a look at some advantages if we use a model hosting pattern for deploying a model to production with Kubeflow.

Advantages of deploying models to production on Kubeflow

A major advantage of having a machine learning model loaded in a model server on Kubeflow is that we can do updates and rollbacks from a single point (e.g., the server process). This allows us to treat a model more like a database table, in that we can apply operations to the model, and then all of the consuming client applications get the updates as soon as the update transaction is complete and they make their next inference request.

Team alignment for model deployment

The model server pattern makes life for the DevOps team considerably easier as they don't have to manually track many model copies. The application engineering team can focus on consuming the model as an internal REST resource on the network, and less on writing specific machine learning API code to integrate a model.

Once the data science team has developed models that the line of business wishes to put into production, the model server pattern allows them to hand the model to the DevOps team to put into production on the model server. This allows the data science team to get out of having to support individual models in production and focus on building the next round of models with the lines of business.

Components of Kubeflow

The logical component groupings of Kubeflow are:

- ML tools
- Applications and scaffolding
- Platforms/clouds

The relationships among the component groups can be seen in Figure 1-5.

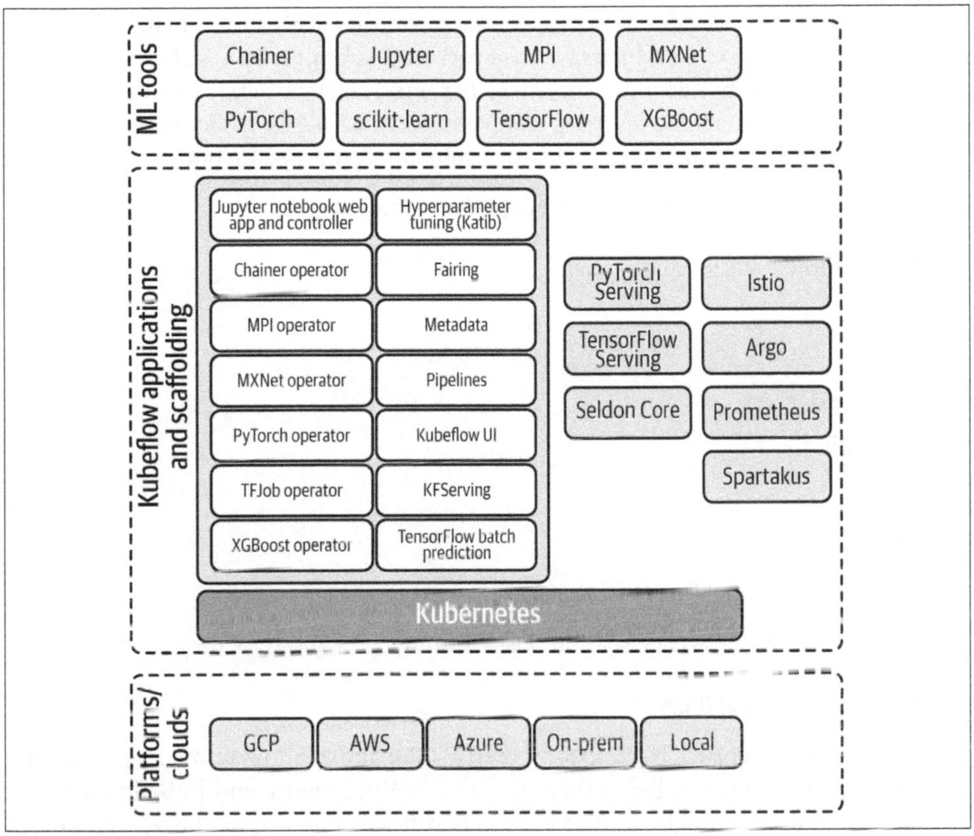

Figure 1-5. Kubeflow platform overview (source: Kubeflow documentation (https:// oreil.ly/QhP2C))

These components work together to provide a scalable and secure system for running machine learning jobs (notebook-based jobs and also jobs outside of notebooks).

Given the rise of Kubernetes as an enterprise platform management system, it makes a lot of sense to have a way to manage our machine learning workloads in a similar manner. In the rest of this section we take a look at each of the component groups, some of their components, and how they are used within the Kubeflow platform.

Machine Learning Tools

Many machine learning frameworks are supported by Kubeflow. In theory, a user could just containerize an arbitrary framework and submit it to a Kubernetes cluster to execute. However, Kubeflow makes Kubernetes clusters aware of the execution nuances that each machine learning library expects or needs to do, such as parallel training on multiple Kubernetes nodes, or using GPUs on specific nodes.

The current training frameworks supported by Kubeflow are:

- TensorFlow
- XGBoost
- Keras
- scikit-learn
- PyTorch
- MXNet
- MPI
- Chainer

Next, we'll give a brief overview about a few frameworks and how they're used.

TensorFlow training and TFJob

TensorFlow is supported by Kubeflow and is the most popular machine learning library in the world today. Being that TensorFlow, Kubernetes, and Kubeflow were all created originally at Google, it makes sense that it was the original library supported by Kubeflow.

As we mentioned, TFJob (*https://oreil.ly/nhiDa*) is a custom component for Kubeflow which contains (*https://oreil.ly/IK69t*) a Kubernetes custom resource descriptor (CRD) and an associated controller (tf-operator (*https://oreil.ly/MSxZa*)). The TFJob CRD (*https://oreil.ly/AqLHm*) is what enables Kubernetes to execute distributed (*https://oreil.ly/wPoTI*) TensorFlow (*https://www.tensorflow.org*) jobs. The TFJob controller (`tf-operator`) is part of the supporting applications and scaffolding included in Kubeflow to enable machine learning libraries on Kubernetes.

Check out the Kubeflow documentation page on TensorFlow (*https://oreil.ly/5LEIb*).

Keras

Keras is supported in the Kubeflow project and can be used in several ways:

- Single-process job run as a custom resource definition (CRD)
- Single-process GPU job run as a CRD
- TFJob as a single-worker job
- TFJob as a distributed-worker job (via the Estimator API)
- Jupyter Notebook (CPU or GPU)
- Kubeflow Pipelines–configured job

Many times, a user may just want to understand how to quickly get a job on the cluster. In Example 1-1, we show the simplest way to run a Keras job on Kubernetes as a job from the command line with kubectl.

Example 1-1. Job example YAML to run a Keras Python script

```
apiVersion: batch/v1
kind: Job
metadata:
  name: keras-job
spec:
  template:
    spec:
      containers:
      - name: tf-keras-gpu-job
        image: emsixteeen/basic_python_job:v1.0-gpu
        imagePullPolicy: Always
      volumes:
      - name: home
        persistentVolumeClaim:
          claimName: working-directory
      restartPolicy: Never
  backoffLimit: 1
```

In the preceding example, Kubernetes would pull the container image from the default container repository and then execute it as a pod on the Kubernetes cluster.

In this example, we're skipping all the other more complex ways of using Kubeflow and running the Keras script as a simple and direct Kubernetes pod. However, when we do this, we lose the advantages of Kubeflow around workflow orchestration and metadata collection.

The Case for Kubeflow Over Just Kubernetes

Without workflow orchestration and metadata tracking, we lose the ability to reliably and consistently execute machine learning workflows and understand how they are performing as we change our training code.

Example 1-1 shows that while you can run simple machine learning scripts easily on Kubernetes, Kubeflow provides further value on top of Kubernetes that may not be immediately recognized.

Applications and Scaffolding

Managing machine learning infrastructure under all of the constraints and goals we've described in this chapter is a tall mountain to climb. Kubeflow provides many subapplications and scaffolding components to help support the full machine learning workflow experience.

Some of the "scaffolding" components that are "under the hood," from the perspective of most users, include:

- Machine learning framework operators
- Metadata
- PyTorch serving
- Seldon Core
- TensorFlow Serving
- Istio
- Argo
- Prometheus
- Spartakus

Many of the above components are never used directly by a normal user, but instead support core functionality in Kubeflow. For example, Istio (*https://istio.io*) supports operations of the Kubeflow distributed microservice architecture by providing functionality such as role-based access control (RBAC) for network endpoints and resources. Argo (*https://argoproj.github.io*) provides continuous integration and deployment functionality for Kubeflow. Prometheus (*https://prometheus.io*) provides systems in Kubeflow with monitoring of components, and the ability to query for past events in monitoring data.

In the following subsections we'll take a closer look at some of the key applications and components in Kubeflow.

Kubeflow UI

The Kubeflow UI is the central hub for a user's activity on the Kubeflow platform. We can see the main screen of Kubeflow in Figure 1-6.

Figure 1-6. The Kubeflow UI

From the Kubeflow UI we can visually performs tasks such as creating Pipelines, running hyperparameter optimization jobs with Katib, and launching Jupyter Notebook servers.

Jupyter Notebooks

Jupyter Notebooks are included with the Kubeflow platform as a core component. These notebooks are popular due to their ease of use and are commonly associated (in machine learning especially) with the Python programming language. Notebooks typically contain code (e.g., Python, Java) and other visual rich-text elements that mimic a web page or textbook.

Notebooks and Different Programming Languages

A notebook kernel is what executes the code in a notebook. There can be different kernels depending on what type of language is embedded in the document.

The Jupyter name is a portmanteau of Julia, Python, and R, the original three languages supported by the Jupyter Ecosystem. While Jupyter Notebooks are only loosely connected to Python, a Python-based notebook will use the IPython kernel, for instance. The Jupyter Notebook App automatically detects the language used for the current running notebook and loads the appropriate kernel for us.

A novel aspect of notebooks is that they combine the concept of a computer program with the notes we typically associate with complex logic in our programs. This in-line documenting property allows a notebook user a better way to not only document what they're doing but to communicate it better to other users that may want to run our code. Given the complexity of machine learning code, this property has been part of the reason we see their explosive popularity in the machine learning space.

Jupyter Notebook integration with Kubeflow. The Kubeflow application deployment includes support for spawning and operating Jupyter Notebooks. Advantages of having Jupyter Notebooks integrated into the Kubeflow platform include:

- Good integration with the rest of the Kubeflow infrastructure from the point of view of authentication and access control
- Ability to share notebooks between users

Notebooks and Fairing

Jupyter Notebooks in Kubeflow also have access to the Fairing library, enabling the notebooks to submit training jobs to Kubernetes from the notebook. This is compelling, because code in a Jupyter Notebook only uses the default single process execution mode. The ability to submit jobs to Kubernetes from the notebook allows us to leverage TFJob to run distributed training jobs.

Sometimes we want separate notebook servers for each user or for a team. Kubeflow allows us to set up multiple notebook servers for a given Kubeflow deployment. Each notebook server belongs to a namespace, and can serve and execute multiple notebooks. Namespaces in Kubeflow also give us multiuser isolation. This means we can have multiple sets of users who can't see one another's resources so that they don't clutter one another's workspaces on the shared multitenant infrastructure.

Kubeflow will launch a container image on Kubernetes for each notebook server. The notebook image containers dependencies such as the libraries for ML and CPU or GPU support in the notebook.

Operators for machine learning frameworks

Each supported machine learning framework on Kubeflow has an associated controller (e.g., `tf-operator` (*https://oreil.ly/qCcmW*)). For example, the TFJob CRD (*https://oreil.ly/zxYwo*) is what makes Kubernetes able to execute distributed (*https://oreil.ly/_K61u*) TensorFlow (*https://www.tensorflow.org*) jobs. The TFJob controller (`tf-operator`) is part of the supporting applications and scaffolding Kubeflow includes to enable machine learning libraries on Kubernetes.

Metadata and artifacts

The metadata (*https://oreil.ly/SCAue*) component in Kubeflow helps users track and manage their ML workflows by collecting and storing the metadata produced by workflows. The information collected about a workflow by the metadata system in Kubeflow includes executions, models, datasets, and other artifacts. Kubeflow defines artifacts in this context as the objects and files that form the inputs and outputs of the components in a machine learning workflow, which we discuss further in Chapter 2.

Once code is run that has the `kubeflow-metadata` API collecting metadata for a workflow, you can go to the Artifacts tab in your Kubeflow UI and see the metadata collected per execution run, as seen in Figure 1-7.

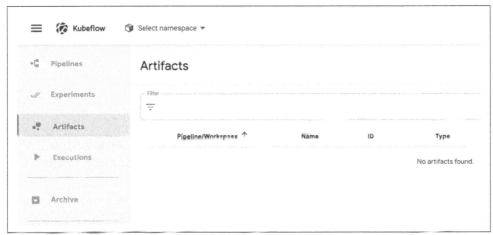

Figure 1-7. The Artifact tab page in the Kubeflow UI

Hyperparameter tuning

Hyperparameter tuning involves exploring the hyperparameter search space to find an optimal (or near optimal) set of hyperparameters for training a machine learning model. Data scientists spend a nontrivial amount of time trying combinations of hyperparameters, and seeing how much more accurate their model can be as a result.

Machine Learning, Parameters, and Hyperparameters

Let's take a quick detour and define some machine learning terminology. Previously in this chapter we defined machine learning as:

> Using algorithms for acquiring structural descriptions from data examples.

In machine learning we are searching for a set of function coefficients that maximize our model's accuracy (or value) with respect to a set of ground-truth labels. This set of function coefficients is sometimes referred to as *parameters*. For example, in neural networks, parameters are the weights on the connections between the artificial neu-rons in the layers.

From the context of machine learning, we can say:

> In machine learning, we have both model parameters and parameters we tune to make networks train better and faster. These tuning parameters are called hyperpara-meters, and they deal with controlling optimization functions and model selection during training with our learning algorithm.
>
> —*Deep Learning* by Josh Patterson and Adam Gibson (O'Reilly)

Examples of hyperparameters include:

- Learning rate
- Regularization
- Momentum
- Sparsity
- Type of loss function
- Optimization algorithm

The process of hyperparameter tuning involves trying different combinations of the above training options to find a combination of parameters for our model that give us the best model accuracy for our target problem.

The included hyperparameter search application with Kubeflow is called Katib (*https://oreil.ly/nhLlg*). Katib, originally inspired by an internal Google system named Vizier, was focused on being machine learning framework agnostic. It lets us create a number of experiments to test trials for hyperparameter evaluation. Currently, Katib supports exploration algorithms such as random search, grid search, and more.

Pipelines

Kubeflow Pipelines (*https://oreil.ly/RG088*) allows us to build machine learning work-flows and deploy them as a logical unit on Kubeflow to be run as containers on Kubernetes. While many times we see machine learning examples in a single Jupyter Notebook or Python script, machine learning workflows are typically not a single script or job.

Previously in this chapter we introduced Figure 1-8, from "Hidden Technical Debt in Machine Learning."

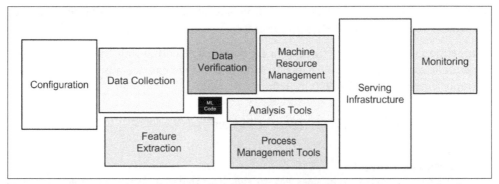

Figure 1-8. Diagram from the paper "Hidden Technical Debt in Machine Learning"

Many of the boxes in this diagram end up as their own subworkflows in practice in a production machine learning system. Examples of this can be seen in how data collection and feature engineering each may be their own workflows built by teams separate from the data science team. Model evaluation is another component we often see performed as its own workflow after the training phase is complete.

Kubeflow Pipelines (see Figure 1-9) simplify the orchestration of these pipelines as containers on Kubernetes infrastructure. This gives our teams the ability to reconfigure and deploy complex machine learning pipelines in a modular fashion to speed model deployment and time to production.

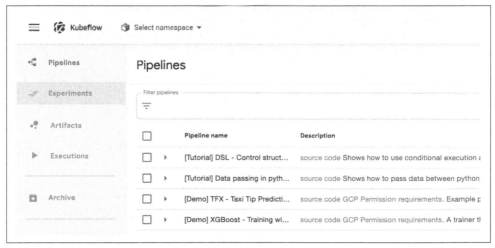

Figure 1-9. Pipeline user interface

Basic Kubeflow Pipeline concepts.   A Kubeflow Pipeline is a directed acyclic graph (DAG) representing all of the components in the workflow. Pipelines define input parameter slots required to run the pipeline, and then how each component's output is wired as input to the next stage in the graph.

A pipeline component is defined as a Docker image containing the user code and dependencies to run on Kubernetes. In Example 1-2 we can see a pipeline definition example (*https://oreil.ly/YdVb7*) in Python.

Example 1-2. Kubeflow Pipeline defined in Python

```
@dsl.pipeline(
  name='XGBoost Trainer',
  description='A trainer that does end-to-end distributed training for XGBoost models.'
)
def xgb_train_pipeline(
    output,
    project,
    region='us-central1',
    train_data='gs://ml-pipeline-playground/sfpd/train.csv',
    eval_data='gs://ml-pipeline-playground/sfpd/eval.csv',
    schema='gs://ml-pipeline-playground/sfpd/schema.json',
    target='resolution',
    rounds=200,
    workers=2,
    true_label='ACTION',
):
    delete_cluster_op = DeleteClusterOp('delete-cluster',
      project, region).apply(gcp.use_gcp_secret('user-gcp-sa'))
    with dsl.ExitHandler(exit_op=delete_cluster_op):
    create_cluster_op = CreateClusterOp('create-cluster', project, region,
      output).apply(gcp.use_gcp_secret('user-gcp-sa'))

    analyze_op = AnalyzeOp('analyze', project, region, create_cluster_op.output, \
      schema,
      train_data, '%s/{{workflow.name}}/analysis' % \
        output).apply(gcp.use_gcp_secret('user-gcp-sa'))

    transform_op = TransformOp('transform', project, region, create_cluster_op.output,
      train_data, eval_data, target, analyze_op.output,
      '%s/{{workflow.name}}/transform' % \
        output).apply(gcp.use_gcp_secret('user-gcp-sa'))

    train_op = TrainerOp('train', project, region, create_cluster_op.output, \
      transform_op.outputs['train'],
      transform_op.outputs['eval'], target, analyze_op.output, workers,
      rounds, '%s/{{workflow.name}}/model' % \
        output).apply(gcp.use_gcp_secret('user-gcp-sa'))
...
```

If we look at this graph in the Pipelines UI in Kubeflow, it would look similar to Figure 1-10.

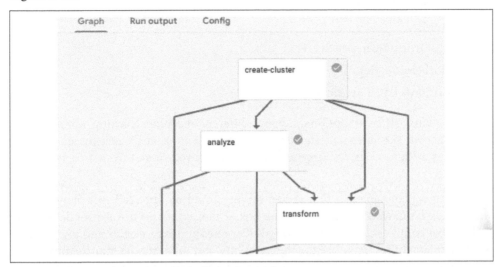

Figure 1-10. Visualization in Kubeflow of a pipeline

The Kubeflow Pipelines UI further allows us to define input parameters per run and then launch the job. The saved outputs from the pipeline include graphs such as a confusion matrix and receiver operating characteristics (ROC) curves.

Kubeflow Pipelines produce and store both metadata and artifacts from each run. Metadata from pipeline runs are stored in a MySQL database, and artifacts are stored in an artifact store such as MinIO (*https://docs.min.io*) server or a cloud storage system. Both MinIO and MySQL are both backed by PersistentVolumes (PV) (*https:// oreil.ly/B0Fvt*) in Kubernetes.

The metadata saved allows Kubeflow to track specific experiments and jobs run on the cluster. The artifacts save information so that we can investigate an individual job's run performance.

Machine Learning Model Inference Serving with KFServing

Once we've constructed a model, we need to integrate the saved model with our applications. Kubeflow offers multiple ways to load saved models into a process for serving live model inference to external applications. These options include:

- KFServing
- Seldon Core Serving
- BentoML
- Nvidia Triton Inference Server
- TensorFlow Serving
- TensorFlow Batch Prediction

The preceding different options support different machine learning libraries, and have their own sets of specific features. Typically, each has a Docker image that you can run as a Kubernetes resource and then load a saved model from a repository of models.

KFServing was designed so that model serving could be operated in a standardized way across frameworks right out of the box. There was a need for a model serving system that could easily run on existing Kubernetes and Istio stacks, and also provide model explainability, inference graph operations, and other model management functions. Kubeflow needed to allow both data scientists and DevOps/MLOps teams to collaborate from model production to modern production model deployment.

KFServing's core value can be expressed as:

- Helping to standardize model serving across orgs with unified data-plane and pre-built model servers
- A single way to deploy, monitor inference services/server, and scale inference workload
- Dramatically shortens time for the data scientist to deploy model to production

---

What Is a Model Inference?

A machine learning model inference server takes new input values and passes them as vectors to a saved model to produce output. This output is referred to as a "model inference."

In some cases, a framework-specific inference server (e.g., TensorFlow Serving) may have specialized features for an associated framework.

Many teams, however, will use different frameworks and will need more flexibility for their model inference serving infrastructure. In this case you should consider KFServing or Seldon Core, as described earlier. In Chapter 8 we cover KFServing in detail, from the core concepts involved in deploying a basic model on KFServing, to building custom model servers for model deployment on KFServing.

Platforms and Clouds

Kubeflow has the flexibility to be deployed anywhere that Kubernetes can be deployed, from a major public cloud, to an on-premise Kubernetes cluster, and also a local single-node Kubernetes deployment on a single machine.

Public clouds

Given that all three major cloud vendors support both managed Kubernetes and then the ability to deploy Kubernetes manually on VMs, Kubeflow can be deployed on any of the major clouds, including:

- Google Cloud Platform (GCP)
- Amazon Web Services (AWS)
- Azure Cloud Platform

Later chapters dig into the specifics of the installation and configurations of each of these clouds. We'll also inform you about what each major cloud offers and how it integrates with the managed Kubernetes offering for the cloud. This will give you a solid view of how appropriate your preferred cloud is for running their Kubernetes and Kubeflow infrastructure.

Installing Kubeflow on a public cloud requires a few things, including:

- Understanding how the cloud vendor integrates with your own infrastructure
- Making sure it's the right version of Kubernetes (and other subcomponents) for your organization
- Security integration themes

Beyond vendor dogmatic themes, a dominant narrative in infrastructure is how a system can be integrated as legacy momentum in enterprise infrastructure. When executed well, this narrative produces consistent value for any enterprise.

> ## Consider the Options for Cloud-Based Kubeflow
>
> Manually running your own Kubeflow installation can be complex. If you are using a single cloud with stock Kubeflow, your team may want to consider using managed notebooks, serverless training and predictions, and a prescriptive pipeline approach like TFX that will do the pipeline steps on serverless infrastructure. Examples would be SageMaker on AWS (*https://oreil.ly/iIWzf*) or CAIP on GCP (*https://oreil.ly/7jJ6m*).
>
> If your install needs complex customizations (e.g., custom container images or custom networking requirements) then managing your own Kubeflow installation on the cloud may make more sense.

Managed Kubernetes in the cloud.   As mentioned previously in this chapter, all three major clouds offer an open source-compatible version of managed Kubernetes:

- Google Kubernetes Engine (GKE)
- Azure Kubernetes Services (AKS)
- Amazon Kubernetes Engine (AKE)

Each system has similarities and differences in how we install and integrate Kubeflow. There are, of course, variations in how to do a Kubeflow installation for every cloud, such as:

- Storage types and strategies
- Identity setup and management
- Container management strategies
- ETL pipeline integration
- Planning infrastructure and modeling cost

Over the course of this book we will introduce you to the core concepts for each cloud offering, and then show how to install Kubeflow specifically for each of the cloud platforms.

On-premise

Kubeflow is supported as deployed on an on-premise Kubernetes cluster. The major differences between Kubeflow on an on-premise cluster and Kubeflow on a major cloud is that an on-premise cluster will have more limitations on how much you can scale resources dynamically. However, an on-premise cluster is not billable by the hour, so there is certainly a trade-off every organization must make.

As we'll see throughout this book, there are also different strategies for identity integration for on-premise Kubernetes versus cloud Kubernetes.

Local

In some cases—mainly testing, development, and evaluation—a user may want to run Kubeflow on a local machine or VM. In this case you can either use VMs to set up a small Kubernetes cluster locally, or you could try a pre-built single-node Kubernetes system such as Minikube (*https://oreil.ly/oRT4P*).

> **Running Kubeflow Locally Can Take a Lot of Resources**
>
> Typically, a Kubeflow on Minikube deployment needs at least 12 GB of memory and 4 CPUs allocated for Minikube. You should also consider how many resources your computer will need, in addition to these requirements, to normally operate.

In Chapter 8 we take you through an exercise in deploying KFServing standalone on Minikube locally to test out model deployment.

Summary

In this introductory chapter we covered the impetus for Kubeflow as a machine learning platform. As we move forward through this book, we'll come to understand how to plan, install, maintain, and develop on the Kubeflow platform as a key cornerstone in our machine learning infrastructure. In the next chapter, we'll take you through the security fundamentals and architecture of Kubeflow to set up the operations content for the rest of the book.

## CHAPTER 2

Kubeflow Architecture and Best Practices

In this chapter we'll continue to build on the introductory concepts from Chapter 1 to dive into the architecture of Kubeflow, and then close out the chapter with best practices for using Kubeflow.

In the first part of this chapter, we'll focus on Kubeflow's architecture and how the components work together to form the platform. When supporting complex distributed systems, DevOps teams need to have an idea which components are talking to which other components in the system. This helps set context when triaging issues with a Kubeflow cluster.

This architectural background sets up the second part of the chapter, where we'll introduce best practices for using Kubeflow. Subsequent chapters will focus on either installing Kubeflow on a specific platform or deploying models on KFServing. In both situations you are better served understanding the architecture and how best to use the system as you build out your custom Kubeflow platform.

Kubeflow Architecture Overview

In Figure 2-1, we can see the high-level architecture of Kubeflow. This diagram shows the request flow from the user into components of Kubeflow via the CLI or `kubectl` to operate the Kubeflow system.

We use the Kubeflow system to set up machine learning workflows that run a job or a series of jobs to build machine learning models. A job in Kubeflow can be a Jupyter Notebook or it can be a Python script in a series of pipeline-connected jobs. A job in Kubeflow can also be as simple as running a Python script in a container on a pod in Kubernetes via `kubectl`.

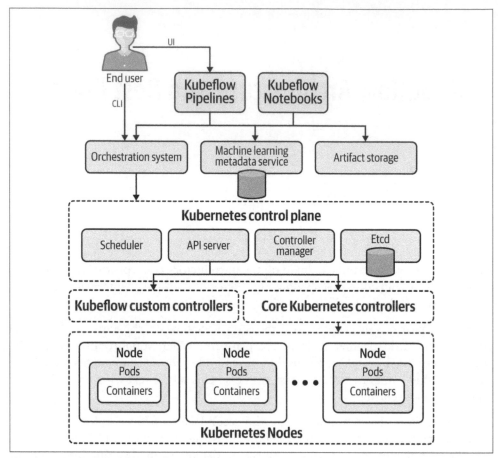

Figure 2-1. High-level Kubeflow architecture

Some components not listed here but which are used "under the hood" by Kubeflow include Istio, Argo, and Prometheus. Istio provides functionality such as RBAC for network endpoints and secures communications between the different components of Kubeflow. Argo provides continuous integration and deployment functionality for Kubeflow. Prometheus provides component monitoring and the ability to query for past events in the captured data.

Kubeflow is built from multiple separate components in a service mesh to provide the full machine learning platform. Istio supports operations of the Kubeflow distributed microservice architecture by providing features such as secure communications, discovery, load balancing, failure recovery, metrics, and monitoring.

Fundamental to operating a Kubeflow cluster is controlling access to resources. Kubeflow is built on the security infrastructure of Kubernetes and Istio, as shown in the user request flow in Figure 2-2.

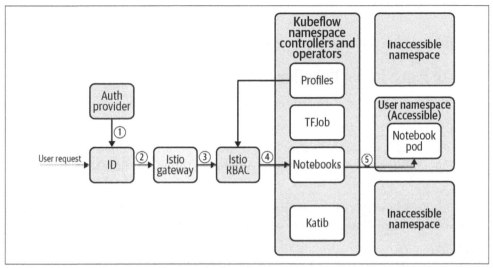

Figure 2-2. Istio usage in Kubeflow for a user request

Let's now take a look at how Kubeflow and Kubernetes work together before we move on to learn how to run and manage jobs on Kubeflow.

Kubeflow and Kubernetes

In Chapter 1, you learned how the Kubeflow architecture solves problems in the machine learning platform space beyond the Kubernetes API. The Kubeflow architecture and components also work together on top of Kubernetes with the communications managed by Istio to operate the Kubeflow system.

Some of the install scripts available with the open source Kubeflow project will create a new Kubernetes cluster for you on specific cloud vendors. In other cases, the install script will only install Kubeflow on an existing Kubernetes cluster. In some instances (e.g., GCP GPU pools), Kubeflow allows for dynamic allocation of Kubernetes resources as needed to be cost efficient. In most on-premise cases, the number of available Kubernetes worker nodes (resources) will be fixed and nondynamic.

Kubeflow provides the orchestration and metadata tracking for the system so that it can leverage the lower-level Kubernetes API to do tasks such as container orchestration. Kubeflow is focused on machine learning specific operations, where Kubernetes is concentrated more generally on secure, scalable, resilient application deployment that is unaware of the specifics of machine learning.

> **More Information About Kubernetes**
>
> For more information about Kubernetes, logging, and debugging, check out Appendices A through C.

Let's now move on to discuss the ways in which we can run jobs on Kubeflow.

Ways to Run a Job on Kubeflow

There are three ways to run a machine learning job on Kubeflow:

CLI
> With the CLI, we can use `kubectl` to launch a Python container to run a Python script. This script may (or may not) write metadata back to the Kubeflow system.

Pipelines
> With Kubeflow Pipelines, we construct a DAG of operations in a configuration file (or via the UI) to schedule a series of orchestrated jobs on Kubeflow.

Notebooks
> With notebooks, we launch a notebook server that may run one or more notebooks. From there each notebook can run different code on the same notebook server. Later in this chapter we dig into the architecture of the notebook server launcher and notebook server system.

Machine Learning Metadata Service

Metadata about the machine learning workflows and jobs in Kubeflow are collected and stored in the Machine Learning Metadata Service. This metadata service is backed by a MySQL database.

The metadata saved allows Kubeflow to track specific experiments and jobs run on the cluster. The artifacts save information so that we can investigate an individual job's run performance.

In the context of Kubeflow, metadata means information about artifacts, including the following:

- Executions (runs)
- Models
- Datasets

Separately, in Kubeflow, *artifacts* refers to pipeline packages, views, and large-scale metrics (time series).

The Kubeflow Pipelines UI further allows us to define input parameters per run and then launch the job. The saved outputs from the pipeline include graphs such as a confusion matrix and ROC curves.

Kubeflow Pipelines produce and store both metadata and artifacts for each run. Metadata from pipeline runs is stored in the Kubeflow Machine Learning Metadata Service.

Storage, Metadata, and Artifacts

Both MinIO and MySQL are backed by PersistentVolumes in Kubernetes.

Artifact Storage

Artifacts in Kubeflow refer to pipeline packages, views, and large-scale metrics (time series). Artifacts are treated differently than metadata and are stored in an artifact store such as MinIO server or a cloud storage system.

Artifacts should end up in an object store (e.g., S3 or GCS). MinIO can either be used to provide a common interface to S3 or GCS, or as a way to create in-cluster object storage (e.g., when running on-premise).

Istio Operations In Kubeflow

Istio is used as a foundational part of Kubeflow, such that Istio secures service-to-service communication in a Kubeflow deployment, using strong identity-based authentication and authorization.

Kubeflow also uses Istio for its policy layer to support quotas and access control. Istio also provides cluster ingress and egress support for automatic logs, metrics, and traces for network traffic.

Looking again at Figure 2-2, we can see how a user request interacts with the different security and Istio components, and the interaction flow for how users work with services in Kubeflow. You can see how the user request is intercepted by the identification proxy ("ID") and (1) communicates with the single sign-on service provider (e.g., Auth Provider, examples include IAM on AWS, or Active Directory and LDAP on-premise). Once the user is authenticated (2), the request is sent on to the Istio gateway. If the user request doesn't have a JSON Web Token (JWT), it gets redirected to an Open ID Connect (OIDC) provider which attaches the JWT.

The redirection can happen in a couple of places. One way the JWT token can be added is before the request hits the Istio gateway. This variant is what happens when something like Identity-Aware Proxy (IAP) is used with Kubeflow. In IAP, when the request goes through the Google Cloud Load Balancer (GCLB), it will redirect the request to have a user login. A cookie then gets cached on the client which is attached in subsequent requests. Subsequent requests will then get the JWT attached by the GCLB.

In other Kubeflow architectures (e.g., with Dex), Istio is configured to redirect requests without JWTs to an identity provider like Dex.

The Istio gateway modifies the request to include the JWT header token containing the user identity. It's worth noting that all associated user requests traveling through the service mesh will also carry this JWT header token.

After the Istio gateway adds the JWT token to the request, Istio RBAC policies are applied (3) to incoming requests to validate access to the service for the given namespace. If the Istio RBAC policy returns DENY, then an error response is sent back for the request.

If the Istio RBAC policy returns ALLOW for the pending request validation, then the request is sent on to the appropriate component of controller. In Figure 2-2 we can see the request being forwarded (4) to the notebook's controller in Kubeflow.

The target controller will then validate authorization with Kubernetes RBAC and creates the resources required within the user-provided namespace. In the case of the example in Figure 2-2, then the notebook controller creates a notebook pod in the user's namespace.

Each further related action by the user will go through the same set of validation steps. In Kubeflow 1.0, the profiles controller manages the creation of profiles, which are covered in more detail later in this chapter. The profiles controller also will apply the appropriate Istio policies for a profile.

Istio and KFServing

In Chapter 1, we introduced you to KFServing and model hosting. KFServing also uses Istio as a foundational part of how it manages models as infrastructure.

In Figure 2-3 we can see an overview of how KFServing uses Istio under the hood.

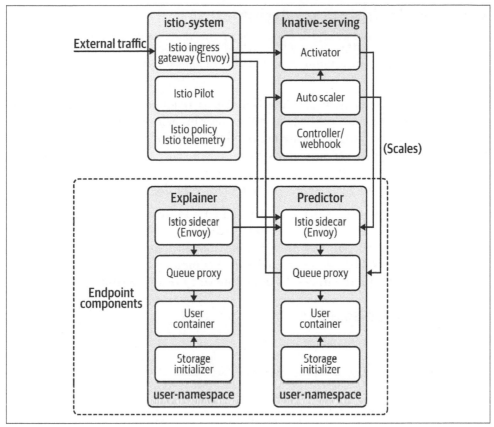

Figure 2-3. Istio traffic management in KFServing

Kubeflow uses Istio to specifically:

- Secure service-to-service communication in a Kubeflow deployment via identity-based authentication and authorization.
- Automate metrics, traces, and logs for traffic within the deployment.

In Chapter 8, we look more closely at KFServing and the need to scale out inference serving. In this context, a service mesh becomes compelling as we may need multiple servers all serving the same model while being represented by the same logical endpoint. These groups of microservices need to be uniformly secured, monitored, and connected. Istio is critical to how this happens in KFServing, as we'll see in Chapter 8.

Kubeflow Multitenancy Architecture

Multitenancy in the context of Kubeflow can be thought of as multiple users sharing a Kubeflow installation or a number of Kubeflow installations within a single Kubernetes cluster.

In the context of security, if absolute isolation is required, it can be achieved by deploying a separate Kubeflow installation per user in their own namespace. To facilitate multitenancy (in part), users are provided with their own namespace in the cluster, and all their pods, services, deployments, jobs, etc., are encapsulated in their namespace. Control plane security is provided at the namespace level, while application-level security is a large motivating factor for this document.

Multitenancy is how we set up a cluster of shared resources and then allow multiple tenants (users) to access the cluster through scheduling. While there is overhead in setting up a multitenant cluster, it is preferable from an operations standpoint in contrast to giving users direct access to individual computers. Let's now take a look at some of the advantages and trade-offs of multitenancy versus isolating users.

Multitenancy and Isolation

Other properties of multitenancy include:

- Isolation of user storage and workloads
- Load balancing
- Users sharing a single machine's resources

Advantages of setting up a shared cluster with Kubernetes include:

- Resource scheduling
- Security integration with Kerberos and Active Directory (AD)
- Heterogeneous GPU support (*https://oreil.ly/p3pL3*)
- More efficient use of expensive resources
- Node-level user access so certain types of jobs have priority over others

Dealing with the implications of multitenancy falls under the direction of the DevOps team, and they obviously have a lot of things to consider, as shown in Figure 2-3. The data science team really only care if they can run their Python job on GPUs; the DevOps team need to make that happen while also worrying about running these container-based workloads in a secure scheduled environment along with other users.

Multiuser Architecture

Kubeflow consists of a number of web applications (e.g., the Kubeflow Dashboard, Jupyter Notebooks, the pipelines UI, etc.) as well as APIs (e.g., the pipelines and Katib APIs) that users need to be able to access from their local machine. To provide a secure, multiuser deployment, we must solve two problems:

- We need to verify a user's identity (authentication).
- We need to restrict access to Kubeflow and services within Kubeflow based on identity (authorization).

At the same time, the goal of the multiuser architecture is for the user to have the same identity and RBAC permissions across both the web applications and the command-line kubectl access points.

Kubeflow provides a pluggable architecture for handling authentication and authorization that makes it easy to integrate the recommended solutions for a particular cloud or on-premise deployment.

A Kubeflow cluster has two user-access routes:

- The Kubeflow central dashboard
- The kubectl CLI

The central dashboard supports UI access to the Kubeflow suite of tools, and kubectl supports command-line access to the Kubernetes API for working with Kubeflow.

The kubectl path still authenticates and authorizes against the Kubernetes API server. However, the browser access path now authenticates with the identity-aware proxy (e.g., Istio gateway, Google Cloud IAP) to get the JWT token that all future session associate transactions will carry in their HTTP headers (e.g., identity).

Authenticated Entities

The authenticated entity here from the IAP can be a user (OIDC, Google IAP) or a ServiceAccount (TokenReview).

Multiuser Authorization Flow

For multiuser authorization in Kubeflow 1.0 for the web application authorization path, the system still consults the Kubernetes RBAC permissions.

A Kubeflow web application does this in one of two ways:

- Via the SubjectAccessReview API (*https://oreil.ly/buK1y*) in the Kubernetes API
- Via impersonation (*https://oreil.ly/6LpP6*) in the Kubernetes API

Kubeflow can use the SubjectAccessReview API to query the Kubernetes RBAC authorizer and check whether a user can perform a given action and that it will work regardless of the authorization mode being used. If the check passes, then the request is made with the web application's credentials.

The other method for authorization from a web application is to use impersonation headers via Kubernetes impersonation. In this case, the check is made by the Kubernetes API server on the impersonated identity. This method only uses one request and it passes through all authorization checks of Kubernetes, as some checks are not caught by the SubjectAccessReview API method.

Issues with Impersonation

While impersonation may sound like a better web application path for authorization, the drawback is that there is no way to scope it down. The Jupyter Notebook web application does not use it because it would have the full permissions of an impersonated user, creating potential for harm.

Given the issues with scope and impersonation, the Kubeflow team recommends the SubjectAccessReview API method as the preferred way to authorize users in web applications. Only use impersonation when the web application has privileged access anyway.

Kubeflow Profiles

Multitenancy in Kubeflow is based on user namespaces (e.g., profiles) and uses Kubernetes RBAC policies to manage access. Profiles govern a user and their access to specific resources, while bindings manage which users can edit a namespace.

Referencing Profiles and Namespaces in Kubeflow

There is a one-to-one correspondence of profiles with Kubernetes namespaces in Kubeflow. Because of this, sometimes you'll see the terms *profile* and *namespace* used interchangeably in the documentation.

Kubeflow profile custom resources control all policies, roles, and bindings for a user, and to guarantee consistency. Sometimes you may want to manage external resources or policies outside Kubernetes, and Kubeflow provides a plug-in interface for that scenario. A profile in Kubeflow owns a Kubernetes namespace with the same name and the associated Kubernetes resources.

Profile access management provides namespace-level isolation based on Kubernetes RBAC and Istio RBAC access control.

The profile custom resource manages the following resources:

- Kubernetes namespace of the profile owner
- Kubernetes RBAC RoleBinding (`namespaceAdmin`)
- Istio RBAC authorization policy (as explained later)
- Resource quota (`v1beta1`)
- Custom plug-ins (`v1beta1`)

The profile also sets up namespace-scoped service-accounts `editor` and `viewer` to be used by user-created pods in the associated namespace.

The Kubernetes RBAC rolebinding makes the profile owner the admin and allows access to the associated namespace via the Kubernetes API (`kubectl`).

Given that Kubeflow cannot run without Istio, the Istio setting for `clusterRbacCon fig` has to be set to `ON` to enable Istio RBAC for all services in Kubeflow. When a Kubeflow user profile is created, Kubeflow also creates an associated Istio authorization policy (`ServiceRole` and `ServiceRoleBinding`, previously covered under Istio RBAC).

Specifically, this Istio authorization policy creates a `ServiceRole` called `ns-access-istio` to allow access to all services in the target namespace via Istio routing.

Also, an Istio namespace-scoped `ServiceRoleBinding` named `owner-binding-istio` binds the `ServiceRole` (`ns-access-istio`) to the profile owner. This allows the profile owner to access services in the associated namespace via Istio, via a browser.

The Future of Profiles in Kubeflow

For now, from the standpoint of the Kubeflow project's evolution, profiles should be considered as the "sugar" to make coordinating namespaces, Kubernetes RBAC, and Istio RBAC all work together. Currently there is work going on in the Kubeflow project to rethink the concept of profiles, and they are likely to change considerably in the future.

Multiuser Isolation

A user should only be able to see resources that they are authorized by Kubeflow to see. This concept is called *multiuser isolation*. Separate users need reliable methods to protect and isolate their own resources with safeties in place to prevent accidentally viewing or changing another user's resources. An example of multiuser isolation is the Jupyter Notebook service.

The administrator account in Kubeflow creates and maintains the Kubeflow cluster. This account has the power to grant access permissions to other users and has the cluster-admin role in the Kubernetes cluster. This allows the administrator to create and modify resources in the cluster. The person or account that deployed Kubeflow will have administration privileges in the Kubeflow cluster.

A normal user account in Kubeflow will have access to a set of resources as specified by the profile resource. The administrator account can grant further access permissions to a user account as needed.

Profile access policies are set by the administrator or the owner of the profiles, and control access to notebooks (and the creation of notebooks). Users can self register to create their own new workspace via the UI. When we log in to Kubeflow and access our primary profile in Kubeflow, the profile associated with our account owns a Kubernetes namespace. You have view and modify access to your primary profile, and you're also allowed to share access to your profile with another user in the Kubeflow system.

Further, you have control over how other users can access your profile with settings such as read or read/modify. The same access created by the profile access policies for notebooks is inherited by resources created by the notebook.

Once a new user is invited to share another user's workspace, they can edit the workspace and operate Kubeflow custom resources.

Kubeflow 1.0 and Isolation

Currently with Kubeflow 1.0.2, not all components have full-fledged integration with isolation. They do, however, have access to the user identity through the headers of the incoming requests. As of the time of writing, notebooks are the first/only service to have multiuser isolation.

Kubeflow 1.0.2 has isolation support, but no hard guarantees around malicious attempts to hack other users profiles.

Notebook Architecture

You can set up multiple notebook servers per Kubeflow deployment. Each notebook server can include multiple notebooks (*.ipynb* files). Each notebook server belongs to a single namespace, which corresponds to the project group or team for that server.

Kubeflow provides a new Web UI to natively spawn Jupyter Notebooks in a Kubeflow environment. The term *notebooks* in Kubeflow refers to two things:

- The actual *.ipynb* notebook *file* the data scientist user will run
- The notebook *server* running the notebook (notebook controller)

The notebook server is launched as a pod in Kubernetes using a container image, and a user can run multiple notebook servers. Further, a notebook server can run multiple notebooks.

> **Kubeflow and JupyterHub**
>
> Kubeflow's notebook architecture does not use the JupyterHub project.

The notebook server has two subcomponents:

- The notebook server launcher UI
- The notebook controller that is run as its own pod, and can run multiple notebook files

Let's now look at both of these subcomponents.

Notebook Server Launcher UI

The notebook server launcher is referred to as the Jupyter Web App in the list of Kubeflow components in the GitHub repository (*https://oreil.ly/8rXFj*). It is a UI within the Kubeflow application that allows the user to launch a notebook custom resource. This interface allows users to create, connect, and delete notebooks from within Kubeflow. The notebook server launcher is a simple web application that provides a UI for creating and deleting Jupyter instances (running as custom resources on Kubernetes in a user's namespace).

The backend of the notebook server launcher uses Python Flask and Angular for the frontend. The pod hosting the Flask server has an associated `ServiceAccount` with proper `RBAC` resources configured. This allows the `jupyter-web-app` pod to manage the notebook custom resources and PVCs in the `kubeflow` namespace.

In Figure 2-4 you can see the notebook server launcher (*jupyter-web-app*) UI.

Figure 2-4. The notebook server launcher UI

From this UI you can click the +NEW SERVER button to create a new notebook server. You can also interact with existing notebook servers by connecting to the server or deleting the existing server.

The UI only executes calls related to notebook custom resources to the Kubernetes API server. Once the call to the Kubernetes API server is made, all calls related to management of child resources (`Deployment`, `Service`, etc.) are performed by the notebook custom resource controller.

When you click +NEW SERVER to create a new notebook server from this form, you are redirected to a form that allows you to configure the `PodTemplateSpec` properties for the new notebook server, as seen in Figure 2-5.

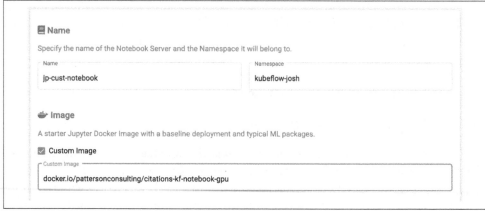

Figure 2-5. Configuring a notebook server with a custom image

The options you can configure are:

- Name
- Namespace
- CPU
- Memory
- Workspace volume
- Data volumes
- Extra resources

When you click the button at the bottom of the notebook server launcher form, a new notebook server is launched with the options set in the form in the kubeflow namespace. For options not specified, a default value will be applied.

Wait a Minute for the Notebook Server to Spawn

Sometimes it takes a few minutes for the notebook server pod to successfully be created. You'll want to wait to connect to the pod correctly or you may see errors such as upstream connect error due to the inability of Kubeflow to route traffic correctly.

Submitting the form causes the notebook server launcher application to emit an instance of the notebook CRD, submitting to the Kubernetes API. The notebook CRD then spawns the notebook server pod via the respective controller.

Older Versions of Kubeflow and Notebooks

Versions of Kubeflow before 0.6 used JupyterHub KubeSpawner to launch notebook servers.

Notebook Controller

The notebook controller (*https://oreil.ly/X6E1J*) allows users to create a custom resource notebook (Jupyter Notebook).

Behind the scenes, the notebook controller creates a StatefulSet to operate the notebook instance and also a service for it. The notebook server design allows for OIDC support and multitenancy for multiple applications. The authenticated JWT is validated in a sidecar by Istio. Further, Istio provides restricted access to Jupyter servers for specific users via HTTP.

The notebook server uses a privileged `ServiceAccount` that is allowed to manage notebook custom resources along with the associated PVCs in all namespaces.

Pipelines Architecture

In Figure 2-6 we can see the Kubeflow Pipelines architecture diagrammed out.

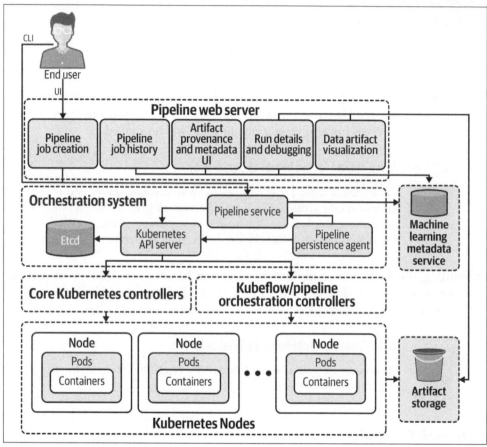

Figure 2-6. Kubeflow pipelines architecture diagram

The high-level execution of a Kubeflow Pipeline involves calling the Pipeline Service to create a static pipeline from a static configuration. For a pipeline configuration we need to use the Python SDK to write a pipeline script in the pipeline domain-specific language (DSL). The DSL compiler then will transform your pipeline configuration into a YAML file (static configuration).

From there, the Pipeline Service calls the Kubernetes API server to set up and execute the required Kubernetes resources (CRDs) to execute the pipeline. Some of these resources are orchestration controllers (e.g., the Argo Workflow Controller) that execute the containers needed to complete the pipeline. Pods in Kubernetes execute the containers that are run from the orchestration controllers on virtual machines in the cluster.

As the containers for the pipeline run on the Kubernetes cluster, they will write metadata and artifacts to the Machine Learning Metadata Service and Artifact Storage systems, respectively.

The Pipelines Persistence Agent tracks Kubernetes resources created by the Pipeline Service and writes the state of these resources in the Machine Learning Metadata Service. The inputs and outputs are tracked by the Pipelines Persistence Agent, which also tracks which containers were executed.

The list of pipelines currently running is maintained by the pipeline web server along with the history of pipeline execution. Other views maintained by the pipeline web server include:

- List of data artifacts
- Debugging information about individual pipeline runs
- Execution status about individual pipeline runs

At this point, we have covered a number of architecture topics; now we'll explore some best practices for users of the platform.

Kubeflow Best Practices

In this section we document some best practices to help users of the system better run their jobs. We cover foundational topics such as:

- Managing job dependencies
- Using GPUs with notebooks
- Writing metadata to the Machine Learning Metadata Service from jobs

Let's start out with the basics of adding dependencies to job.

Managing Job Dependencies

Many times we will be able to use stock Docker images for quick TensorFlow jobs. In the case that we're just running a container of Python code on Kubernetes via `kubectl`, we can just build in the dependencies in the container.

Some notebook users, however, who are less familiar with tools such as Docker, may still need to launch notebook servers with custom dependencies. There are two main methods for managing dependencies for notebooks in Kubeflow:

- Use `pip` to dynamically install dependencies from inside a notebook cell.
- Build a custom notebook Docker image with the dependencies already built in.

You'll choose one of these options based on the constraints you have for your execution context.

If you know you'll be using this same set of dependencies over and over, you may want to build your own Docker image for this specific Kubeflow Jupyter Notebook. Other reasons to build your own Docker images include:

- If you don't have permissions in your environment to run `pip` from the notebook
- If your Kubeflow cluster does not have internet access

Many Kubeflow clusters will have internet access, but in some cases with enterprise on-premise clusters you may see a Kubeflow cluster that has no internet connectivity for security considerations.

Dependency Best Practice

In both of these methods (building a new Docker image versus installing inside the notebook), installing dependencies from a *requirements.txt* file is a best practice.

Ideally we'd just pull in our dependencies inside the notebook. However, in some cases our code may depend on dependencies that are persnickety[1] about installing, so we need more control about how it is installed in the local image environment. In this case, we're going to have to build a custom Docker image based to run our GPU notebook on Kubeflow, as you will see in the next section.

Building a custom notebook Docker image

In Example 2-1, you can see the `dockerfile` code we need to build our new Docker image.

---

1 `rtree` comes to mind here, not to point any fingers.

Example 2-1. Hello World in Python

```
# Create Docker image for the demo
#
# This Docker image is based on existing notebook image
# It also includes the dependencies required for training and deploying
# This way we can use it as the base image

FROM gcr.io/kubeflow-images-public/tensorflow-2.1.0-notebook-gpu:1.0.0

COPY requirements.txt .

# We want to install the requirements in the system directory so we need to
# switch to root
USER root
RUN apt -y install libspatialindex-dev
RUN pip3 --no-cache-dir install -r requirements.txt
USER jovyan
```

In this code listing we're just using an existing TensorFlow 2.1 notebook image that already has support for GPUs. Leveraging this existing image allows us to benefit from all of the work the Kubeflow team already did in their image build process and simply add in the dependencies (here: `rtree` via `libspatialindex-dev`) that we need.

From here, we can build our custom Kubeflow notebook container locally with the command:

```
docker build dockerfile
```

Then we can push this new container image to the repository of our choice (e.g., Docker Hub). Once the container is in a repository, we can use it in the Custom Image field in the notebook server configuration page in Kubeflow, as seen in Figure 2-7.

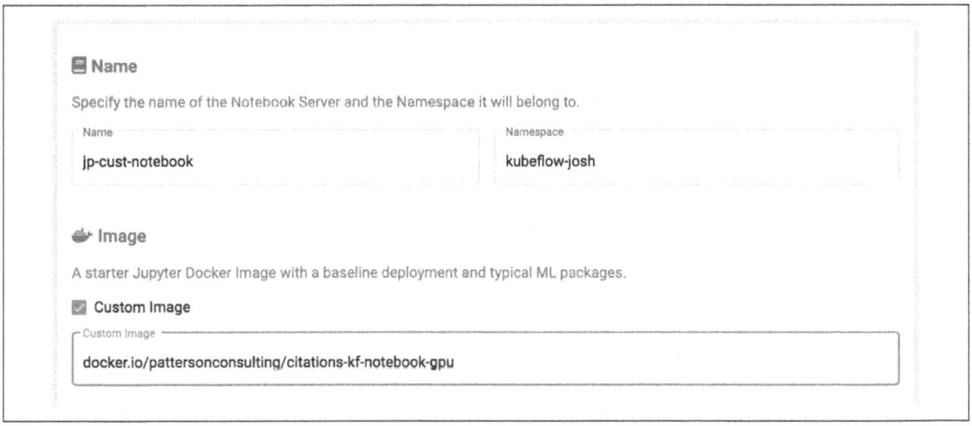

Figure 2-7. Configuring a notebook server to use a custom container image

This is a good point at which to talk about best practices for using GPUs with Kubeflow.

Using GPUs

GPUs are a key way that data scientists accelerate their model training. Kubeflow allows a team of data scientists to share GPU resources across the team, managed by Kubeflow and Kubernetes.

Using GPUs with notebooks

To use GPUs with notebooks on Kubeflow, we need to do the following:

1. Verify there are GPUs physically present in the hardware cluster managed by Kubernetes.
2. Use the correct notebook container image for GPUs and notebooks.

To launch notebooks with the correct notebook container image, we would navigate to the notebook server launch page in the Kubeflow user interface. From there, once you click the New Server button from the Notebooks tab in Kubeflow, you will see a page to configure the new notebook server, as shown in Figure 2-8.

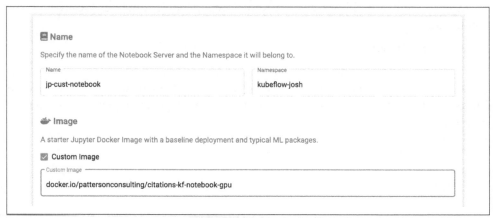

Figure 2-8. Notebook server configuration page

You'll need to use a container image with GPU support. There are standard container images that come prepackaged with Kubeflow that support GPUs.

GPUs and Custom Images

If you are building a custom image to use with GPUs and notebooks, it's a best practice to use one of the standard Kubeflow GPU container images as a base image in your Dockerfile.

Once you've configured the rest of your notebook server, you can click the Submit button at the bottom of the form. Once the notebook server is finished loading, you will be able to click the Connect button on the row for your server on the Notebook Servers page. This will launch a Jupyter Notebook in your browser for you to write code to execute on the GPU.

Validating that notebook code is using the GPU

To try out the notebook server with a GPU, we can load up the provided notebook on our GitHub repository (*https://oreil.ly/vtHmf*). Once you download this notebook and then upload it to the notebook server, you will be able to see it, as shown in Figure 2-9.

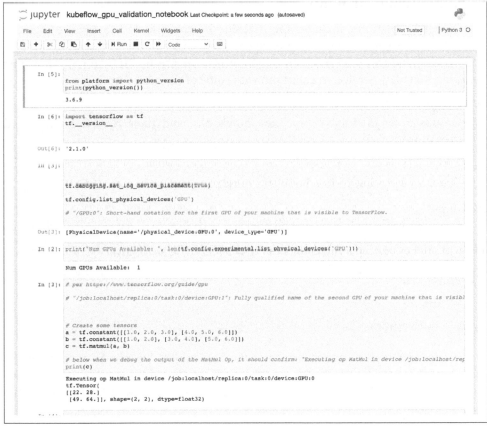

Figure 2-9. GPU validation notebook

You likely won't have to spend much time with this notebook, it's just meant as a quick check to confirm that we're on the right version of TensorFlow with a Docker image that can see the local GPU.

In the bottom cell in the notebook, you will also see some basic tensor operations executing and being run on `/job:localhost/replica:0/task:0/device:GPU:0`, indicating that the code is running physically on the local GPU.

Multiple Notebooks and GPUs

Before the NVIDIA A100 and MIG, if multiple notebooks tried to access a single GPU on a notebook server, you would likely see the notebooks lock up or crash. Try to have only a single notebook active at a time while on a single GPU notebook server if you are not using the A100 and MIG with Kubeflow.

Experiment Management

The Kubeflow platform includes the Machine Learning Metadata Service that can track multiple aspects of the jobs and experiments you run on the system. In this section we'll introduce some basic concepts on how to use the SDK for the Machine Learning Metadata Service. We start out with some of the basic terminology:

Workspace
Groups a set of runs of pipelines, notebooks, and their related artifacts and executions.

Run
Captures a pipeline or notebook in a workspace and group executions.

Execution
Captures a run of pipeline or notebooks in a workspace and group executions.

These three key concepts relate together in the hierarchy as follows:

- Workspace
  - Run
    - Execution

Other concepts include `store`, which is the SDK object we use to connect to the metadata gRPC service. We'll also note that an Execution also serves as the object for logging artifacts as its input or output. Let's move on and look at how to set up the metadata SDK.

Install the metadata SDK

To install the metadata SDK for a given notebook, we know from the previous dependency management section that we can either create a custom notebook image or we can install the dependencies at the top of the notebook.

To install at the top of the notebook, use the commands in Example 2-2.

Example 2-2. Pip commands to install Kubeflow metadata SDK

```
# To use the latest publish `kubeflow-metadata` library, you can run:
!pip install kubeflow-metadata --user
# Install other packages:
!pip install pandas --user
# Then restart the Notebook kernel.
```

Once we have the metadata SDK installed for our notebook, we can begin writing metadata into the Kubeflow system.

Basic metadata SDK usage

The code snippet in Example 2-3 shows the basic Python header code you might use to get your code set up to use the metadata SDK.

Example 2-3. Basic SDK usage example

```
import pandas
from kubeflow.metadata import metadata
from datetime import datetime
from uuid import uuid4

METADATA_STORE_HOST = "metadata-grpc-service.kubeflow"
  # default DNS of Kubeflow Metadata gRPC service.
METADATA_STORE_PORT = 8080
```

For further examples on how to use specific objects within the metadata SDK, check out the notebook (*https://oreil.ly/vwCpw*).

Once you get a feel for the metadata SDK, you'll be able to track metadata about not only your Kubeflow Pipelines but also your notebooks and raw container-based Python code running on Kubeflow.

Summary

In this chapter we covered a series foundational topics around the architecture of Kubeflow and some of its subsystems such as notebooks and pipelines. We then transitioned into best practices on how to advise your users to best run their jobs on Kubeflow.

Let's move on to the next chapter, where we look at the ways we need to think about planning out Kubeflow deployment for our organizational needs.

## CHAPTER 3

Planning a Kubeflow Installation

Planning a new Kubeflow installation is key to having a successful platform for your machine learning operations. This chapter introduces and covers the topics your team needs to consider in the process of planning your new Kubeflow cluster.

It's important to keep in mind that Kubeflow itself runs atop of Kubernetes, and though a deep understanding of Kubernetes is not a prerequisite to following the various topics and installation and configuration steps outlined, a working knowledge of Kubernetes may be beneficial.

Additionally, though Kubeflow can be deployed on top of an existing Kubernetes deployment, the assumption in this chapter will be that a new Kubernetes deployment is being created specifically for Kubeflow. Although the narrative outlined is for a dedicated Kubeflow installation, these topics can be easily transferred if Kubeflow is being deployed to an existing Kubernetes environment.

This chapter discusses the various types of users of a Kubeflow installation, which components of Kubeflow to deploy, how storage will be allocated to users, installation on-premise versus the cloud, security requirements, and hardware considerations.

Security Planning

This section reviews the current state of enterprise security integration (authentication and authorization) for Kubernetes, and then specifically for Kubeflow and associated components. Ideally, we want to provide a holistic and fully encompassing security approach with regard to the aforementioned components. For the purposes of this section, the term *security* will mean authentication and authorization generally, and not things such as container security, digital signatures, encryption, and so on.

Understanding the various Kubeflow components and how they interact with the underlying Kubernetes system provides a keen perspective on knowing how to operate, secure, and otherwise manage a Kubeflow installation. At a very high level, the distinct Kubeflow components can be broken into two broad categories:

- Components that *extend* the Kubernetes API
- Components that are applications that run atop of Kubernetes

Later in this chapter, the importance of this distinction will become apparent, especially in regard to planning to secure the Kubeflow installation, and/or integrate it with other security systems.

Components That Extend the Kubernetes API

Most, if not all, of the training components of Kubeflow, be it Chainer Training, MPI Training, TensorFlow Training, etc., provide Kubernetes custom resource definitions (CRDs). The purpose of CRDs is to *extend* the Kubernetes API so that a desired state of infrastructure, beyond what Kubernetes provides out of the box, can be declaratively written and achieved.

As an example, the TensorFlow training CRD defines a TFJob that describes the number of TensorFlow chiefs, workers, and parameter servers that should be run for a given training job. By simply declaring the desired state, and defining the container that will run, Kubernetes is given the knowledge on how to deploy the desired number of chiefs, workers, and parameter servers for a training job. In the example of TFJob, it is the role of a TF Operator component to continuously monitor Kubernetes for the addition of (or changes to) TFJob objects, and act accordingly, by requesting Kubernetes to deploy additional containers, inject TensorFlow specific primitives to the container, and so on.

By virtue of providing a CRD, it can be stated that a the TFJob *extends* the Kubernetes API, so that a user deploying a TensorFlow training job (or, conversely a Chainer Training Job, or an MPI Training Job, etc.) needs to only submit a declaration to Kubernetes on the desired state, and Kubernetes (with help of the controller watching the CRDs) moves to keep the components deployed to the desired state.

Components Running Atop Kubernetes

Other components of Kubeflow, namely Jupyter Notebooks, Hyperparameter Training (Katib), Pipelines, and others, are applications that are deployed *atop* of Kubernetes. These are applications that in theory can be deployed standalone and are not Kubernetes-specific. Rather, they are a collection of tooling that has been specifically chosen to integrate with other areas of Kubeflow, to weave together an end-to-end system for machine learning.

Background and Motivation

A direct consequence of there being various components of Kubeflow is that the way that users access the environment can differ dramatically between the components.

Kubeflow has the following major usage patterns:

- Interacting with Kubeflow components via the API, using the CRDs that *extend* the Kubernetes API
- Interacting with Kubeflow components that are applications, that are deployed *atop* Kubernetes

Each of these workflows has a series of specific steps that are required to have them execute in a Kubeflow environment—especially if they are to run in a secure manner. Though not a concrete requirement, a gateway machine is often used to access the Kubernetes cluster that Kubeflow is running atop.

Before discussing how to these access patterns translate to Kubeflow, it's important to take a moment to review some of the methods used to access Kubernetes itself—as well as applications that run atop Kubernetes.

All access to the Kubernetes control plane happens via the Kubernetes API. Two of the most common ways to access the API would be via the Kubernetes command-line utility (kubectl), and the Kubernetes dashboard.

When an application has been deployed to Kubernetes, access to that application is governed by how the application was exposed when it was deployed. For example, a simple web application can be exposed via a load balancer, or via a Kubernetes ingress. The distinction between the two is rather subtle: in the load balancer scenario, requests to the application will typically bypass Kubernetes itself (that is on

Layer 7—networking and networking policies aside); while in the ingress scenario, access is piped through a Kubernetes primitive (the ingress controller).

Kubeflow is an application that, in some ways, extends Kubernetes. Kubeflow also deploys applications atop Kubernetes and is an important point when thinking through a security strategy. To properly secure a Kubeflow installation, the Kubernetes API—the "control plane"—must be secured, in addition to, or as well as, the deployed Kubeflow applications (Jupyter Hub, etc.).

Whichever access pattern a user takes, the security goal would be that the cluster is to be accessed securely. The root of the requirements can be anything from corporate policy to auditability to securing customer data. A key motivator (besides the obvious) is data security. Users in a Kubeflow installation will (or should) have access to highly sensitive information—it is key to building accurate models—and their ability to share any information (intentionally or accidentally) should be extremely limited.

As such, controls must be in place so that, regardless of how a user deploys Kubeflow-specific infrastructure, data shouldn't be inadvertently exposed by things such as the HTTP service.

Kubeflow and Deployed Applications

Once an application has been deployed to Kubernetes (e.g., a user has the necessary authorization to deploy a deployment, or a pod, or a service), and has in turn launched, for example, a web server, it is the responsibility of that server or service to provide its own methods of authentication and authorization. That is, Kubernetes only authenticates and authorizes the *infrastructure* aspect here—whether a user is allowed to submit a desired state of an application's infrastructure. However, once that has been authorized, if an application requires any level of authentication and authorization, it must provide it on its own. Kubernetes does not facilitate that at all.

Take for example the Kubernetes Dashboard. The Dashboard is a JavaScript application that allows users to interact with the Kubernetes API via a GUI. As previously mentioned, the API server requires requests to be authenticated. The Dashboard can pass along authentication tokens (e.g., bearer tokens), but it itself has no native method of obtaining such tokens. While a client-go credential plug-in can be used for kubectl commands, no such method is available out of the box for the Dashboard.

To provide a similar experience, the HTTP endpoint of the Dashboard is exposed to the "world" (that is, anything outside the Kubernetes cluster) via an ingress, which is typically a reverse proxy. Prior to forwarding requests to the Dashboard application itself, the Ingress has an OAuth Proxy which it invokes to check if a user is authenticated. It is the OAuth Proxy (filter) that checks to see if a token is present, and if not, initiates an OIDC flow. Once a token is obtained (browser-based), that token is presented to the ingress, which in turn copies it to the upstream request to the

Dashboard. The Dashboard then simply forwards that request to the API server with the obtained token, and the flow continues the same as the `kubectl` interaction.

It is important to once again note that the Kubernetes Dashboard is *not* a core component of Kubernetes or the control plane, and is not even required. It is merely a JavaScript application that interacts with the API server, which is deployed like any other application.

Conversely, Kubeflow is a set of applications deployed atop Kubernetes. For example, part of the Kubeflow deployment is JupyterHub (and Jupyter Notebooks), which are themselves exposed as HTTP servers. These exposed servers require authentication and authorization to be configured independently. The Kubeflow Dashboard (another HTTP service) is also deployed as part of Kubeflow; it, too, requires that authentication and authorization be configured for it.

The challenge at this juncture is precisely the security around these applications: it is to be ensured that only authorized users can and should be allowed to access these applications exposed by Kubeflow. This cannot be handled by the control plane level, and must be addressed for each component (or via a higher/rolled-up method, which is yet to be determined).

There is an additional component to be considered: when users deploy their own containers and potentially expose an HTTP service via that container. These endpoints also required security, with (ideally) little to no configuration requirements on the user's part.

For certain Kubeflow components, this can be handled using Istio integration, and in other parts may require custom integrations.

Integration

At the control plane level, many forms of integration are available, including:

- X509 certificates
- OIDC connectors

X509 certificates work as any other PKI certificate infrastructure, and clients require a valid certificate to authenticate to the Kubernetes control plane. Management, issuing, revoking, and other aspects of a PKI infrastructure are topics of their own, and well documented.

OIDC integration can be achieved with an existing Identity Provider installation, such as one that authenticates Kerberos tickets and exchanges them for OIDC tokens. Additionally, Kubeflow integrates well with Dex, which is an open source OIDC Federation—or bridge—that allows users to use various authentication methods.

Some of the integrations that Dex provides include:

- LDAP
- GitHub
- SAML 2.0
- OIDC
- LinkedIn
- Microsoft

For more background on security-related technologies, check out Appendix A.

Users

Prior to planning a Kubeflow installation, it is important to take a moment to consider the user community that will be using Kubeflow on a day-to-day basis for machine learning, as well as the users responsible for the installation, managing, and overseeing the operation of it.

Understanding the varying skill sets of these different user communities, and considering how Kubeflow can bridge potential gaps between them, helps foster input and buy-in from each of these groups.

Profiling Users

Historically, data science has been an insular practice in which a data scientist has been huddled away with their own laptop or personal server, many times using tools like Anaconda locally. Eventually, after considerable effort by the data scientist, a machine learning model emerges that, ideally, is useful to the line of business in the organization. The data scientist looks to incorporate their model into the production pipeline or application, for example by integrating the model or its outputs in an application.

As data science workflows and model deployment expectations have grown more complex, organizations have struggled with the inherent overhead of maintaining the infrastructure to facilitate model training and model deployments. This complexity is further compounded when the data scientist has been off on their own, eventually emerging with a model produced using their own tooling that operations teams may struggle to integrate and support.

A classic example of this would be a data scientist building a model with a specific version of TensorFlow and then sending the frozen model graph to the operations team. The operations team, not being experts in TensorFlow, are unable to load the model in a standardized manner, such as in the workflow of deploying to an ordinary web server or database system, and now are faced with two options:

- Design, deploy, and maintain a custom model-serving process.
- Duplicate the model to each application that wants to integrate with the model outputs.

Often this scenario puts the data science teams and the operations teams at odds: the data scientist has certain specific expectations for their models, while the operations team will attempt to generalize the deployment for ease of maintainability.

Other factors that might complicate the relationship between the data scientists and the operations teams include:

- Versions of tooling that the data scientists want to use in their workflows
- Shared access to GPUs for modeling jobs
- Secure access to sensitive corporate and customer data
- Data scientists wanting to run distributed training jobs on shared infrastructure
- Container management
- Portability: data scientists wanting to try out a workload on the public could then move it back on-premise, or vice versa

From a higher level, we can roll most of these issues into the following requirements:

- Provide secure access to data.
- Provide a shared multitenant compute infrastructure (e.g., CPU, GPU).
- Allow for flexibility in versioning of tools.
- Use a generally supportable method to deploy and integrate models.
- Manage portability as to where model training and inference can be run (on-premise versus cloud, etc.).

Fortunately, a properly installed and working Kubeflow system alleviates many of the aforementioned potential issues. Kubeflow provides tooling to all of these items, and as an operator, our focus should mostly be on the Kubeflow system itself and how it affects the various users.

Varying Skillsets

To better characterize our users, we can roll users into three major groups:

- Data scientists
- Data engineers (*https://oreil.ly/S0GTp*)
- DevOps engineers

The data scientists typically want to take Python code that is running locally and run it on more powerful hardware with access to data they cannot move to their own laptop or server.

Data scientists typically know the basics of:

- Working with a terminal and shell scripting
- Python
- Jupyter Notebooks
- Machine learning fundamentals

The data scientists are supported by both data engineers and then DevOps engineers.

A data engineer (*https://oreil.ly/Xp2FV*) works with a data scientist (*https://oreil.ly/pZsQG*) (though from an organizational perspective they may be under the data warehouse team, or may be attached to the data science team). A data engineer typically knows:

- Where to get certain data from the system of record
- How to build ETL jobs to get the data in a form that can be vectorized
- SQL, Hadoop, Kafka, Spark, Hive, Sqoop, and other ETL tooling

Data engineers are many times the interface between the data warehouse system (where the system of record is located) and consumers of that system and its data. Though both data engineers and data scientists need a platform they can work together on, this system or platform is built and supported by yet another team: the DevOps team.

A DevOps engineer typically has the following skills:

- Hardware management (GPUs, drivers, storage, network)
- Networking
- Shared infrastructure management for clusters (e.g., Kubernetes, Hadoop)
- Container management

- General Linux (or other operating system) skills
- General overview of application and network security

A DevOps engineer (though more widely applied to DevOps teams) faces a range of challenges. One challenge is the need to support multiple versions of machine learning libraries. Further complicating matters is the challenge of providing ways to secure sensitive customer data, while also allowing data engineers the flexibility to build workflows that support data scientists.

Managing infrastructure for different workflow strategies, such as notebooks versus straight Python code, becomes a trick to balance, and then some teams will also want the capability to run a software (and hardware) stack that provides portability between on-premise and the cloud. Supporting hardware (and associated software drivers) for new emerging hardware, such as ASICs and TPUs in a shared multitenant environment is becoming a more common task DevOps engineers also need to tackle. Finally, DevOps teams are almost always needed to provide secure and separate storage on a per-user basis within a multitenant environment.

In some ways, DevOps is the hardest job of the lot. They are required to provide an agnostic infrastructure that satisfies the machine learning requirements, the data security requirements, and portability of a system. It is for this reason that a container management system such as Kubernetes has grown to where it is today. It is also for this reason that we believe it will continue to grow as a platform.

Workloads

Thinking about the target workloads that Kubeflow will be supporting aids in considering the placement of the infrastructure—how to allocate storage. We need to think about how to allocate storage and other ongoing operational needs.

In this section, two major usage patterns are outlined. The first describes Kubeflow as being used more along the lines of a dedicated platform to ingest and house data, as well as doing machine learning. The other pattern considers Kubeflow as more utilitarian, and as a tool that provides machine learning capabilities, but not as a data silo; utilitarian by choice in that it provides machine learning infrastructure with a "bring your own data" mindset.

Cluster Utilization

Depending on what types of components are installed on the Kubeflow cluster, Kubeflow can be used to solve a number of problems. As a thought exercise, we can group these into three subpatterns:

- Ad hoc exploratory data science workflows
- ETL and data science modeling workflows that are run daily (or on some temporal pattern (*https://oreil.ly/amRYO*))
- Model serving (inference) transactions

Analyzing these patterns further, we can put them into two groups:

- Batch (or analytical) workloads
- Transactional workloads

Both the exploratory data science workflows and the temporal ETL and data science workflows are considered batch workloads. Batch workloads are workloads that start up and run for a few minutes or even hours. While they tend to consume a set of resources for longer periods of time than transactional workloads, they are (typically) more efficient in terms of how they use the hardware in contrast to transactional workloads. Batch workloads deal in larger amounts of data, typically, so they are able to do things like "read data sequentially from disk and operate at the transfer rate of the disk," which is more effective than lots of small disk seeks.

Jeff Dean's "Numbers Everyone Should Know"

To learn more about writing software to use hardware more effectively in distributed systems, check out Jeff Dean's (*https://oreil.ly/f0BlY*) page, "Numbers Everyone Should Know" (*https://oreil.ly/N0lsL*).

If Kubeflow is serving inferences to external applications, then it can be considered a typical pattern of transactional operations, which are short-lived and tend to do quick (e.g., sub-500 ms) data operations (e.g., pull data from a database and send it back over an HTTP connection). It's a challenge in itself to make transactional operations more efficient (and many books have been written on this topic).

Model inferences are transactions in which input data (or vector/tensor) is sent to a model server hosting the copy of the model we wish to query for prediction output. The model server uses the incoming data as input to the model and then sends the result back across the network. With smaller models (e.g., 100k parameters in a neural network) the inference latency is not bad (and in some cases can be dominated by the time required to deserialize the input and then re-serialize the output). However, when we are dealing with larger models (e.g., an R-CNN (*https://oreil.ly/cVaxC*) in TensorFlow), we can see inference latencies in the hundreds of milliseconds, even when using a GPU such as an Nvidia Titan X. Planning for inference loads for applications is covered in more detail in Chapter 8. Model server instances are typically pinned to a specific set of resources (e.g., a single machine with a GPU), so in most cases we can just forecast the load, then set aside a specific number of instances to run model server processes.

Data Patterns

Depending on the type of utilization, the amount of data required varies. In planning an installation, it is important to consider whether Kubeflow will act as a dedicated repository of data (a "data silo") or will only provide transient storage for immediate processing needs.

Dedicated versus transient

In the case where users want to have large amounts of data housed within Kubeflow, a dedicated data storage story is needed. Questions arise as to space-provisioning needs, quotas, and other traditional data issues.

When considering whether to have Kubeflow function as a data repository, it should be considered whether other data lakes or larger data repositories exist, and if Kubeflow is the right place to store the data. If there are other existing data warehouses or data lakes, then it makes less sense to duplicate this data in various places, and Kubeflow should only house the data it needs when utilized for machine learning purposes. Thought of another way: the data should live in a data warehouse or data lake, and either a subset of data should be brought into Kubeflow for processing—or perhaps only vectorized data should arrive in Kubeflow, and the vectorization be prepared elsewhere.

On the flip side, if the data being used within Kubeflow is derived data—or other data that doesn't already have a home, or perhaps data that has been specifically engineered from machine learning purposes—then the long-term storage of the data within Kubeflow might be appropriate.

Ultimately, deciding on whether data should live in Kubeflow or elsewhere is a function of considering whether Kubeflow will be functioning merely as an application layer or as a more über-like infrastructure, providing data storage, compute, and processing power all together.

GPU Planning

Part of the planning process for a Kubeflow cluster involves understanding what users will need to support their workflows in terms of processing power. The base case in processing is the CPU, but newer workloads are more hungry for linear algebra processing, so we see GPUs becoming more common every day. As the industry grows, we're seeing new processing chips such as FPGAs and ASICs (Tensor Processing Units, or TPUs). While they are not as common today in usage, it's likely we'll have to consider them in our modeling forecasts at some point. In the rest of this section we'll take a look at the considerations for GPU workloads on a Kubeflow cluster.

Planning for GPUs

A core use case for Kubeflow is to have scheduled and secure access to a cluster of GPUs in a multitenant environment. There are three major ways to use GPUs with TensorFlow:

- Single machine, single GPU
- Single machine, multiple GPUs
- Multiple machines each with a single GPU
- Multiple machines each with multiple GPUs with Horovod (*https://oreil.ly/Ehxij*)

Deciding on which GPU training strategy depends on considerations such as:

- Training data size
- GPU hardware setup

Many times, when we are dealing with data that fits on a single machine, we will use a single or multiple GPUs on a single machine. This is because a single machine with multiple GPUs can utilize inter-GPU communication which would outperform distributed training. This is attributed to how distributed training's network overhead is more expensive in terms of latency compared to inter-GPU communication.

However, if we are dealing with a huge amount of data (say 1 PB) that is too large to fit in a single machine, then distributed training may be the only option.

> **Multiple GPUs and Scaling**
>
> Not all model architectures will demonstrate roughly linear scalability as we add more GPUs during machine learning training runs.

GPU use cases

GPUs can help your workloads in three major areas:

- Traditional HPC applications (e.g., fluid dynamics and protein folding)
- Deep learning and machine learning modeling
- Applications ported to use GPUs specifically (e.g., using Nvidia's RAPIDS (*https://rapids.ai*) system)

Most deep learning models are valid candidates for use with GPUs, as we'll give more detail further on in this section. Some traditional machine learning models are also candidates for speedup with GPUs, and we cover certain known cases for a few popular models below as well. There are also cases where workloads that are not HPC or machine learning are being ported to GPUs for speedup with Nvidia's new RAPIDS system.

The best way to leverage GPUs in your jobs is to first confirm your task is a good candidate for GPU acceleration. If the task is not a great candidate for GPU, but still needs access to data only on the cluster, then you could still run the job via Kubeflow as a container but on CPU, and yet still be able to process the data securely.

Should I Write CUDA Code Directly?

We'd advise against trying to write Compute Unified Device Architecture (CUDA) code directly, as there are already a lot of machine learning and deep learning libraries with CUDA backends for linear algebra acceleration.

GPU anti-use cases

The most common error we see is where someone assumes that since GPUs sped up their complex linear algebra problem, it can by extension speed up any arbitrary system. If the system is not written with some sort of CUDA-aware libraries (*https://oreil.ly/L7513*), then it most likely will not be able to take advantage of GPUs out of the box.

Models that Benefit from GPUs

In terms of GPU usage, we largely need to consider how interconnected the "model" is, and how large the model's memory space is. If your model is thousands of completely independent algorithms/equations, then each GPU can work on its own problem as fast as it can, and then come back to the workload manager with its results and get another batch of work to do. Think of the SETI@Home model, where you can take chunks and distribute the chunks across the internet. These workloads just need lots of GPUs, but the GPUs don't need to talk to each other.

Most deep learning models are extremely interconnected, so that the interconnect between GPUs becomes important (when we're using multiple GPUs on a single model). Nvidia's NVLink gives GPUs massive bandwidth to talk to each other. So if you're doing simulations where millions of particles are bouncing off each other, or convolutional neural networks (CNNs) where neurons are sending stuff between them, this interconnect becomes important. The DGX-1, DGX-2, and other eight-way V100 NVLink boxes like Cisco's or HPE's box have this capability.

For reference, the DGX-2 is unique right now in that it has NVSwitch, which gives maximum bandwidth between each GPU (each having six NVLink "lanes"). Instead of having point-to-point links between GPUs where you might only have one or two lanes between GPUs, the nonblocking switch gives six lanes from any GPU to any other GPU. This secondarily has the benefit of exposing a single memory space of 512 GB for the whole system, so GPUs can transparently access memory on another GPU without having to use CUDA memory management functions where they copy stuff between memory spaces. If you have a particular model (like NLP) where your GPU memory is the bottleneck, this can speed up training by ten times.

Major deep learning architectures to note would be:

- Convolutional neural networks (CNNs)
- Transform architectures (e.g., bidirectional encoder representations from transformers (BERT))
- Long short-term memory (LSTM) networks

Long Short-Term Memory Networks and GPUs

It's worth noting that LSTM network's training GPU speedup is only true with Nvidia optimizations. LSTM networks are by definition sequential networks, which can't be parallelize like the filter computation in CNNs.

These are models that we see in common use today and are tremendous candidates for GPU usage. We touch on details around GPU usage for both architectures in the subsections that follow.

While you can train any deep learning model with CPU, certain workloads just take much less time to train using GPUs. Given the dense parameter count and connection counts in deep learning, that's why we typically associate deep learning in general with GPU usage.

Distributed versus multi-GPU training

When discussing multi-GPU training, it is, at times, important to make the distinction between between training in a distributed manner—versus using multiple physical machines together, versus multi-GPU training—using a single machine with multiple GPUs.

As an example, in the case of distributed TensorFlow, it is typically referring to the situation where the user uses Kubeflow and the TFJob CRD to run a distributed training job across *multiple machines*, with or without GPUs. That is, the training (regardless of CPU or GPU, can be distributed to many machines). To further clear up the differences, we can think of it another way: we can define "multi-GPU" in the context of a single machine with multiple GPUs directly attached, and "distributed-GPU" as a many machines with zero or more GPUs.

We want to highlight these definitions because sometimes these are conflated with the scenario where a distributed training job, and specifically when using TensorFlow, has multiple hosts and each has a GPU (which we differentiate by calling it "distributed-multi-gpu"). In the case of distributed-multi-gpu, it is *technically* a multi-GPU setup, but we consider this to have different execution semantics so we give it a different moniker.

For most cases (defined as "use cases using eight GPUs or fewer" (*https://oreil.ly/5gWpv*)), training on a single machine with multiple GPUs is going to outperform both a single GPU and distributed TensorFlow (*https://oreil.ly/2XADm*) with GPUs. Due to network overhead, for instance, we see that it takes more than 16 distributed GPUs to equal the performance of a single machine with 8 GPUs on board.

The point at which distributed training across multiple machines comes into play is when there is a need to leverage more than 8 GPUs at once, and then we are ready to amortize the cost of the network overhead to jump up above 16 GPUs and gain the added scale.

Infrastructure Planning

When planning a Kubeflow installation, consideration must be given to the underlying infrastructure that will be running Kubeflow. Though Kubeflow is running on top of Kubernetes, and as such many of the topics discussed in this section will, to a certain degree, overlap with core Kubernetes concepts, the requirements and thought process are framed more from a Kubeflow perspective, and less from a general Kubernetes one.

Kubernetes Considerations

To frame our discussion on how we want to set up our Kubeflow installation, be it on-premise or the cloud, we'd first look at how Kubernetes clusters are typically arranged from a logical standpoint. In Figure 3-1 (from the Kubernetes documentation site (*https://oreil.ly/HDQmq*)), we can see different types of clusters broken up into logical layers.

The route chosen—cloud, on-premise, etc.—drives the amount of investment required to stand up and manage Kubernetes, and consequently Kubeflow.

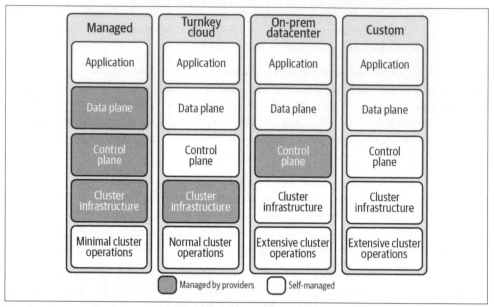

Figure 3-1. Production environment options for Kubernetes clusters

On-Premise

Installation of Kubeflow using on-premise infrastructure comes with all the requirements of any other on-premise hardware: it requires the datacenter, the workforce to manage the hardware, the network, the software, etc. Deploying Kubeflow on-premise generally means we want to use our existing hardware in a multitenant way such that many users can share expensive infrastructure.

In this section we'll look at some of the various ways an on-premise cluster can be set up to give more context around what "on-premise" really means.

The Nvidia DGX

Nvidia DGX (*https://oreil.ly/bKVsj*) is a line of Nvidia-produced servers and workstations which specialize in using general-purpose computing on GPUs to accelerate deep learning applications. The servers feature eight GPUs based on the Pascal or Volta daughter cards with HBM 2 memory, connected by an NVLink mesh network.

The product line is intended to bridge the gap between GPUs and AI accelerators in that the device has specific features that make it specialized it for deep learning workloads. Nvidia recommends Kubernetes as a great way to manage a DGX between users:

For Nvidia DGX servers, Kubernetes is an especially useful way of efficiently allowing users to distribute their work across a cluster. For example, a deep learning (DL) training job can be submitted that makes the request to use eight GPUs and Kubernetes will schedule that job accordingly as GPUs become available in the cluster. Once the job is complete, another job can start using the same GPUs. Another example is a longstanding service can be set up to receive live input data and output inferenced results.

Deploying Kubernetes and forming DGX servers as a cluster requires some setup, but it is preferable to giving users direct access to individual machines. Instead of users needing to ensure that they reserve a server, Kubernetes handles scheduling their work. It also can split up a single node so that multiple users can use it at the same time. All of this ensures that GPUs are being used as efficiently as possible. User access to the cluster can still be managed, certain nodes can be tagged for privileged use, specific jobs can have resource priority over others, and jobs can write to network storage.

Normally, if you were using TensorFlow (as an example) and GPUs locally, you could set up TensorFlow configuration (*https://oreil.ly/wR4V2*) to run directly on the GPUs.

However, when running on Kubeflow and GPUs on the DGX-1, you can simply set up your custom job CRD YAML file with certain flags and a container with CUDA dependencies built in.

Datacenter considerations

GPUs consume an enormous amount of power and generate a tremendous amount of heat. Depending on the amount of power and heat dissipation available per rack, the amount of GPUs (and specifically the number of DGXs) varies. It is not uncommon to find only two DGXs in a 42U rack. In addition to the DGX-1, Nvidia also offers the DGX-2 and the DGX-A100 (*https://oreil.ly/HYaQF*).

Depending on the layout and storage, additional considerations need to be made. For example, if using Flash-backed storage served over InfiniBand, consideration needs to be given to the distance of the interconnects, the required switching hardware, etc.

Cloud

Given that GPU workloads tend to be ad hoc (e.g., "every so often we'll want to run a GPU for two days solid"), running a machine learning workload on the cloud with GPUs makes a lot of sense. All three major clouds offer GPUs:

- Google Cloud (*https://oreil.ly/Z_srd*)
- Microsoft Azure (*https://oreil.ly/Lg2xG*)
- AWS (*https://oreil.ly/Vc0Xh*)

The common Nvidia GPUs offered on the cloud are:

- K80
- P4
- T4
- P100
- V100
- A100

We should also consider what kind of instance (for example, Azure GPUs (*https://oreil.ly/zH2Mz*)) we're running our workloads on, beyond just what kind of GPU.

Getting a Cloud Image Running with Deep Learning

While it's common to hear about data scientists just "running GPUs on the cloud," it can actually be a pain to get an image up and running. A great tip when starting out is to look for a pre-built image (for example, "Deep Learning VM" (*https://oreil.ly/aiMTf*)) on your cloud of choice to skip over a lot of the install headaches.

By nature of being the cloud, there are no traditional datacenter considerations. Though consideration does need to be given to the transport of data to the cloud (assuming the data is coming from another datacenter or another form of on-premise). Many cloud providers have dedicated interconnects to their cloud for exactly such purposes.

Another consideration for using GPUs in the cloud is the speed GPUs can consume data. In a fully decked out on-premise installation, where the GPU cluster is interconnected with flash-backed, super low-latency high-speed storage, GPUs can obtain data pretty fast. In the cloud, and certainly dependent upon the cloud provider, there may be additional overhead—by orders of magnitude. The consequence of this relates more to training time, and might only be an issue on very large models, or when training on very large amounts of data.

Placement

The choice of where to place the infrastructure for Kubeflow, and conversely Kubernetes, can boil down to capital versus operational costs (CapEx versus OpEx). Certainly, the cloud provides enormous benefit in terms of elasticity and flexibility, while an on-premise solution may solve other business or regulatory requirements.

Ultimately, no matter where the underlying infrastructure is placed, given that Kubeflow runs on top of Kubernetes, this provides a rather large degree of portability. It would be a safe bet to say that at any given point a Kubeflow installation can be moved from the cloud to on-premise, from an on-premise installation to the cloud, or even extended between the two.

Container Management

There are public and private registries for container images. Docker is currently the most popular container platform, and Dockerhub.com is currently a major repository for public containers. Docker Hub provides a repository for container images to be stored, searched, and retrieved.

Other repositories include Google's Container Registry and on-premise Artifactory installs. Unless specified otherwise, Docker Hub is the default location from which Docker will pull images.

For many types of jobs (e.g., a basic TensorFlow model training job in Python), we can just leverage a public container repository like Docker Hub or the Google container registry (*https://oreil.ly/M3Boj*). However, in other cases where our code may be more sensitive, we need to consider other measures, such as an on-premise container registry such as Artifactory.

Serverless Container Operations with Knative

A core component that Kubeflow uses under the hood is Knative. We give Knative light coverage in this section so that the user is generally aware of its role in Kubeflow.

Knative provides building blocks that enable serverless, declarative, container-based workloads on Kubernetes. The provided primitive building blocks include:

- Event-triggered functions on Kubernetes
- Scale to and from zero
- Queue-based autoscaling for GPUs and TPUs

Traditional workload scaling operates in a step-function method for scale versus cost. This contrasts with Knative's ability to enable serverless scaling in a linear fashion. Knative provides middleware components from core to building modern, source-centric, and container-based applications that can run anywhere (on-premise, cloud).

Knative is also used in Kubeflow for routing and managing traffic with blue-green deployment. Kubeflow makes use of Knative to autoscale workloads up and down dynamically as traffic dictates in KFServing.

Core components of Knative include:

- Eventing: management and delivery of events
- Serving: request-drive compute (that can scale to zero)

With Knative Eventing we can create subscriptions to event sources declaratively, and then also route events to Kubernetes endpoints. Knative Serving provides stateless services on Kubernetes more easily. Knative Serving makes autoscaling, network, and rollouts easier to manage.

Sizing and Growing

Forecasting would be the exercise of taking the concepts from the previous sections and applying them in a sizing heuristic. If we summarize the user group–profiled workloads from the preceding section that we're likely to see on our cluster, e.g., "multitenancy," we could say:

- There will be periods when a set of users will be trying different ideas in data science and will be kicking off a batch training job that could take minutes or hours.
- There will be a group of jobs (ETL, data science) that run every day that are batch workloads.
- There will be transactional workloads that are sustained by a set amount of resources and are always running the model server processes.

So if we carve off the model server (transactional) portion of things, we can focus on modeling the batch workloads for the ad hoc jobs and then the scheduled jobs.

For the ad hoc exploratory data science jobs, ideally we'll create lanes for different subgroups of users in our data science teams, so a single user cannot hog the cluster with a "super-job." These exploratory jobs represent future output from the data science organization, but we cannot run them at the expense of the present output of the organization. So we'll also want to create a lane for the scheduled jobs that need to run every day and probably need to finish by a set time.

Forecasting

As a compute-planning exercise, it's generally a good idea to build a spreadsheet with 24-hour buckets on it, where each row on the spreadsheet represents a user group (see Figure 3-2). We'll consider the daily (temporal) jobs as their own group and enter them as the first group.

	A	B	C	D	E	F	G
1							
2							
3		Hours	1:00 AM	2:00 AM	3:00 AM	4:00 AM	5:00 AM
4		Daily Jobs	5	5	5	0	0
5		Exploratory DS	0	0	2	2	8
6							
7							

Figure 3-2. Example cluster forecasting spreadsheet

List the other groups you can think of as subsequent rows in the spreadsheet. In each cell, add up the number of GPU instances you think the group will need for that time block. It's good to do this exercise over a 24-hour set of time blocks because of different overlapping time zones, and then also at the times that the workday teams tend to run jobs.

Once you have all the groups as rows, and all the time blocks filled out per group, sum up the columns across the 24-hour windows. Look for the cell that has the largest number, and this number is your peak GPU usage for a typical day in your organization.

To forecast what your team will need a year from now, make a copy of the spreadsheet and then add in a growth metric per cell (may be different per group, etc.). These two spreadsheets will give you cluster usage today and then a peak usage a year from now.

These two numbers will give you a decent estimate on how to plan for GPUs for either a cloud budget for running Kubeflow in the cloud, or for an on-premise infrastructure hardware budget.

Storage

Kubeflow clusters tend to cater to compute-hungry workloads, and so far in this section we've focused on sizing with respect to the compute budget our users will need. However, compute cannot exist without data, so we need to consider how much data we'll be processing.

Key storage considerations are:

- Ingest rate of data (per day, per year)
- Current total data size in the storage system
- Average data size per job
- Average intermediate data size per job
- Compression impact on file size on disk
- Replication factor (*https://oreil.ly/rz7Mk*) (if any) of the storage system

An example spreadsheet of these factors in use is shown in Figure 3-3.

Consideration	Value	Unit
Ingest rate of data (per day, per year)	100	MB / day
Current total data size in the storage system	30	GB
Average data size per job	500	MB
Average intermediate data size per job	100	MB
Compression impact on file size on disk	0%	no compression
Replication factor of the storage system	1	
Average Concurrent Users	5	
Projected total data size at end of year	65.64	GB
Forecasted yearly growth rate of data stored	118.82	%
Projected Amount of Job Data Storage Needed	2.93	GB
Total Forecasted Storage Required	68.57	GB

Figure 3-3. Example spreadsheet forecasting storage required for cluster

If we multiply the incoming daily ingest rate by 365 days, and then add the existing data stored, we have a storage number that roughly tells us how much space we'll need at the end of the year. Beyond just data stored, we want to consider space for running jobs (potentially a copy of the data as it is processed) and then any intermediate data the job produces. If we add all three of these numbers together, we get a total forecast for storage required at the end of the year.

Obviously this number won't be perfect, but it gets us in the ballpark. We also should consider the fact that we want to have extra space for operations beyond just what we're storing, so when we go to make the hardware purchase (or cloud provision) we'll likely allocate more space than this number directly.

Scaling

For most systems that are running constantly, we build a sizing and growth plan (as shown previously in this chapter) and then make direct considerations for how many machines we need of which type. We'll call this "planned scaling" based on a direct growth forecast, and most systems require this type of planning.

We contrast this to dynamic scaling systems that automatically provision "most hosts" for a certain type of code or function deployed to a system. An example of dynamic scaling would be how AWS (*https://oreil.ly/jGyRL*) can add more web servers to a group to handle more traffic load as a response to changing demand.

Although there are some emerging design patterns where workloads can "burst" to the cloud from on-premise under the guise of needing more capacity, most of the time when we're dealing with enterprise infrastructure we're talking about a planned scaling situation.

 Situations Where Scale Is Overmarketed

Often the term *scale* is thrown around and has conflated meanings. Some vendors in the enterprise arena want to give the idea that their application (somehow) has no limit to scale. This typically is just not true, because "network switches have limits." Parallelizing an operation on more compute nodes can hit other bottlenecks such as:

- Algorithm design
- GPU memory transfer rates
- Neural network architecture design
- Communication overhead

There really is just no free lunch here, so always take scale guarantees with a grain of salt.

Summary

In this chapter we started out by continuing our security conversation and then worked our way through a series of topics we want to think about when planning a Kubeflow deployment. Portions of this chapter are situational or background material but serve to give you insight into scenarios to watch out for as you design your Kubeflow deployment.

We'll shift gears in our next chapter, and move into actually deploying Kubeflow.

## CHAPTER 4

Installing Kubeflow On-Premise

In this chapter we take a look at the basics for installing Kubeflow on an existing on-premise Kubernetes cluster. The assumption in this chapter is that you already have some background knowledge with Kubernetes and that you also have access to an existing Kubernetes cluster either on-premise or managed in the cloud. There are also options for learning environments such as Minikube (*https://oreil.ly/qxcMk*), kubeadm-dind (*https://oreil.ly/-_kn1*).

We also assume that you're comfortable with software infrastructure install processes and can work from a command-line interface. If you need a quick refresher, in the next section we review some basic commands for Kubernetes.

Kubernetes Operations from the Command Line

Given that Kubeflow is tightly integrated with Kubernetes, we need to know a few Kubernetes core commands to perform any type of install. In this section we review the commands:

- kubectl
- docker

This chapter will give you the specifics around what parts of Kubernetes we need to worry about for an on-premise install. Let's start out by getting some of our core command-line tools installed.

Installing kubectl

kubectl controls the Kubernetes cluster manager and is a command-line interface for running commands against Kubernetes clusters. We use kubectl to deploy and manage applications on Kubernetes. Using kubectl, we can:

- Inspect cluster resources
- Create components
- Delete components
- Update components

For a more complete list of functions in kubectl, check out this cheat sheet (*https://oreil.ly/_7vWy*).

kubectl is a fundamental tool for Kubernetes and Kubeflow operations, and we'll use it a lot in the course of deploying components and running jobs on Kubeflow.

Installing kubectl on macOS

An easy way to install kubectl on macOS is to use the brew command (*https://oreil.ly/wpoIr*):

```
brew install kubernetes-cli
```

Once we have kubectl, we need permission for it to talk to our Kubernetes cluster.

Understanding kubectl and contexts

kubectl knows how to talk to remote clusters based on a local context file stored on disk. We define a kubectl context as an entry in a kubectl file used to identify a group of access parameters under a common ID. Each of these groups of access parameters, or contexts, has three parameters:

- Cluster
- Namespace
- User

The default location for the local kubeconfig file is *~/.kube/config* (or *$HOME/.kube/config*). We can also set this location with the KUBECONFIG environment variable or by setting the --kubeconfig (*https://oreil.ly/kYaR0*) flag (*https://oreil.ly/n5oV6*).

We can also use multiple configuration files, but for now, we'll consider the case of the default configuration file. In some cases, you will be working with multiple clusters, and their context information will also be stored in this file.

To view the current `kubectl` config, use the command:

```
kubectl config view
```

The output should look something like this:

```
apiVersion: v1
clusters:
- cluster:
    certificate-authority: /home/ec2-user/.minikube/ca.crt
    server: https://172.17.0.3:8443
  name: kubeflow
contexts:
- context:
    cluster: kubeflow
    user: kubeflow
  name: kubeflow
current-context: kubeflow
kind: Config
preferences: {}
users:
- name: kubeflow
  user:
    client-certificate: /home/ec2-user/.minikube/profiles/kubeflow/client.crt
    client-key: /home/ec2-user/.minikube/profiles/kubeflow/client.key
```

The output can vary depending on how many contexts are currently in your local file, but it tells us things like what clusters we have attached and what the configuration is for the current context. For more information on operations we can perform on the context system for kubectl, check out the online resource (*https://oreil.ly/v1TNQ*).

We use `kubectl` context files to organize information about:

- Clusters
- Users
- Namespaces
- Authentication mechanisms

Let's now look at a few specific ways to use the context file and `kubectl`.

Getting the current context. If we want to know what the current context is, we would use the command:

```
kubectl config current-context
```

The output should look similar to the following console log output:

```
kubeflow
```

This gives us the ID of the context group in our context file; kubectl currently will send Kubernetes commands to the cluster represented by that ID.

Adding clusters to our context file.   To add a new Kubernetes cluster to our local context file we use the set-cluster, set-credentials, and set-context commands (*https:// oreil.ly/wBBBY*), as seen in the following example:

```
kubectl config \
  set-cluster NAME \
  [--server=server] \
  [--certificate-authority=path/to/certificate/authority] \
  [--insecure-skip-tls-verify=true]

kubectl config \
  set-credentials NAME \
  [--client-certificate=path/to/certfile] \
  [--client-key=path/to/keyfile] \
  [--token=bearer_token] \
  [--username=basic_user] \
  [--password=basic_password] \
  [--auth-provider=provider_name] \
  [--auth-provider-arg=key=value] \
  [--exec-command=exec_command] \
  [--exec-api-version=exec_api_version] \
  [--exec-arg=arg][--exec-env=key=value] \
  [options]

kubectl config \
  set-context [NAME | --current] \
  [--cluster=cluster_nickname] \
  [--user=user_nickname] \
  [--namespace=namespace] \
  [options]
```

Note that in the set-context command, the NAME parameter is the name of the credential set in using the set-credentials command.

In the next chapter we'll look at how to pull credentials for a public cloud and automatically add the Kubernetes context to our local context file.

Switching contexts.   To change the default context to point to another Kubernetes cluster, use the command:

```
kubectl config use-context [my-cluster-name]
```

All commands issued via kubectl now should be routed to the cluster we previously added with the ID [*my-cluster-name*].

Using kubectl

Let's get used to using kubectl by trying a few commands to get information from the cluster, such as the following:

- The current running services
- The cluster information
- The current running jobs

Getting running services

To confirm our cluster is operational and the components are running, try the following command:

```
kubectl -n kubeflow get services
```

We should see a list of components running that match the components we just installed on our cluster (see Example 4-1).

Example 4-1. List of services from the command line

NAME	TYPE	PORT(S)	AGE
admission-webhook-service	ClusterIP	443/TCP	2d6h
application-controller-service	ClusterIP	443/TCP	2d6h
argo-ui	NodePort	80:30643/TCP	2d6h
centraldashboard	ClusterIP	80/TCP	2d6h
jupyter-web-app-service	ClusterIP	80/TCP	2d6h
katib-controller	ClusterIP	443/TCP,8080/TCP	2d6h
katib-db-manager	ClusterIP	6789/TCP	2d6h
katib-mysql	ClusterIP	3306/TCP	2d6h
katib-ui	ClusterIP	80/TCP	2d6h
kfserving-controller-manager-metrics-service	ClusterIP	8443/TCP	2d6h
kfserving-controller-manager-service	ClusterIP	443/TCP	2d6h
kfserving-webhook-server-service	ClusterIP	443/TCP	2d6h
metadata-db	ClusterIP	3306/TCP	2d6h
metadata-envoy-service	ClusterIP	9090/TCP	2d6h
metadata-grpc-service	ClusterIP	8080/TCP	2d6h
metadata-service	ClusterIP	8080/TCP	2d6h
metadata-ui	ClusterIP	80/TCP	2d6h
minio-service	ClusterIP	9000/TCP	2d6h
ml-pipeline	ClusterIP	8888/TCP,8887/TCP	2d6h
ml-pipeline-ml-pipeline-visualizationserver	ClusterIP	8888/TCP	2d6h
ml-pipeline-tensorboard-ui	ClusterIP	80/TCP	2d6h
ml-pipeline-ui	ClusterIP	80/TCP	2d6h
mysql	ClusterIP	3306/TCP	2d6h

notebook-controller-service	ClusterIP	443/TCP	2d6h
profiles-kfam	ClusterIP	8081/TCP	2d6h
pytorch-operator	ClusterIP	8443/TCP	2d6h
seldon-webhook-service	ClusterIP	443/TCP	2d6h
tensorboard	ClusterIP	9000/TCP	2d6h
tf-job-operator	ClusterIP	8443/TCP	2d6h

This lets us confirm which services that we've deployed are currently running.

Get cluster information

We can check out the status of the running cluster with the command:

```
kubectl cluster-info
```

We should see output similar to Example 4-2.

Example 4-2. kubectl cluster-info output

```
Kubernetes master is running at https://172.17.0.3:8443
KubeDNS is running at https://172.17.0.3:8443/api/v1/namespaces/kube-system...

To further debug and diagnose cluster problems, use kubectl cluster-info dump.
```

Get currently running jobs

Typically we'd run a job based on a YAML file with the kubectl command:

```
kubectl apply -f https://github.com/pattersonconsulting/tf_mnist_kubflow_3_5...
```

We should now have the job running on the Kubeflow cluster. We won't see the job running and writing to our console screen because it is running on a remote cluster. We can check the job status with the command:

```
kubectl -n kubeflow get pod
```

Our console output should look something like Example 4-3.

Example 4-3. kubectl output for currently running jobs

NAME	READY	STATUS	RESTARTS	AGE
admission-webhook-deployment-f9789b796-95rfz	1/1	Running	0	2d6h
application-controller-stateful-set-0	1/1	Running	0	2d6h
argo-ui-59f8d49b9-52kn8	1/1	Running	0	2d6h
centraldashboard-6c548fc6dc-pzskh	1/1	Running	0	2d6h
jupyter-web-app-deployment-657bf476db-v2xgl	1/1	Running	0	2d6h
katib-controller-5c976769d8-fcxng	1/1	Running	1	2d6h
katib-db-manager-bf77df6d6-dgml5	1/1	Running	0	2d6h
katib-mysql-7db488768f-cgcnj	1/1	Running	0	2d6h
katib-ui-6d7fbfffcb-t84xl	1/1	Running	0	2d6h
kfserving-controller-manager-0	2/2	Running	1	2d6h
metadata-db-5d56786648-ldlzq	1/1	Running	0	2d6h

```
metadata-deployment-5c7df888b9-gdm5n            1/1   Running    0    2d6h
metadata-envoy-deployment-7cc78946c9-kcmt4      1/1   Running    0    2d6h
metadata-grpc-deployment-5c8545f76f-7q47f       1/1   Running    0    2d6h
metadata-ui-665dff6f55-pbvdp                    1/1   Running    0    2d6h
minio-657c66cd9-mgxcd                           1/1   Running    0    2d6h
ml-pipeline-669cdb6bdf-vwglc                    1/1   Running    0    2d6h
ml-pipeline-ml-pipeline-visualizationserver...  1/1   Running    0    2d6h
ml-pipeline-persistenceagent-56467f8856-zllpd   1/1   Running    0    2d6h
ml-pipeline-scheduledworkflow-548b96d5fc-xkxdn  1/1   Running    0    2d6h
ml-pipeline-ui-6bd4778958-bdf2x                 1/1   Running    0    2d6h
ml-pipeline-viewer-controller-deployment...     1/1   Running    0    2d6h
mysql-8558d86476-xq2js                          1/1   Running    0    2d6h
notebook-controller-deployment-64b85fbc84...    1/1   Running    0    2d6h
profiles-deployment-647448c7dd-9gnz4            2/2   Running    0    2d6h
pytorch-operator-6bc9c99c5-gn7wm                1/1   Running    30   2d6h
seldon-controller-manager-786775d4d9-frq9l      1/1   Running    0    2d6h
spark-operatorcrd-cleanup-xq8zb                 0/2   Completed  0    2d6h
spark-operatorsparkoperator-9c559c997-mplrh     1/1   Running    0    2d6h
spartakus-volunteer-5978bf56f-jftnh             1/1   Running    0    2d6h
tensorboard-9b4c44f45-frr76                     0/1   Pending    0    2d6h
tf-job-operator-5d7cc587c5-tvxqk                1/1   Running    33   2d6h
workflow-controller-59ff5f7874-8w9kd            1/1   Running    0    2d6h
```

Given that a TensorFlow job is run as an extension of the TensorFlow operator, it shows up as a pod alongside the other Kubeflow components.

Using Docker

Docker is the most common container system used in container orchestration systems such as Kubernetes. To launch a container we run an image. An image includes everything needed to run an application (code, runtime, libraries, etc.) as an executable image. In our TensorFlow job's cases, it includes things like the TensorFlow library dependencies and our Python training code to run on each container.

Docker Hub (*https://hub.docker.com*) provides a repository for container images to be stored, searched, and retrieved. Other repositories include Google's Container Registry (*https://oreil.ly/mhxjQ*) and on-premise Artifactory installs (*https://oreil.ly/vy458*).

Basic Docker install

For information on how to install Docker, check out their documentation page (*https://oreil.ly/g0PVW*) for the process.

For the remainder of this chapter we assume that you have Docker installed. Let's now move on to some basic Docker commands you'll need to know.

Basic Docker commands

For details on using the build command, see the Docker documentation page (*https://oreil.ly/n-z8a*).

The command that follows builds the image from the dockerfile contained in the local directory and gives it the tag [account]/[repository]:[tag]:

```
docker build -t "[account]/[repository]:[tag]" .
```

To push the container we built in this Docker command, we'll use a command of the following form:

```
docker push [account]/[repository]:[tag]
```

The following command takes the container image we built in the previous step and pushes it to the mike account in Artifactory under the Kubeflow repo. It also adds the tag dist_tf_estimator.

```
docker push mike/kubeflow:dist_tf_estimator
```

Now let's move on to building TensorFlow containers with Docker.

Using Docker to build TensorFlow containers

When building Docker container images based on existing TensorFlow container images, be cognizant of:

- The desired TensorFlow version
- Whether the container image will be Python2- or Python3-based
- Whether the container image will have CPU or GPU bindings

We're assuming here that you'll either build your own base existing TensorFlow container or pull an existing one from gcr.io or Docker Hub. Check out the TensorFlow repository at Docker Hub (*https://oreil.ly/F-sF_*) for some great examples of existing TensorFlow container images.

> **Containers, GPUs, and Python Version**
>
> Check out each container repository for its naming rules around Python 2 versus Python 3, as it can be different per repository. For GPU bindings within the container image, be sure to use the correct base image with the -gpu tag.

Now let's move on to the install process for Kubeflow from the command line.

Basic Install Process

The basic install process for Kubeflow is:

1. Initialize Kubeflow artifacts.
2. Customize any artifacts.
3. Deploy Kubeflow artifacts to the cluster.

We break down each of these in the following sections.

Installing On-Premise

To install Kubeflow on-premise, we need to consider the following topics:

- Considerations for building Kubernetes clusters
- Gateway host access to the cluster
- Active Directory integration and user management
- Kerberos integration
- Learning versus production environments
- Storage integration

We start off by looking at variations of ways to set up Kubernetes clusters.

Considerations for Building Kubernetes Clusters

To frame our discussion on how we want to set up our Kubeflow installation on-premise, we'll revisit the diagram for how clusters are broken up into logical layers (Figure 4-1).

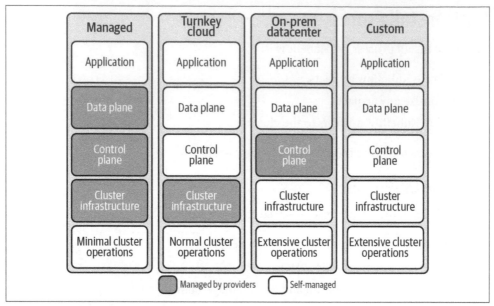

Figure 4-1. Production environment options for Kubernetes clusters (source: Kubernetes documentation (https://oreil.ly/xR_Mf))

Kubeflow lives in the application layer for our cluster, and we'll install it as a set of long-lived pods and services.

Kubernetes Glossary

Kubernetes has a lot of terms and concepts to know. If you ever get confused, just check out the Kubernetes standardized glossary (*https://oreil.ly/OgQVr*) in the documentation on the Kubernetes project website.

Given this context, we understand that we need to install Kubeflow on an existing Kubernetes cluster. The location of things such as the control plane and the cluster infrastructure may greatly impact install design decisions, such as:

- Networking topologies
- Active Directory integration
- Kerberos integration

Let's look further at what goes into setting up a gateway host to access our cluster.

Gateway Host Access to Kubernetes Cluster

In most shared multitenant enterprise systems, we have a gateway host that is used for access to the cluster. For the purposes of installing Kubeflow on a Kubernetes system, your cluster will likely need the same pattern setup.

Typically, the gateway host machine needs the following resources:

- Network access to the Kubernetes cluster
- kubectl installed and configured locally

Network access to the Kubernetes cluster where Kubeflow resides is required as we need access for kubectl to send commands across the network. There are variations where container building is done on a machine that is not the gateway host, but it typically is a function of how your IT department sets things up.

It is perfectly fine for a gateway host to be a local machine that meets these requirements.

Active Directory Integration and User Management

In most organizations, users are managed by an Active Directory installation. Most enterprise software systems will need to integrate with this Active Directory installation to allow users to use systems such as Kubernetes or Kubeflow.

Let's start off by looking at the typical user experience in an organization for accessing a Kubernetes cluster integrated with Active Directory.

Kubernetes, kubectl, and Active Directory

To access a Kubernetes cluster, users typically will have to formally request access to the cluster from their enterprise IT team. After an approval process has been successfully cleared, users will be added to the appropriate Active Directory group for access to the cluster.

Users access the gateway host (which again, can be their local machine) using a set of credentials, and immediately after logging in with the generic credentials, will be granted a Kerberos ticket. That ticket can later be used to authenticate to the Kubernetes cluster.

The necessary binaries (kubectl, and plug-ins—as we mention in the following text), as well as the required kubeconfig (Kubernetes configuration) will need to be configured by users. Once the kubeconfig has been configured, users only need to concern themselves with executing the appropriate kubectl commands.

Kerberos Integration

Enterprise IT teams commonly use Kerberos for a network authentication protocol as it is designed to be used by client/server applications (such as Kubernetes nodes) to provide strong authentication using secret-key cryptography. As described on the Kerberos website:

> Kerberos was created by MIT as a solution to these network security problems. The Kerberos protocol uses strong cryptography so that a client can prove its identity to a server (and vice versa) across an insecure network connection. After a client and server has used Kerberos to prove their identity, they can also encrypt all of their communications to assure privacy and data integrity as they go about their business.

By default, Kubernetes does not provide a method to integrate with Kerberos directly, because it relies on a more modern approach—OpenID Connect, or OIDC for short.

One method of using Kerberos with Kubernetes is to exchange an existing Kerberos ticket for an OIDC token, and to present that token to Kubernetes upon authentication. This works by first authenticating to an OIDC token provider using an existing Kerberos credential, and obtaining an OIDC token in exchange for the Kerberos authentication. This can be accomplished by using a `kubectl` plug-in, with an example here (*https://oreil.ly/7SWux*).

Storage Integration

Out-of-the-box Kubeflow does not have a notion of a specific datastore and lets the underlying Kubernetes cluster define what storage options are available.

When setting up our Kubeflow installation and running jobs, we need to consider:

- What kind of storage our cluster has available
- Data access patterns that are best suited for our job
- Security considerations around the data store

How we store data is intricately linked to how we access data, so we want to make sure that we think about how we're going to access the data as we design our storage. The job types we'll consider with regard to our data access patterns are:

- Python (or other) code in a single container run on Kubernetes
- A container is run on a specific Kubeflow operator (e.g., TFOperator, or PyTorchOperator) in normal single node execution or in distributed mode
- Python code run from a Jupyter Notebook

There are two facets to consider across these three job variants:

- Are we providing enough bandwidth to the job such that we're not starving the modeling power of the code that is running?
- Are we integrating with the storage layer via filesystem semantics or via network calls?

Let's start off by looking at the job bandwidth and storage for Kubeflow jobs.

Thinking about Kubeflow job bandwidth

If you'll recall, in Chapter 2 we talked about how GPUs can affect jobs, from single GPUs to multi GPUs and even distributed GPUs. GPUs can be hungry for data, so having an extremely fast storage subsystem is critical. We don't want the GPUs waiting on data.

If a given job is going to be training on a lot of data, we can think about that job requiring a high-bandwidth storage solution that can satiate the needs of the GPUs. On the other hand, if a job was heavily computation bound, without a smaller dataset, the speed at which the initial data is received by the GPUs may not be that important. In the latter scenario, we can think of that as a lower-bandwidth job.

Common access storage patterns with Kubeflow jobs

There are two major ways Kubeflow jobs access storage:

- Using network calls across the network or internet
- Using filesystem semantics

If the job is going to pull data across the network/internet with the user's own credentials (that we don't mind putting in the configuration/code somewhere), then we don't have to worry about filesystem semantics and mount points for Kubernetes at the Kubernetes level.

In this case, the code handles all network calls to get the data locally, but our cluster's hosts need external network connectivity. Such examples might be accessing storage from S3, SFTP, third-party systems, etc.

If you want to use a local mount point to access a partition of the data (e.g., in a manner similar to how a local filesystem will be used by Python and notebooks on a local laptop), then you will need to provision storage using persistent volume claims (PVCs) at the Kubernetes pod and container level.

Options for Kubeflow storage

Kubernetes itself provides a plethora of storage mechanisms, more of which can be found here (*https://oreil.ly/Kw49W*). At the most basic level, storage can be thought of as being locally attached storage on a particular Kubernetes worker node (e.g., a locally attached and ephemeral volume), or a layer of persistent storage, typically provided by a storage subsystem.

In the context of Kubeflow, a high-speed storage subsystem is preferred, such as a fiber-connected storage array. This provides a consistent high-bandwidth storage medium that can satiate the GPU needs.

Several examples of such high-bandwidth systems include:

- NetApp AFFA800
- Cisco FlexPod
- FlashBlade

In Chapters 5 through 7 we provide further details for each of the core storage systems for managed Kubernetes for the public clouds.

Persistent volume claims and Kubeflow storage

Kubeflow, by default, will use persistent volumes (*https://oreil.ly/Hv2Im*) (PVs) and persistent volume claims (PVCs) for its storage needs. As an example, when a user deploys a notebook server, they will be given the option of dynamically allocating storage (out of a storage class), or to use an existing persistent volume claim.

The key distinction to understand between PVs and PVCs is that a PV is simply a representation of storage "somewhere," such as an allocated "1 GB of space." To actually utilize that storage space, a claim must be made against that storage. Once a claim is made, Kubernetes provides certain guarantees that for the lifespan of the claim, the underlying storage will not be released. Hence, in the context of Kubernetes, it's not enough to simply have a PV, but a PVC must be acquired against that storage as well.

If a user dynamically provisions storage, Kubeflow will automatically create a PVC against the newly allocated storage, which can later be used and reused for various pods, notebooks, etc. If a user would like to provide an *existing* PVC when setting up a Kubeflow environment, such as Notebook, it is the PVC that is provided to Kubeflow (and not the PV itself).

Container Management and Artifact Repositories

Container management is key to Kubeflow and Kubernetes (or any container orchestration system) because we have to have some place for container images to live.

We should be clear here how container images differ from configuration files (e.g., Dockerfiles) that define container images. We can push our configuration files (Dockerfiles) to a source control repository such as *github.com*, but we need a different repository to manage application binary artifacts (e.g., container images).

Specifically, we need a place to store and manage all of our container application images for later deployment to Kubernetes.

There are two types of artifact repositories for container images:

- Public container image repositories (or registries)
- Private (and perhaps on-premise) container image repositories (or registries)

Public repositories/registries are typically accessed across the internet and allow everyone to see your containers (at least at the free tier). The most popular public artifact repository is *hub.docker.com*, also known as Docker Hub.

Private repositories/registrie can also be hosted on the internet, or be hosted on-premise. The details and implementation of creating and managing private repositories and registries are specific to each implementation.

The important key for Kubeflow is to understand that all container images must be *pulled* from a container repository somewhere. By default, Kubeflow is preconfigured to pull all container images from the Google Container Registry (gcr.io). Kubeflow provides a mechanism for setting the location of the container registry.

Setting up an internal container repository

JFrog Artifactory OSS (*https://oreil.ly/qkP4c*) is an open source option for an on-premise container application registry (there are also commercial upgrades over the open source version (*https://oreil.ly/bI57S*)).

To download Artifactory (or get a Docker image), check out their website (*https://oreil.ly/gQi7W*). To install Artifactory on-premise, see their Confluence documentation (*https://oreil.ly/25K8f*). Artifactory includes support for:

- Solaris
- MacOS
- Windows
- Linux

Artifactory dependencies include a local database (default is an embedded Derby database), a filestore (local FS is the default), and integration with an HTTP server.

Accessing and Interacting with Kubeflow

There are two major ways to work with Kubeflow:

- The CLI, primarily using the kubectl tool, as well as the kfctl tool
- With a web browser, using the Kubeflow web UI

We cover the details of each in the next subsections.

It's important to keep in mind that the Kubeflow management operations—such as deploying a Kubeflow installation, upgrading components of Kubeflow, etc.—are done using the kfctl tool, while seeing what the cluster is currently "doing" is done via the kubectl tool.

Common Command-Line Operations

kubectl is the fundamental tool we are interested in for command line options on Kubeflow. In a previous section in this chapter we reviewed some of the key things we can do on a Kubernetes-based cluster with kubectl. The relevant operations on Kubeflow we are interested in with kubectl are:

- Running a basic container with some code, typically Python, on our cluster
- Running a group of containers on a special Kubernetes operator such as TFJob

For the first case, many times our practitioners have some Python code they'd like to run on GPUs. In these cases we create a container with the appropriate dependencies and run it on our Kubernetes cluster with Kubeflow.

In the second case, we need to set up our job YAML file to specify a targeted Kubernetes customer operator, such as TFJob, so we can leverage special container coordination modes such as TensorFlow distributed training.

Accessible Web UIs

The key web resource Kubeflow provides is the Kubeflow Dashboard UI that has links to all the other web-accessible resources Kubeflow provides. In Figure 4-2, we can see what the dashboard looks like.

As discussed in Chapter 1, this dashboard is effectively a quick table for the other relevant resources available via a web browser for Kubeflow users.

Figure 4-2. Kubeflow UI

Installing Kubeflow

In this section, we will discuss the steps required to install Kubeflow.

System Requirements

As of the time of writing, the Kubernetes cluster must meet the following minimum requirements:

- 4 CPUs
- 50 GB storage
- 12 GB memory

The recommended Kubernetes version is 1.14. Kubeflow has been validated and tested on Kubernetes 1.14. Your cluster must run at least Kubernetes version 1.11, and Kubeflow does not work on Kubernetes 1.16.

Set Up and Deploy

Installing Kubeflow requires these steps:

1. Download the `kfctl` tool.
2. Prepare the Kubeflow artifacts.
3. Deploy the artifacts to a cluster.

Using a compatible system (such as Linux, or macOS), you acquire the `kfctl` tool by downloading it from the Kubeflow releases pages on GitHub (*https://oreil.ly/vwCYT*). See Example 4-4.

Example 4-4. Download and unpack the kfctl binary[1]

```
$ cd ~/bin
$ curl -LOJ https://github.com/.../kfctl_v1.0.2-0-ga476281_linux.tar.gz
$ tar zxvf kfctl_v1.0.2-0-ga476281_linux.tar.gz
```

Once the tool has been downloaded, a working directory is created which will hold the artifacts and any customizations done for Kubeflow. In Example 4-5, we will use the `kf` directory in the user's home directory (~/kf).

Example 4-5. Create working directory

```
$ mkdir ~/kf
$ cd ~/kf
```

We are not ready to prepare the Kubeflow installation. This is done by specifying an initial manifest to download and prepare from, as in Example 4-6.

Example 4-6. Prepare Kubeflow installation[2]

```
$ cd ~/kf
$ ~/bin/kfctl build -V -f "https://raw.githubusercontent.com/..."
```

This will create a `kustomize` directory, which will hold all the templates Kubeflow will deploy. At this stage, any additional customizations can be done.

As an example, to set a custom container registry to use, we can use the `kfctl` tool. The command in Example 4-7 will change the default container registry from `gcr.io` to `hub.docker.com`.

Example 4-7. Set a custom container registry

```
$ ~/bin/kfctl alpha set-image-name hub.docker.com
```

---

1 The URL here has been shortened for space reasons; the full URL is *https://github.com/kubeflow/kfctl/releases/download/v1.0.2/kfctl_v1.0.2-0-ga476281_linux.tar.gz*.

2 The URL here has been shortened for space reasons; the full URL is *https://raw.githubusercontent.com/kubeflow/manifests/v1.0-branch/kfdef/kfctl_istio_dex.v1.0.2.yaml*.

Once we're ready, Kubeflow can be deployed using the `kfctl apply` command as seen in Example 4-8.

Example 4-8. Deploy Kubeflow

```
$ ~/bin/kfctl apply -V -f kfctl_istio_dex.v1.0.2.yaml
```

 Kubernetes Context

Keep in mind that Kubeflow will use the default Kubernetes context, and this will dictate to which Kubernetes cluster Kubeflow will be installed.

Summary

In this chapter we looked at the practical steps to deploying Kubeflow on-premise. While many users will want to jump to the cloud (as we will in the next chapters), on-premise installations are still relevant for many enterprise situations. As we move into the next chapter, we'll see how we begin to build on many of the concepts introduced in this chapter while evolving the install for a cloud deployment.

## CHAPTER 5

Running Kubeflow on Google Cloud

In this chapter we'll continue to apply concepts and themes from the book so far, but now we'll shift gears and look at deploying to the cloud. Most organizations will have some sort of preference for one of the three major clouds, based on technology differentiators or dogma around history with a particular vendor. It really comes down to, very often, "which is your organization's preferred cloud?"

There are many places that offer hosted VMs, but for the purposes of talking about Kubeflow operations we're going to focus on the "big three" cloud vendors:

- Google Cloud Platform (GCP)
- Azure Cloud Platform
- Amazon Web Services (AWS)

Other vendors offer managed Kubernetes as a service, and are probably good candidates for deploying Kubeflow, but, for the sake of brevity, we'll focus on the big three clouds. Our focus for each cloud offering is how their managed Kubernetes is deployed, and then what products on the cloud are relevant for integration.

In this chapter, we give a review of the relevant components to Kubeflow operations for Google Cloud, and then point out the specific aspects of the cloud to keep in mind. Kubeflow can run on GCP via the managed Google Kubernetes Engine (GKE). Let's start off by taking a tour of GCP.

Overview of the Google Cloud Platform

The Google Cloud Platform is a suite of modular services that include:

- Computing
- Data storage
- Data analytics
- Machine learning

These services represent a set of physical assets such as servers, memory, hard disks, and virtual resources such as virtual machines. These assets live in Google datacenters around the world, and each datacenter belongs to a global *region*.

Each *region* is a collection of *zones*, which are separate and distinct from other zones in the same region (*https://oreil.ly/Jus_-*). A zone identifier is a combination of the region ID and a letter representing the zone within the region. An example would be zone "c" in the region "us-east1": its full ID would be `us-east1-c`.

Some regions have different types of available resources (e.g., some regions do not have GPUs of certain types available, different storage options, etc.).

Check Out Google Cloud Locations Around the World

To see all of the regions and zones available, check out Google Cloud's page on locations (*https://oreil.ly/k4T1Y*).

Some of the major services offered on top of the base cloud infrastructure include:

- App Engine
- Compute Engine
- Google Kubernetes Engine (GKE)
- Cloud Storage
- Cloud DNS
- Cloud Console
- Cloud Shell
- Cloud APIs
- Cloud Identity and Access Management (IAM)
- Cloud Identity-Aware Proxy (IAP)

This is not an exhaustive list of services, but we want to highlight a few relevant services for operating Kubeflow and Kubernetes on GCP. In the following subsections we'll dig deeper in some of the services that are relevant to Kubeflow.

Storage

Google Cloud Storage is an object store service for the Google Cloud Platform that allows us to store and access data. It is considered Infrastructure as a Service (IaaS) and is a combination of scalability and performance along with the security functionality of the Google Cloud Platform. Similar to how Amazon's S3 is set up, Google Cloud Storage is organized into buckets that are identified by a unique key. Within each unique bucket, we can have individual objects.

All objects are addressable using HTTP URLs with patterns such as:

- *http://bucket.storage.googleapis.com/object*
- *https://storage.cloud.google.com/bucket/object*
- *https://storage.googleapis.com/bucket/object*

Four classes of storage (*https://oreil.ly/MOnfD*) are offered by the Google Storage service:

- Multi-regional Storage
- Regional storage
- Nearline storage (*https://oreil.ly/TmzVQ*)
- Coldline storage (*https://oreil.ly/0B5hM*)

All of these storage classes offer low latency and high durability. The main consideration for what type of storage offering we want to use for a particular dataset is how often we'd want to access the dataset.

You would use multi-regional storage if you were building a global service and accessing the same data from multiple regions. For example, if you were serving video files in a global service then you'd want a multiregional bucket because you don't want users in Europe fetching from a US datacenter. If you're only running in a single region (typical for training) then regional storage should be sufficient.

When we're processing data with Google Cloud DataProc or a Google Compute Engine instance, then we'd want to use regional storage. In cases where we're only going to access the data once a month, we can opt to use the nearline storage offering. In the case that we only plan on accessing a dataset once a year (e.g., disaster recovery), then we can go with the coldline storage offering, which is the cheapest of the four offerings.

Object Storage Versus Block Storage

In the situation where you are looking at both GCP object storage (*https://oreil.ly/1gf9Z*) and GCP block storage, the main advantage for block storage is that it can be mounted via PVC in Kubernetes. As a result, block storage provides POSIX semantics and works with POSIX-compliant file libraries (e.g., File library in Python)— in contrast, reading/writing GCS requires special libraries.

Google storage upload operations are atomic, providing a consistency model that has strong read-after-write consistency for our upload operations. As we've described, the Google storage API is consistent regardless of the storage class selected for the dataset.

Understanding GCP Cloud Storage Pricing

For more details on how pricing works for the Google Cloud Storage offering, check out the Google Cloud page (*https://oreil.ly/v_cvq*).

Google Cloud Identity-Aware Proxy

Kubeflow consists of a number of web applications (e.g., the Kubeflow Dashboard, Jupyter Notebooks, the pipelines UI, etc.) as well as APIs (e.g., the pipelines and Katib APIs) that users need to be able to access from their local machine. To provide a secure, multiuser deployment, we need to solve two problems:

Authentication
> We need to verify a user's identity and know the identity of the user so we can show information specific to that user (e.g., only show a user the notebooks or pipelines they created).

Authorization
> We need to restrict access to Kubeflow and services within Kubeflow based on the user's identity.

Kubeflow provides a pluggable architecture for handling authentication and authorization that makes it easy to integrate the recommended solutions for a particular cloud or on-premise deployment.

On Google Cloud Platform, using Cloud IAP is the recommended solution for authentication and authorization. When Kubeflow is secured with IAP, only users with the IAP-secured web app user IAM role will be allowed to access Kubeflow; all other requests will be rejected. Furthermore, all of this is handled by Google Cloud's highly scalable IAM service without ever hitting the actual Kubeflow services running in your project.

In Figure 5-1 we can see how Cloud IAP manages the authentication and authorization flow.

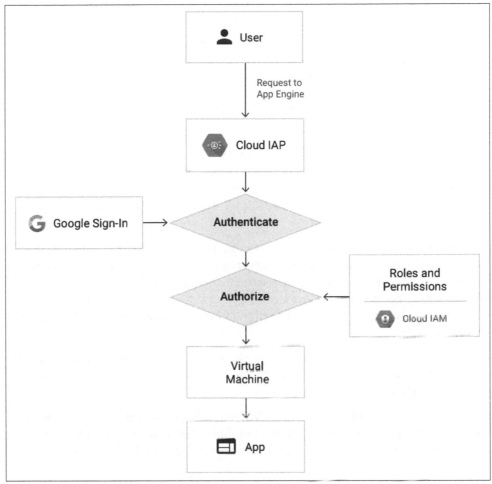

Figure 5-1. The Google Cloud IAP authentication and authorization flow

IAP will attach a signed JSON Web Token (JWT) to the request. Kubeflow services use this JWT to:

- Identify the user (e.g., to create custom views of resources specific to the user).
- Perform fine-grained authorization.

Once we've granted a user access to an application, Cloud IAP will execute authentication and authorization checks when the user tries to access the Cloud IAP-secured application, as we can see in Figure 5-1.

Kubeflow uses Istio to provide fine-grained access control to individual services within a Kubeflow cluster. For example, Kubeflow relies on Istio to ensure that Alice can only access her notebooks and not notebooks owned by Bob.

A major advantage of IAP over traditional VPN solutions is that access can be restricted based on a user's context. For example, we may want to allow Alice access to Kubeflow but only if she is running on a trusted corporate device that has all of the latest security patches, and not from untrusted devices (e.g., a hotel's business center).

Google Cloud Security and the Cloud Identity-Aware Proxy

To manage access to applications running in Google Cloud's App Engine standard environment, App Engine flexible environment, Compute Engine, and GKE, Google recommends we use the Cloud IAP. We are able to use an application-level access control model as Cloud IAP establishes a central authorization layer for applications such as Kubeflow that are accessed by HTTPS. This allows us an alternative to using network-level firewalls.

We want to use Cloud IAP when we want to keep our users using access control policies for applications and resources. This means we can set up a group policy for members of one group to access the system, such as our data scientists, and then another group policy for engineers working on another system such that they cannot use Kubeflow. In Figure 5-2 we can see how Cloud IAP manages the authentication and authorization flow.

Once we've granted a user access to an application, Cloud IAP will execute authentication and authorization checks when the user tries to access the Cloud IAP-secured application, as we can see in Figure 5-2.

Roles in the Cloud IAM (*https://oreil.ly/Y37Nt*) control who can access systems protected by Cloud IAP. This allows us to set up fine-grained access controls for users of a product or resource such as Kubeflow without requiring a VPN.

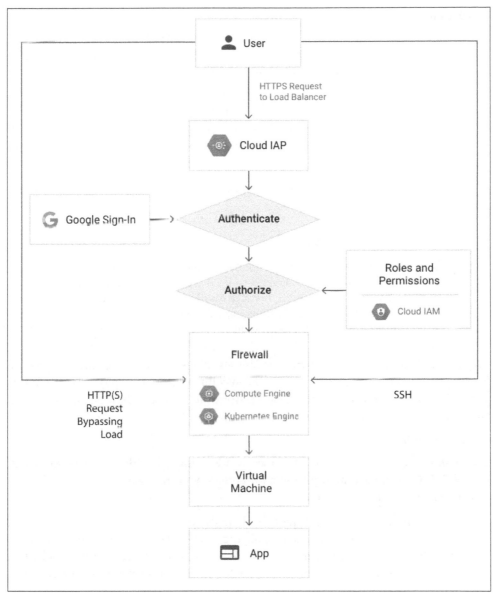

Figure 5-2. Google Cloud IAP authentication and authorization checks flow (source: Google Cloud documentation (https://oreil.ly/OF0hD))

Authentication

A system determines a client's identity through methods of authentication. We can authenticate to a GCP API by either using a normal user account or by using a GCP service account. We cover service accounts later in this chapter.

For GKE applications such as Kubeflow, HTTPS requests to Kubeflow are sent to the load balancer and then routed to Cloud IAP. If Cloud IAP is enabled, then the Cloud IAP Authentication Server is queried for information on Kubeflow, such as GCP project number, request URL, and Cloud IAP credentials in the request headers or cookies.

OAuth 2.0 manages the Google Account sign-in system and sets a token in the Kubeflow user's browser cookie for later use.

Cloud IAP and OAuth 2.0

Cloud IAP uses OAuth 2.0 to manage the Google Account sign-in flow that the user is directed to if no credentials are found. Once the user signs in, a token is stored locally for future use. All Google Cloud Platform applications use the OAuth 2.0 protocol for authentication and authorization.

The Cloud IAP checks for browser credentials of the current user and if none are found, it redirects the user to the Google Account sign-in web page. Typically this access flow is kicked off by authenticating from the gcloud sdk tools on your local laptop with the command:

```
gcloud auth login
```

This command will bring up a browser window loaded with the page shown in Figure 5-3. (If you have multiple Gmail accounts, you may see an account selection screen before you see this screen.)

The system checks to see if the request credentials are stored in the system and, if so, the system uses these credentials to pull the user's identity. The user identity is defined as both their email address and user ID. Beyond pulling the user's identity, the system checks the user's Cloud IAM role to see if the user has access to the given resource.

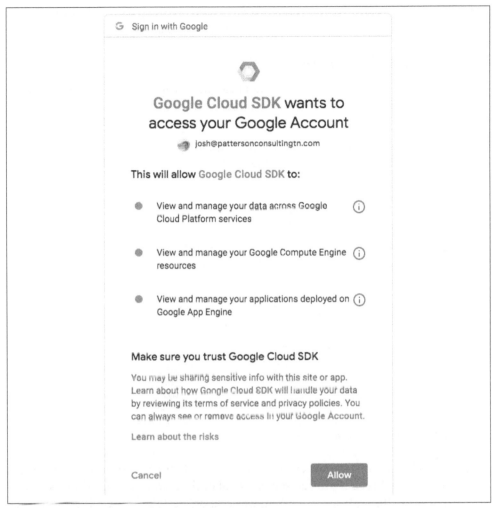

Figure 5-3. Google Cloud SDK access confirmation screen

Authorization

Authorization (*https://oreil.ly/U8uGn*) checks to see if a user has access to certain resources, and determines what an authenticated client can access with respect to GCP resources. In the world of authorization we want to create policies showing which user can access which resource and to what extent.

On GCP, the relevant Cloud IAM policies are applied to by Cloud IAP to confirm whether the user is allowed to access the desired resource. For example, when we log in to the GCP Console project, the system checks to see if we have the IAP-secured web app user role. If so, we can access the GCP Console project.

A Kubeflow user will need the proper IAP-secured web app user role in our GCP Console project if they want to access the Kubeflow application.

GCP Projects for Application Deployments

We need a GCP project to contain any application that we want to run on GCP. We can access GCP from either the command line or from the web UI, which we see in Figure 5-4.

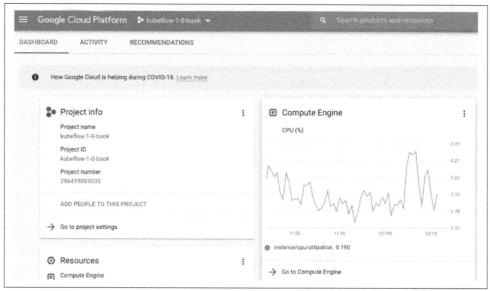

Figure 5-4. Main GCP Console screen

From the GCP Console we can create a project that holds any arbitrary application. For Kubeflow, we'll need a project to contain all of the resources related to the Kubeflow application. To see a list of current projects or create a new GCP project, click the project drop-down menu in the top bar to the right of the "Google Cloud Platform" logo. We will see a dialog pop-up similar to the image in Figure 5-5.

We'll use both the GCP Console and GCP project screen later on in this chapter when we start to set up Kubeflow on our own GCP account. Let's continue our overview of the GCP platform by taking a look at service accounts.

Figure 5-5. Project selection dialog screen in the GCP Console application

GCP Service Accounts

Sometimes we want an account to represent an application on GCP as opposed to a user on GCP. For this purpose we use *service accounts* on GCP. These service accounts allow our application to access other GCP APIs on our behalf. Service accounts are supported by all GCP applications and are recommended to be used for most server applications.

Using Service Accounts

When deploying server applications on GCP it is recommended to use service accounts as a best practice. No matter if we are developing locally or as a production system, we should consider using service accounts so we don't end up hardcoding in transient user accounts or private API keys (e.g., "a Google project ID").

Given that Kubeflow runs as a long-lived application in a GCP project, it is a good candidate for using service accounts, as we'll see later in this chapter.

Beware Leaving Instances Running

Kubeflow can quickly consume GCP resources. Once you get going it's easy to set up Kubeflow and then forget you allocated all of those GCP resources. If you don't plan on using Kubeflow for an extended period of time, you'll likely need to tear down the Kubeflow install or you may get an unexpected GCP bill at the end of the month.

Signing Up for Google Cloud Platform

If you don't already have an account on Google Cloud Platform (GCP), sign up on the home page (*https://cloud.google.com*).

Kubeflow 1.0 Won't Install on GCP with Free-Tier Account

The free-tier accounts won't allow enough resources to run Kubeflow. You'll need to provide billing information to deploy Kubeflow 1.0 on GCP.

Installing the Google Cloud SDK

The Google Cloud SDK is a set of client-side tools that allow us to work with the GCP. Some of the main command-line tools include:

- gcloud
- gsutil
- bq

These tools allow us to use services such as:

- Google BigQuery
- Google Cloud Storage
- Google Compute Engine

There is also a robust set of web UIs for the Google Cloud Platform, and we have the option to do most functions from either the command-line or the web UI.

Update Python

Before you install Google Cloud's SDK, make sure and upgrade Python to the latest version to avoid issues (e.g., Secure Sockets Layer (SSL) issues). There are multiple ways to manage Python and its dependencies, and the ways will vary depending on what platform you are running on. For macOS users (a typical client), this may be a number of package managers, including:

- Anaconda
- The package installer from *python.org*
- brew

For other operating systems there will be other options; however, we simply want to remind the user that Python should be updated to the latest version regardless of what platform you are using.

Download and Install Google Cloud SDK

After you have Python updated, take a look at the instructions (*https://oreil.ly/YOzZW*) for getting the GCloud SDK working. For macOS users, a simple way to do this is to use the interactive installer (*https://oreil.ly/otbmm*).

Once you have the GCloud SDK working, log in to your GCloud account from the command line with the gcloud auth tool (*https://oreil.ly/X2BgF*):

```
gcloud auth login
```

Following this, a sequence of screens will pop up in your web browser, asking for permission via OAuth for GCloud tools to access the Google Cloud Platform.

Installing Kubeflow on Google Cloud Platform

The high-level version of the Kubeflow install process is covered in these steps:

1. Create a GCP Project.
2. Configure the project (billing, APIs, etc.).
3. Check resource quotas.
4. Set up OAuth credentials.
5. Deploy Kubeflow.

To set up a basic Kubeflow install on GCP, we have the option of allowing the Kubeflow installation scripts to handle the GKE cluster part for us as part of the Kubeflow install.

Production Kubeflow Installations

Production enterprise installations of Kubeflow likely will want more control over how Kubernetes is set up, so we include instructions in this chapter about how to set up Kubeflow both ways.

Now we'll take a closer look at how to perform each step from the Kubeflow install step list.

Create a Project in the GCP Console

We need to create a new GCP project to contain our Kubeflow installation. In Figure 5-6 we can see the project's dialog window from earlier in this chapter, but with a focus on the top half.

Figure 5-6. Google Compute Platform Project dialog window

To create a new project, we click the New Project button in the top right of the dialog window, bringing up the New Project dialog window, as seen in Figure 5-7.

Figure 5-7. New Project dialog window

Once we have a new project created for GCP, we need to do some configuration work. Specifically, we need to enable certain APIs, as we'll see in the next section.

 Optional: Manually Create a Managed GKE Cluster

The easiest install of Kubeflow does the GKE cluster installation for us, so we'll skip those instructions for now.

Enabling APIs for a Project

We need to enable the following APIs for our new project:

- Compute Engine API (*https://oreil.ly/lfVEY*)
- Kubernetes Engine API (*https://oreil.ly/Xn1rl*)
- Identity and Access Management (IAM) API (*https://oreil.ly/3_Fj3*)
- Deployment Manager API (*https://oreil.ly/j2UJe*)
- Cloud Resource Manager API (*https://oreil.ly/seu3f*)
- Cloud Filestore API (*https://oreil.ly/Z_hrC*)
- AI Platform Training and Prediction API (*https://oreil.ly/69spv*)
- Cloud Build API (*https://oreil.ly/L-_98*) (required if you plan to use Fairing (*https://oreil.ly/ocB0r*) in your Kubeflow cluster)

The Compute Engine API creates and runs VMs on GCP. The Kubernetes Engine API allows our tools to create and manage Kubernetes clusters on GCP, and the Identity APIs allow us to manage users. Finally, the Google Cloud Deployment Manager API allows our tools to programmatically configure, deploy, and view Google Cloud services.

By default, most of the APIs for a project are disabled for new GCP projects, so we need to enable each of these APIs so that Kubeflow can operate correctly. To find the page for enabling APIs, go to the main page for "APIs and Services" on GCP by using the top left drop-down navigation panel.

Once there, we'll see a page similar to Figure 5-8, with an Enable APIs and Services button at the top.

Figure 5-8. APIs and Services screen on GCP

When we click this button, it will take us to the GCP API Library page. We can either use the preceding links to find the specific API pages to enable, or use the search box on the API library, as seen in Figure 5-9.

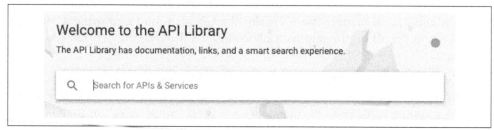

Figure 5-9. GCP API library search box

When we enable each API, we'll see a screen as shown in Figure 5-10.

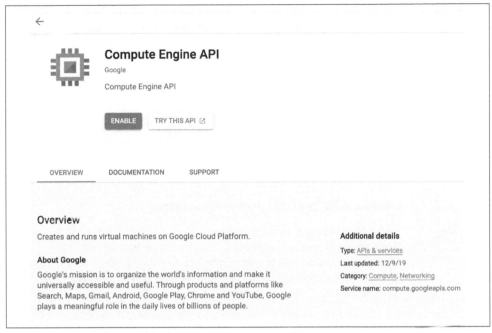

Figure 5-10. Panel to enable the Compute Engine API

Resources and Quotas

Some resources have quotas on them, and you will hit those quotas periodically, which will limit what you can do with Kubeflow. As you hit the limitations on a project, you'll have to request increases in services quotas. For more information on how to check and adjust resource quotas, check out the Google Cloud documentation (*https://oreil.ly/c3MsJ*).

Set Up OAuth for GCP Cloud IAP

The next step in the Kubeflow install process for GCP is to set up Cloud IAP (previously mentioned in this chapter). Cloud IAP is what we'll want to use for production Kubeflow installations.

When we set up Cloud IAP, we create an OAuth client for Cloud IAP on GCP that uses the email address to verify the user's identity. We need to do four tasks to get Cloud IAP working with Kubeflow:

1. Set up our OAuth consent screen.
2. Configure the Credentials tab.
3. Confirm the redirect URI.
4. Save the client ID and client secret to use later to enable Cloud IAP.

Let's now work through each of those four steps.

Kubeflow on GCP and Password-Only Authentication

Earlier versions of Kubeflow allowed you to use basic authentication (e.g., username and password) with Kubeflow instead of Cloud IAP. Future versions will completely remove the password-only functionality. Cloud IAP is the recommended way to deploy Kubeflow on GCP.

Set up the OAuth consent screen

To get Cloud IAP working we first need to set up our consent screen. We can find this page in the GCP portal (*https://oreil.ly/uuMnv*).

We want to create an OAuth client ID that identifies Cloud IAP when requesting access to a user's email account. The user's identity is verified by Kubeflow using the email address.

This screen will allow a user of Kubeflow to choose whether or not to grant access to their private data. All applications in the associated GCP project will work through this consent screen. The OAuth consent screen configuration panel is pictured in Figure 5-11.

We need to fill out a few specific fields:

- Application name (a name you give the application)
- Support email (likely your own email address, or the organization's IT support email address)
- Authorized domains

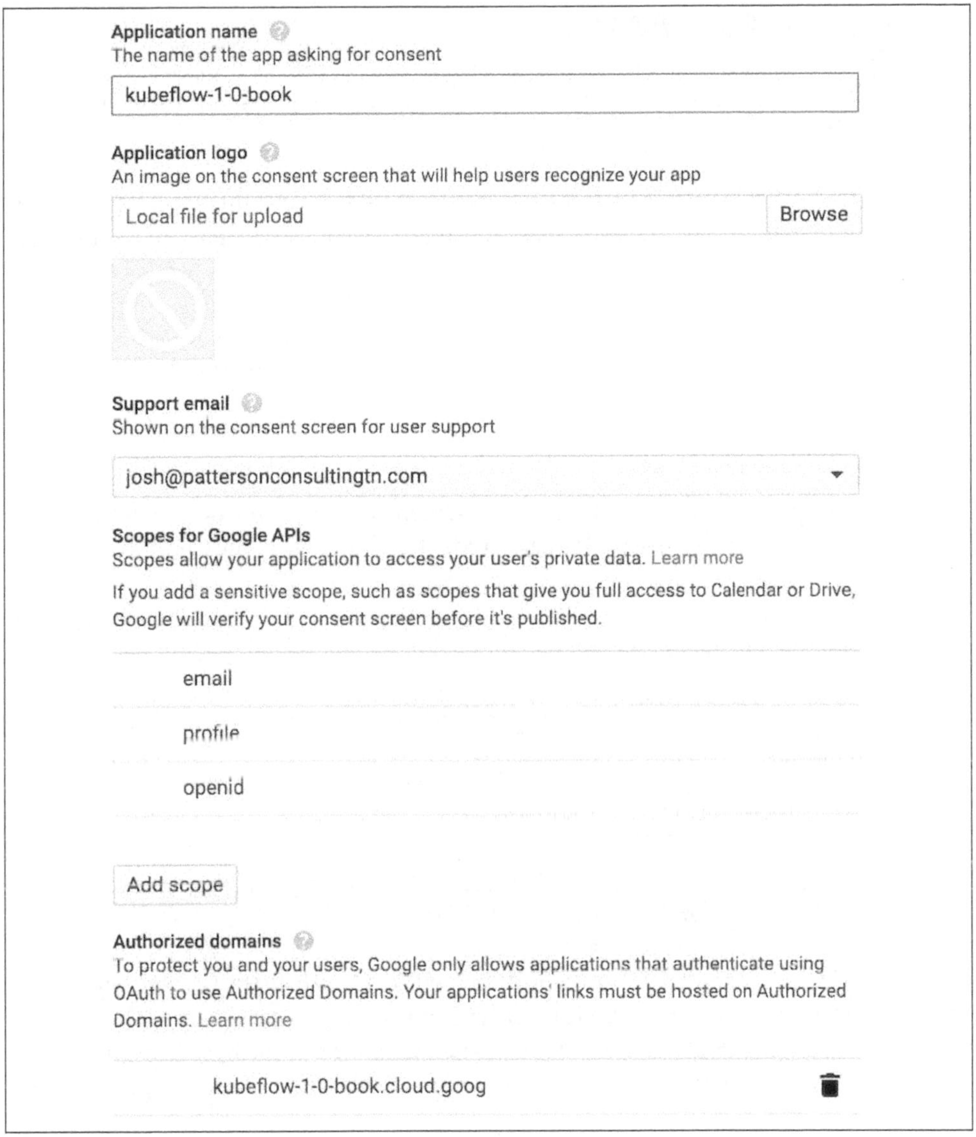

Application name ⊘
The name of the app asking for consent

> kubeflow-1-0-book

Application logo ⊘
An image on the consent screen that will help users recognize your app

| Local file for upload | Browse |

Support email ⊘
Shown on the consent screen for user support

| josh@pattersonconsultingtn.com | ▼ |

Scopes for Google APIs
Scopes allow your application to access your user's private data. Learn more

If you add a sensitive scope, such as scopes that give you full access to Calendar or Drive, Google will verify your consent screen before it's published.

email

profile

openid

Add scope

Authorized domains ⊘
To protect you and your users, Google only allows applications that authenticate using OAuth to use Authorized Domains. Your applications' links must be hosted on Authorized Domains. Learn more

kubeflow-1-0-book.cloud.goog   🗑

Figure 5-11. OAuth consent screen

For authorized domains, we want to use something of the pattern: *<GCP Project ID>.cloud.goog*. Where the *<GCP Project ID>* is the GCP Project ID for the project containing the Kubeflow deployment, as we saw in Figure 5-11. In that image, we can see an authorized domain entered for the project ID `kubeflow-1-0-book`.

Finding the Project ID

We can find the project ID at any time in the GCP Console by clicking on the "project settings" link in the top right drop-down menu.

Some project configurations will not present the authorized domains configuration. If you are using your own domain, then add that as well. In this case, the authorized domain would be:

```
kubeflow-1-0-book.cloud.goog
```

Once you have filled out the configuration fields for the OAuth consent screen, click the Save button.

Configuring the Credentials tab

On the same page for the OAuth consent screen tab we have the Credentials tab. When we click this tab we'll see a "Create credentials" dialog, as shown in Figure 5-12.

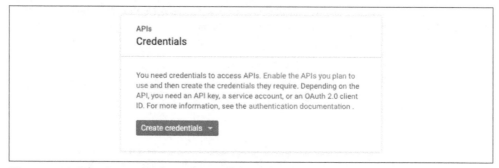

Figure 5-12. The Create credentials panel for GCP

Click the "Create credentials" button and then click "OAuth client ID." We then select "Web application" under the "Application type" and in the "Name" box we'll enter any name we choose for the OAuth client ID. (The name we choose here is not the name of the application nor the name of the Kubeflow deployment, but a handy label for the OAuth client ID.)

Next let's configure the "Authorized redirect URIs" field with the following URI:

```
https://iap.googleapis.com/v1/oauth/clientIds/<CLIENT_ID>:handleRedirect
```

Here `<CLIENT_ID>` is the OAuth client ID (similar to: "abc.apps.googleusercontent.com"). To get the `CLIENT_ID` we need to first create the OAuth Client ID and save it. Then we will see a dialog similar to the image in Figure 5-13.

Figure 5-13. GCP OAuth client secret page

The post-creation pop-up dialog will give us the client ID we need to update the redirect URL. We'll want to save both the client ID and the client secret to enable Cloud IAP in our environment variables during the Kubeflow install process later in the chapter.

To complete our authorized redirect URI, we need to find our newly created OAuth credential in the credential list. See Figure 5-14.

Figure 5-14. OAuth credentials panel

To complete the Redirect URI entry, you'll need to click the pencil button on the lower right of the screen for the newly created OAuth 2.0 client ID. When we click the pencil icon, it takes us back to the client ID edit page. There we can insert the new client ID in the template of:

```
https://iap.googleapis.com/v1/oauth/clientIds/<CLIENT_ID>:handleRedirect
```

This ends up looking like the image in Figure 5-15 based on the client ID in the image in Figure 5-14.

Figure 5-15. OAuth 2.0 client configuration panel

Once you enter the URI and press Return, this should complete the entry of the Authorized redirect URI. This should complete your OAuth 2.0 setup.

Now we're ready to continue our installation of Kubeflow.

Authorized Redirect URIs

The URI for the authorized redirect URI is not dependent on the Kubeflow deployment or endpoint. We may have multiple Kubeflow deployments using the same OAuth client and we would not have to modify the redirect URIs.

Deploy Kubeflow Using the Command-Line Interface

To deploy Kubeflow from the command line on GCP, we'll use the `kfctl` command-line tool included with the Kubeflow project. The command-line install process gives us more control over how the deployment process works.

Deploying Kubeflow with a GUI

If you'd like to use a GUI for the install, check out the online resource on deploying Kubeflow using the deployment UI (*https://oreil.ly/4e6b8*).

The prerequisites for the command-line installation are:

- `kubectl` installed
- `gcloud` SDK installed

GCP Cloud Shell and Boost Mode

If you are using Cloud Shell (*https://oreil.ly/tibiM*) for certain command-line operations, you should enable boost mode (*https://oreil.ly/dSFFY*). Boost mode temporarily boosts the power of your Cloud Shell VM, which helps with certain install operations.

To install Kubeflow on GCP, we have to complete the following steps:

1. Create user credentials.
2. Create environment variables.
3. Set up `kfctl`.
4. Run `kfctl` comands.
5. Confirm deployment.

Let's now work through each of these high-level steps in detail.

Creating user credentials

We need to authenticate our local client with OAuth2 credentials for the Google Cloud SDK tools. We do this with the command:

```
gcloud auth application-default login
```

This command will immediately make the Google Authentication web page pop up in your web browser, as in Figure 5-16.

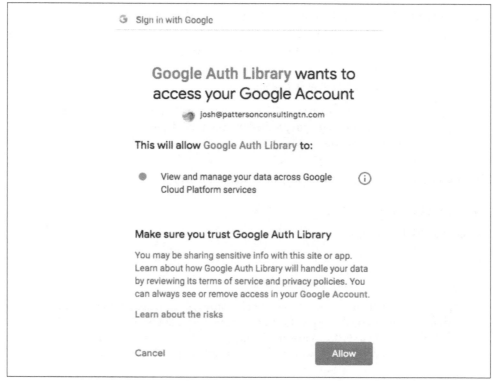

Figure 5-16. The GCP authentication confirmation web page

When we click the Allow button, the command line will show output similar to Example 5-1.

Example 5-1. The command-line console output post-authentication confirmation

```
(base) Joshs-MacBook-Pro-2:kubeflow_book_tests josh$ gcloud auth \
   application-default login
Your browser has been opened to visit:

http://accounts.google.com/o/oauth2/auth?redirect_uri?http%3A%2F%2Flocalhost%3A \
8085%2F051850-6qr4p6hn506pt8ejuq83di341hur.apps.googleusercontent.com&scope?https \
%3A%2F%2Fwww.googleapis.com%Fauth%2Fcloud-platform&access_type=offline
```

```
Credentials saved to file: \
  [/Users/josh/.config/gcloud/application_default_credentials.json]

These credentials will be used by any library that requests \
Application Default Credentials.

To generate an access token for other uses, run:
  gcloud auth application-default print-access-token
```

Now let's move on and create the required local environment variables.

gcloud auth Login Variations

Normally, as a developer we interact with GCP via the gcloud command with the auth command:

```
gcloud auth login
```

Once we run this command from our terminal, the system gets our credentials and stores them in *~/.config/gcloud/* and these credentials will be found automatically. However, any code or SDK running code will not automatically pick up these credentials.

However, when we want our code to interact with GCP via the SDK in a system such as Kubeflow, we want to use the variation of the auth command:

```
gcloud auth application-default login
```

The difference in this variation of the auth command is that the credentials are stored in "the well-known location for Application Default Credentials" (*https://oreil.ly/3dkcw*). This enables our SDK-based code to find the credentials in a consistent fashion (*https://oreil.ly/0G-ue*) automatically.

Create required environment variables

Now that we have our Cloud IAP system set up on GCP, we need to configure the local kfctl tool to be able to use it. Let's create environment variables for CLIENT_ID and CLIENT_SECRET, as we can see in the following sample code. This is where we'll use the information we saved previously for the OAuth client ID on GCP.

```
export CLIENT_ID=<CLIENT_ID from OAuth page>
export CLIENT_SECRET=<CLIENT_SECRET from OAuth page>
```

We can see the same information that was saved previously being used for CLIENT_ID:

```
josh$ export CLIENT_ID=1009144991723-3hf8m978i03v1tfep28302afnilufe1i.apps. \
googleusercontent.com
josh$ echo $CLIENT_ID
1009144991723-3hf8m978i03v1tfep28302afnilufe1i.apps.googleusercontent.com
```

And then the same export command being used for CLIENT_SECRET:

```
josh$ export CLIENT_SECRET=fLT_u5KnCc1oQVYKbMmkoh0d
josh$ echo $CLIENT_SECRET
fLT_u5KnCc1oQVYKbMmkoh0d
```

We now have our environment variables set up for Cloud IAP authentication on GCP.

Now let's set up the kfctl tool.

Set up kfctl

We need to download and set up the kfctl tool before we can continue our Kubeflow installation. kfctl is similar to kubectl but is specialized for Kubeflow.

Download the kfctl v1.0.2 release from the Kubeflow releases page (*https://oreil.ly/u-x1O*). Now unpack the downloaded tarball for the release with the command:

```
tar -xvf kfctl_<release tag>_<platform>.tar.gz
```

Optionally, we can add the kfctl location to our path, which is recommended unless we want to use the full path for kfctl each time we use it:

```
export PATH=$PATH:<path to kfctl in your kubeflow installation>
```

Now when we type the kfctl command from anywhere, we should see what appears in Example 5-2.

Example 5-2. kfctl command default output

```
A client CLI to create Kubeflow applications for specific platforms or 'on-prem'
to an existing Kubernetes cluster.

Usage:
  kfctl [command]

Available Commands:
  alpha       Alpha kfctl features.
  apply       deploys a Kubeflow application.
  build       Builds a KF App from a config file
  completion  Generate shell completions
  delete      Delete a Kubeflow application.
  generate    'kfctl generate' has been replaced by 'kfctl build'
Please switch to new semantics.
To build a KFAPP run -> kfctl build -f ${CONFIG}
Then to install -> kfctl apply
For more information, run 'kfctl build -h' or read the docs at www.kubeflow.org.
  help        Help about any command
  init        'kfctl init' has been removed.
Please switch to new semantics.
To install run -> kfctl apply -f ${CONFIG}
For more information, run 'kfctl apply -h' or read the docs at www.kubeflow.org.
```

```
version     Print the version of kfctl.

Flags:
  -h, --help   help for kfctl

Use "kfctl [command] --help" for more information about a command.
```

We're now ready to configure kfctl for our specific environment.

Set up environment variables for kfctl

We need to set up the following environment variables for use with kfctl:

- ZONE
- PROJECT
- KF_NAME
- BASE_DIR
- KF_DIR
- CONFIG_URI

The first environment variable we need is the zone where we want to deploy our GKE cluster and Kubeflow installation.

Setting the ZONE environment variable. If you'll recall from earlier in the chapter, a zone identifier (*https://oreil.ly/ELsmj*) is a combination of the region ID and a letter representing the zone within the region. An example would be zone "c" in the region "us-east1": its full ID would be us-east1-c. To configure our zone, check out the options in the Google Cloud documentation (*https://oreil.ly/yXKXS*).

 Not All Zones Are Created Equal

Some regions have different types of available resources (e.g., some regions do not have GPUs of certain types available, different storage options, etc.).

Once you have selected a zone ID to use, set up the $ZONE environment variable with the following command:

```
export ZONE=<your target zone>
```

Now that we have a zone selected, let's move on and configure the project ID for the GCP project.

Setting the PROJECT environment variable. We'll do this with this command:

```
export PROJECT=<your GCP project ID>
```

We can find our GCP project ID (not to be confused with the project name) by clicking on the line of three vertical dots in the upper-righthand corner of the Google Cloud Console screen, as in Figure 5-17.

Figure 5-17. GCP Console drop-down

When we click "Project settings," we should see a panel similar to Figure 5-18.

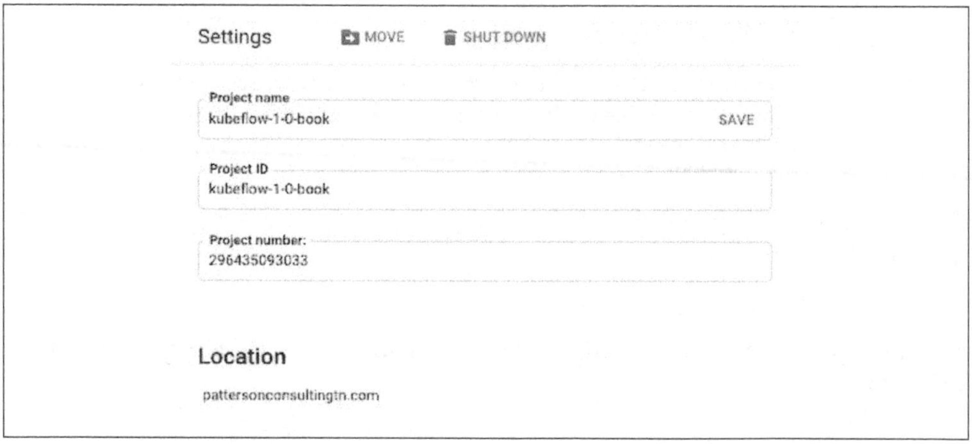

Figure 5-18. GCP project settings

Grab the Project ID from the middle input box and paste it into this export line. Once you execute this line in your local terminal, you should have your project ID as an environment variable.

Set GCloud configuration variables.   We also want to set the local `gcloud` tool variables:

```
gcloud config set project ${PROJECT}
gcloud config set compute/zone ${ZONE}
```

kfctl and gcloud Tools

`kfctl` by default uses the `gcloud` defaults for zone and project.

Setting the CONFIG environment variable.   We need to specify a configuration file during the "init" phase of the Kubeflow install, and set our CONFIG environment variable to point to the Kubeflow deployment configuration:

```
export CONFIG_URI=<url of your configuration file for init>
```

Kubeflow deployment configuration files are YAML files for specific ways to deploy Kubeflow (such as "on GCP with IAP enabled" (*https://oreil.ly/VEJL0*)). In this case, we want the CONFIG_URI for Kubeflow 1.0.2 on GCP, which is.

```
export CONFIG_URI="https://raw.githubusercontent.com/kubeflow/manifests/ \
    v1.0-branch/kfdef/kfctl_gcp_iap.v1.0.2.yaml"
```

Setting the Kubeflow deployment environment variables.   Now we need to set the environmental variable for the name of the directory where we want Kubeflow configurations to be stored. We do this with the following three environment variables:

- `$KF_NAME`
- `$BASE_DIR`
- `$KF_DIR`

The command to set the `KF_NAME` environment variable i as follows:

```
export KF_NAME=<your choice of application directory name>
```

Building on this environment variable, we further define:

```
export BASE_DIR=<path to a base directory>
export KF_DIR=${BASE_DIR}/${KF_NAME}
```

This gives us a full directory path to our new Kubeflow deployment subdirectory. With these environment variables set, we can use `kfctl` to deploy Kubeflow on GCP.

Kubeflow deployment with kfctl

Kubeflow deployment on GCP with `kfctl` at this point is only the following commands now that we have our variables set up:

```
mkdir -p ${KF_DIR}
cd ${KF_DIR}
kfctl apply -V -f ${CONFIG_URI}
```

When we run this, we should see output similar to the listing in Example 5-3.

Example 5-3. Sample output of kctl apply -V -f ${CONFIG_URI}

```
INFO[0481] Creating service account profiles-controller-service-account in...
INFO[0481] Service account already exists...              filename="gcp/gcp.go:1721"
INFO[0481] Setting up iam policy for serviceaccount: kf-1-0-book-deployment-admin...
INFO[0481] New policy: {[] [0xc000c1f200 0xc000c1f260] BwWpdeVmj8M= 1 {200 map...
INFO[0481] New policy: {[] [0xc000c1f200 0xc000c1f260] BwWpdeVmj8M= 1 {200 map...
INFO[0482] Downloading secret user-gcp-sa from namespace kubeflow filename=...
INFO[0482] Creating secret user-gcp-sa to namespace kubeflow-josh filename=...
INFO[0482] Generating PodDefault in namespace kubeflow-josh; APIVersion...
E0702 10:08:57.816996   14659 memcache.go:199] couldn't get resource list for...
E0702 10:08:57.885694   14659 memcache.go:111] couldn't get resource list for...
INFO[0484] Applied the configuration Successfully!        filename="cmd/apply.go:72"
```

The Kubeflow application should now be deployed on GCP. It may take a few minutes to show up as deployed in the GCP Console, but from the administrator's end of things, you are done with deployment commands.

Confirm Kubeflow deployment

To confirm we successfully deployed Kubeflow, we can use the command:

```
kubectl -n kubeflow get  all
```

This should show output similar to Example 5-4.

Example 5-4. kubectl -n kubeflow get all sample output

NAME	READY	STATUS	RESTARTS	AGE
pod/admission-webhook-bootstrap-stateful-set-0	1/1	Running	0	7m15s
pod/admission-webhook-deployment-64cb96ddbf-nhqxw	1/1	Running	0	6m47s
pod/application-controller-stateful-set-0	1/1	Running	0	7m47s
pod/argo-ui-778676df64-wkhc	1/1	Running	0	7m18s
pod/centraldashboard-f8d4bdf96-tlflp	1/1	Running	0	7m17s
pod/cloud-endpoints-controller-7764d66f9b-zjskn	1/1	Running	0	6m38s
pod/jupyter-web-app-deployment-5f954cd95c-6lv66	1/1	Running	0	7m13s
pod/katib-controller-6b789b6cb5-qqbr2	1/1	Running	1	6m51s
pod/katib-db-manager-64f548b47c-7lrlj	1/1	Running	1	6m51s
pod/katib-mysql-57884cb488-zztcx	1/1	Running	0	6m50s
pod/katib-ui-5c5cc6bd77-wqbwm	1/1	Running	0	6m50s

```
pod/kfserving-controller-manager-0                          2/2   Running     1   6m55s
pod/metacontroller-0                                        1/1   Running     0   7m19s
pod/metadata-db-76c9f78f77-zt4lw                            1/1   Running     0   7m9s
pod/metadata-deployment-674fdd976b-t475s                    1/1   Running     0   7m9s
pod/metadata-envoy-deployment-5688989bd6-v882g              1/1   Running     0   7m9s
pod/metadata-grpc-deployment-6d5b69bf44-cjm9l               1/1   Running     4   7m9s
pod/metadata-ui-9b8cd699d-6z6rh                             1/1   Running     0   7m8s
pod/minio-d56488484-8dznh                                   1/1   Running     0   6m48s
pod/ml-pipeline-768488fd9-l7gwd                             1/1   Running     0   6m49s
pod/ml-pipeline-ml-pipeline...                              1/1   Running     0   6m39s
pod/ml-pipeline-persistenceagent-5cf98c69df-gj2fx           1/1   Running     0   6m46s
pod/ml-pipeline-scheduledworkflow-5c594867c6-c2gcs          1/1   Running     0   6m40s
pod/ml-pipeline-ui-7cb547b666-ww9m6                         1/1   Running     0   6m43s
pod/ml-pipeline-viewer-controller...                        1/1   Running     0   6m40s
pod/mysql-67cb6fcdfc-s5gxb                                  1/1   Running     0   6m47s
pod/notebook-controller-deployment...                       1/1   Running     0   7m6s
pod/profiles-deployment-7c7fc789f4-xx8wp                    2/2   Running     0   6m37s
pod/pytorch-operator-5fd5f94bdd-cvtdh                       1/1   Running     0   7m5s
pod/seldon-controller-manager-679fc777cd-ktds9              1/1   Running     0   6m32s
pod/spark-operatorcrd-cleanup-vcjvs                         0/2   Completed   0   7m11s
pod/spark-operatorsparkoperator-c7b64b87f-8wrzb             1/1   Running     0   7m11s
pod/spartakus-volunteer-8579dbb8c-nft2g                     1/1   Running     0   6m55s
pod/tensorboard-6544748d94-kpcpb                            1/1   Running     0   6m54s
pod/tf-job-operator-7d7c8fb8bb-ddpc7                        1/1   Running     0   6m53s
pod/workflow-controller-945c84565-4fsm2                     1/1   Running     0   7m18s

NAME                                TYPE        CLUSTER-IP      PORT(S)              AGE
service/admission-webhook-service   ClusterIP   10.39.250.60    443/TCP              7m17s
service/application-controller...   ClusterIP   10.39.243.252   443/TCP              7m48s
service/argo-ui                     NodePort    10.39.250.187   80:32741/TCP         7m19s
service/centraldashboard            ClusterIP   10.39.242.15    80/TCP               7m18s
service/cloud-endpoints-controller  ClusterIP   10.39.254.242   80/TCP               6m40s
service/jupyter-web-app-service     ClusterIP   10.39.249.144   80/TCP               7m14s
service/katib-controller            ClusterIP   10.39.248.50    443/TCP,8080/TCP     6m52s
service/katib-db-manager            ClusterIP   10.39.244.156   6789/TCP             6m52s
service/katib-mysql                 ClusterIP   10.39.245.26    3306/TCP             6m52s
service/katib-ui                    ClusterIP   10.39.240.120   80/TCP               6m52s
service/kfserving-controller...     ClusterIP   10.39.243.191   8443/TCP             6m57s
service/kfserving-controller...     ClusterIP   10.39.244.157   443/TCP             6m57s
service/kfserving-webhook...        ClusterIP   10.39.250.37    443/TCP             6m4s
service/metadata-db                 ClusterIP   10.39.252.165   3306/TCP             7m11s
service/metadata-envoy-service      ClusterIP   10.39.249.146   9090/TCP             7m11s
service/metadata-grpc-service       ClusterIP   10.39.240.236   8080/TCP             7m11s
service/metadata-service            ClusterIP   10.39.249.11    8080/TCP             7m11s
service/metadata-ui                 ClusterIP   10.39.241.147   80/TCP               7m10s
service/minio-service               ClusterIP   10.39.252.113   9000/TCP             6m50s
service/ml-pipeline                 ClusterIP   10.39.251.159   8888/TCP,8887/TCP   6m50s
service/ml-pipeline-ml...           ClusterIP   10.39.247.130   8888/TCP             6m40s
service/ml-pipeline-tensor...       ClusterIP   10.39.240.173   80/TCP               6m45s
service/ml-pipeline-ui              ClusterIP   10.39.241.6     80/TCP               6m45s
service/mysql                       ClusterIP   10.39.240.174   3306/TCP             6m48s
service/notebook-controller...      ClusterIP   10.39.242.76    443/TCP             7m8s
```

```
service/profiles-kfam          ClusterIP   10.39.247.3     8081/TCP      6m39s
service/pytorch-operator       ClusterIP   10.39.243.225   8443/TCP      7m7s
service/seldon-webhook-service ClusterIP   10.39.251.78    43/TCP        6m33s
service/tensorboard            ClusterIP   10.39.251.89    9000/TCP      6m55s
service/tf-job-operator        ClusterIP   10.39.248.38    8443/TCP      6m54s

NAME                        DESIRED CURRENT READY UP-TO-DATE AVAILABLE AGE
daemonset.apps/nvidia-driver...  0      0      0      0          0      6m38s

NAME                                                READY UP-TO-DATE AVAILABLE AGE
deployment.apps/admission-webhook-deployment        1/1   1          1         7m17s
deployment.apps/argo-ui                             1/1   1          1         7m20s
deployment.apps/centraldashboard                    1/1   1          1         7m19s
deployment.apps/cloud-endpoints-controller          1/1   1          1         6m40s
deployment.apps/jupyter-web-app-deployment          1/1   1          1         7m15s
deployment.apps/katib-controller                    1/1   1          1         6m53s
deployment.apps/katib-db-manager                    1/1   1          1         6m53s
deployment.apps/katib-mysql                         1/1   1          1         6m52s
deployment.apps/katib-ui                            1/1   1          1         6m52s
deployment.apps/metadata-db                         1/1   1          1         7m11s
deployment.apps/metadata-deployment                 1/1   1          1         7m11s
deployment.apps/metadata-envoy-deployment           1/1   1          1         7m11s
deployment.apps/metadata-grpc-deployment            1/1   1          1         7m11s
deployment.apps/metadata-ui                         1/1   1          1         7m11s
deployment.apps/minio                               1/1   1          1         6m51s
deployment.apps/ml-pipeline                         1/1   1          1         6m51s
deployment.apps/ml-pipeline-ml-pipeline...          1/1   1          1         6m41s
deployment.apps/ml-pipeline-persistenceagent        1/1   1          1         6m48s
deployment.apps/ml-pipeline-scheduledworkflow       1/1   1          1         6m42s
deployment.apps/ml-pipeline-ui                      1/1   1          1         6m45s
deployment.apps/ml-pipeline-viewer-controller...    1/1   1          1         6m42s
deployment.apps/mysql                               1/1   1          1         6m49s
deployment.apps/notebook-controller-deployment      1/1   1          1         7m8s
deployment.apps/profiles-deployment                 1/1   1          1         6m40s
deployment.apps/pytorch-operator                    1/1   1          1         7m7s
deployment.apps/seldon-controller-manager           1/1   1          1         6m34s
deployment.apps/spark-operatorsparkoperator         1/1   1          1         7m13s
deployment.apps/spartakus-volunteer                 1/1   1          1         6m57s
deployment.apps/tensorboard                         1/1   1          1         6m56s
deployment.apps/tf-job-operator                     1/1   1          1         6m55s
deployment.apps/workflow-controller                 1/1   1          1         7m20s

NAME                                          DESIRED CURRENT READY AGE
replicaset.apps/admission-webhook-deployment...   1       1      1    7m17s
replicaset.apps/argo-ui-778676df64                1       1      1    7m20s
replicaset.apps/centraldashboard-f8d4bdf96        1       1      1    7m19s
replicaset.apps/cloud-endpoints-controller...     1       1      1    6m40s
replicaset.apps/jupyter-web-app-deployment...     1       1      1    7m15s
replicaset.apps/katib-controller-6b789b6cb5       1       1      1    6m53s
replicaset.apps/katib-db-manager-64f548b47c       1       1      1    6m53s
replicaset.apps/katib-mysql-57884cb488            1       1      1    6m52s
replicaset.apps/katib-ui-5c5cc6bd77               1       1      1    6m52s
```

```
replicaset.apps/metadata-db-76c9f78f77              1    1    1    7m11s
replicaset.apps/metadata-deployment-674fdd976b      1    1    1    7m11s
replicaset.apps/metadata-envoy-deployment...        1    1    1    7m11s
replicaset.apps/metadata-grpc-deployment...         1    1    1    7m11s
replicaset.apps/metadata-ui-9b8cd699d               1    1    1    7m11s
replicaset.apps/minio-d56488484                     1    1    1    6m50s
replicaset.apps/ml-pipeline-768488fd9               1    1    1    6m51s
replicaset.apps/ml-pipeline-ml-pipeline...          1    1    1    6m41s
replicaset.apps/ml-pipeline-persistenceagent...     1    1    1    6m48s
replicaset.apps/ml-pipeline-scheduledworkflow...    1    1    1    6m42s
replicaset.apps/ml-pipeline-ui-7cb547b666           1    1    1    6m45s
replicaset.apps/ml-pipeline-viewer-controller...    1    1    1    6m42s
replicaset.apps/mysql-67cb6fcdfc                    1    1    1    6m49s
replicaset.apps/notebook-controller-deployment...   1    1    1    7m8s
replicaset.apps/profiles-deployment-7c7fc789f4      1    1    1    6m40s
replicaset.apps/pytorch-operator-5fd5f94bdd         1    1    1    7m7s
replicaset.apps/seldon-controller-manager...        1    1    1    6m34s
replicaset.apps/spark-operatorsparkoperator...      1    1    1    7m13s
replicaset.apps/spartakus-volunteer-8579dbb8c       1    1    1    6m57s
replicaset.apps/tensorboard-6544748d94              1    1    1    6m56s
replicaset.apps/tf-job-operator-7d7c8fb8bb          1    1    1    6m55s
replicaset.apps/workflow-controller-945c84565       1    1    1    7m20s

NAME                                                    READY   AGE
statefulset.apps/admission-webhook-bootstrap-stateful-set   1/1   7m18s
statefulset.apps/application-controller-stateful-set    1/1   7m50s
statefulset.apps/kfserving-controller-manager           1/1   6m58s
statefulset.apps/metacontroller                         1/1   7m22s

NAME                               COMPLETIONS  DURATION  AGE
job.batch/spark-operatorcrd-cleanup  1/1         28s      7m15s
```

After we have confirmed that Kubeflow deployed on GKE, we can take a look at the main user interface and check out the Kubeflow application.

Accessing the Kubeflow UI Post-Installation

Once we have Kubeflow installed, we can use a web browser to log in to the main user interface included with Kubeflow, as seen in Figure 5-19.

We can access this page from the following URI (typically several minutes after the deployment process completes on GCP):

```
https://<KF_NAME>.endpoints.<project-id>.cloud.goog/
```

The delay on the URI being available is attributed to Kubeflow's need to provision a signed SSL certificate and register a DNS name on GCP.

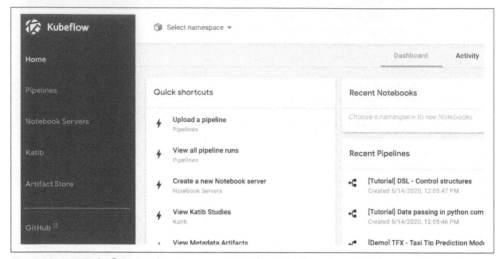

Figure 5-19. Kubeflow application user interface (deployed on GCP)

Getting the ingress URI for your deployment

To get the URI for your new Kubeflow deployment on GCP, use the following command from the command line:

```
kubectl -n istio-system get ingress
```

The output of this command should be similar to what you see in Example 5-5.

Example 5-5. Output for the URI ingress command

```
NAME            HOSTS                           ADDRESS         PORTS AGE

envoy-ingress   kf-1-0-book-deployment.endpoints... 34.120.141.194 80    3h26m
```

Summary

In this chapter we showed you, step by step, how to deploy Kubeflow 1.0 on GCP from the command line. Kubeflow on GCP has many similarities with the on-premise install, but also uses different components for identity and for components such as Istio. Over the next two chapters we go into the further differences of how AWS and Azure handle a Kubeflow install.

## CHAPTER 6

Running Kubeflow on Amazon Web Services

Kubeflow can be deployed on Amazon Web Services (AWS) via the managed Amazon Elastic Kubernetes Service (EKS). First, we will introduce the Amazon Web Services platform and the services it provides.

Overview of Amazon Web Services

Amazon Web Services is a cloud platform that provides organizations with over 165 services and products. Organizations use AWS for many use cases such as storage, compute, database management, networking, management and monitoring, and artificial intelligence, as well as data analysis, deployment management, and application services.

The availability of these services varies based on your location. Amazon cloud covers 21 geographic regions around the world. *Regions* are defined as geographic areas. Within each region are independent subregions called *Availability Zones* that divide the area of a single region into smaller, more manageable sections. These zones allow organizations to deploy their applications across multiple Availability Zones within the same region. In the case of zone failure, applications will stay online because zones are completely isolated from each other.

Some of the most popular services provided by AWS include:

- Amazon EC2
- Amazon RDS
- Amazon CloudFront
- Amazon VPC

- Amazon SNS

- Amazon Elastic Beanstalk

- Amazon Lambda

- Amazon Auto Scaling

- Amazon ElastiCache

This list only scratches the surface. For our needs, we will utilize some of AWS's offerings in order to deploy and run Kubeflow.

Storage

AWS offer storage as Infrastructure as a Service (IaaS), much like Google's Cloud Storage. AWS also offers a wide variety of storage options. Each option aims to provide a solution for specific storage use cases. These options include:

- Amazon Elastic Block Store

- Amazon Elastic File System

- Amazon FSx for Lustre

- Amazon FSx for Windows File Server

- Amazon Simple Storage Service (S3)

- Amazon Glacier

- AWS Storage Gateway

Each product targets specific use cases for the data stored. Data access patterns may determine what type of storage is appropriate. The performance of your storage has largely to do with the storage service you choose. For example, some use cases require frequent data access and low-latency response times, while some may rarely need to access data at all. In low-latency use cases, Amazon S3 or Amazon Elastic Block Store may be the appropriate storage that you should consider, depending on your requirements. Amazon S3 is a popular option for storage. AWS S3 storage is organized into buckets that are identified by a unique key. This is a common approach used by Google Cloud and other cloud providers.

On the other hand, there is Amazon Glacier which provides long-term storage at low cost. Choosing Amazon Glacier should indicate the data is rarely accessed. Amazon Glacier storage falls into a storage category known as *cold storage*. Data stored in cold storage is rarely accessed and may never be accessed again. As a result, Amazon Glacier provides three retrieval options just for accessing data that will affect the cost. Accessing data in cold storage can take up to five hours to retrieve in some cases.

Amazon Storage Pricing

For more information on Amazon cloud storage pricing, you should first determine what type of storage you require (*https://oreil.ly/JHsYR*). Data access patterns, latency requirements, and overall size of the data should be taken into consideration when making this decision.

From AWS's offerings, select which storage product you plan to use to see a pricing tab on the top right corner of the page. This will allow you to calculate your expected storage costs.

Amazon Cloud Security

Security is a critical component of all cloud-based services. To ensure your applications running on Amazon Cloud services are secure you will need to utilize Amazon's IAM service. IAM is a free service that provides a wide variety of security measures for applications and data hosted on AWS services. These measures include:

Granular Permissions
> Allow you to easily manage users' access to resources

Identity Federation
> Provides the ability to link other identity management systems

Financial Transaction Support
> AWS IAM is PCI DSS compliant

Multifactor Authentication
> User accounts can be set up with two-factor authentication

Application Permissions
> Using IAM applications and resources can be granted access to the other resources deployed within the AWS ecosystem

AWS Compute Services

In addition to the storage services described earlier, AWS offers a wide variety of cloud-based compute resources. In this section, we will briefly discuss these services and how they differ from each other.

Cloud-based compute resources are desired for large-scale deployments because of their availability, scalability, and low maintenance. By using these services you can reduce the up-front costs of deploying your application while knowing that you have on-demand resources available to scale up when needed.

Following is a list of compute resources offered by AWS:

- Amazon EC2
- Amazon Lightsail
- Amazon ECS
- Amazon Fargate
- AWS Lambda

Managed Kubernetes on EKS

Amazon Elastic Kubernetes Service (EKS) is a managed service provided by Amazon. Managed Kubernetes is a Kubernetes cluster that is usually hosted and maintained by a cloud services provider. Managed services allow your Kubernetes cluster to easily scale because it is running in a large datacenter with many resources. EKS also makes deploying and managing your Kubernetes cluster much easier.

We will be using EKS later in this chapter to deploy our Kubeflow applications to the EKS cluster. First, we will set up your AWS account, configure our EKS cluster, and deploy our Kubeflow applications.

Signing Up for Amazon Web Services

Before getting started, you will need to have an Amazon Web Services account. If you do not, you can sign up for the free tier (*https://oreil.ly/usXGh*). You should see what appears in Figure 6-1.

Figure 6-1. AWS account management screen

In the top right of your screen, click Create an AWS Account.

The free tier account never expires and gives you 12 months of limited usage. Your usage depends on what service you are using. For example, under the free tier you are allowed 750 hours on an EC2 micro instance. This is great for users who are just getting their feet wet with AWS.

Installing the AWS CLI

The AWS CLI allows you to manage your AWS services. In this section, we will set up the AWS CLI on your local machine. We'll use the AWS CLI to create projects, deploy code, configure instances, and manage the infrastructure. Then we will set up your local computer with the prerequisites for provisioning and deploying Amazon EKS and Kubeflow.

Update Python

Next, before moving on, you need to make sure you have the latest version of Python. If you do not have Python already installed, you will need to install it before moving forward.

There are numerous Python package-management frameworks that exist to help manage dependencies. However, we recommended that you consider using pip (*https://pypi.org/project/pip/*) as it is the most convenient and will simplify some of the steps later on. The only requirement is that your system's Python version be at least 2.7.9.

You can check which version of Python is on your system by executing:

```
$ python --version
```

Install the AWS CLI

Now that you have an AWS account you will need to install the AWS CLI on your local machine. The AWS CLI is a command-line interface tool that allows you to manage your Amazon cloud resources. The CLI provides off-the-shelf commands for all Amazon Web Services in a single package. The type of AWS service you are using will determine what commands you will need to become familiar with.

As a side note, the AWS Management Console is a web user interface that provides much of the same functionality as the CLI. However, the CLI enables developers to write scripts for a higher level of control and automation while adding functionality.

There are three ways to install the AWS CLI:

- Via `pip`
- Virtual Environment
- Bundled installer

We recommend using `pip` if possible. To install the AWS CLI via `pip`, you can follow these detailed instructions (*https://oreil.ly/bnGXd*). To install using one of the other installation methods, take a look a these AWS instructions (*https://oreil.ly/yJvdF*) for installing the CLI using a virtual environment or a bundled installer.

Configuring AWS CLI

After you have installed the AWS CLI, you will need to set up your AWS profile. To do this, execute:

```
$ aws configure
```

You should be prompted to enter your AWS Access Key, AWS Secret Access Key, region, and output format.

Your output should resemble:

```
$ aws configure
AWS Access Key ID [None]: ACCESSKEYEXAMPLE
AWS Secret Access Key [None]: SECRET/ACCESS/KEY
Default region name [None]: us-east-2
Default output format [None]: json
```

If you do not already have your AWS keys, you can generate them in the AWS Management Console under My Security Credentials. Hover over your account name in the top right corner of the AWS console and select My Security Credentials. Then select Users on the left menu bar.

Now you should see the screen shown in Figure 6-2.

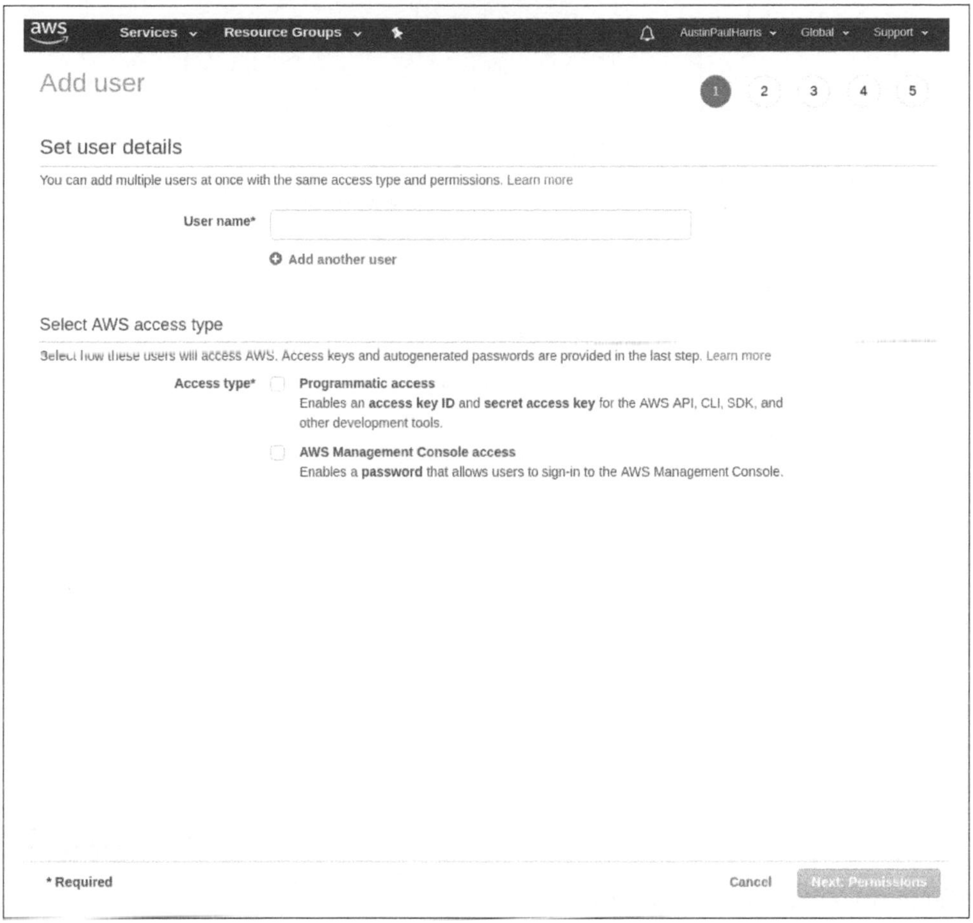

Figure 6-2. AWS account management screen

Enter your desired username in the text box. More than likely, the second option should be Programmatic Access unless you are creating an account that needs access to the AWS management console. When you have finished, click Next on the bottom of your screen. This will take you to the permissions screen shown in Figure 6-3.

Here you can add your user to an existing permissions group. If you do not already have a security group, you can click Create Group in the middle of the page. Once you have successfully added the user's permissions, click Next at the bottom of your screen. You will see a preview of the user's details; if this is correct, click Create User at the bottom of your screen. The user's AWS Access Key and AWS Secret Access Key should be displayed. You need to copy these details over to your local terminal where you are configuring the AWS CLI to complete the process.

Figure 6-3. AWS account management screen

Kubeflow on Amazon Web Services

The next sections will cover the Kubeflow install process using the CLI. First, we will need to install some packages on your local machine, the first being kubectl. We'll use the kubectl CLI to execute commands against our Kubernetes cluster hosted on AWS.

Installing kubectl

As mentioned earlier, we will use kubectl to execute commands against our Kubernetes cluster. To install kubectl, execute:

```
curl -LO https://storage.googleapis.com/kubernetes-release/release/`curl -s \
    https://storage.googleapis.com/kubernetes-release/release/stable.txt`/bin/linux/ \
    amd64/kubectl
```

Install the eksctl CLI for Amazon EKS

Next, you will need to install the eksctl command-line tool. The eksctl tool is a binary package used to create Kubernetes clusters on Amazon EKS.

Depending on your OS, you can use your preferred package manager to download the latest release. Here we use curl:

```
$ curl --silent --location "https://github.com/weaveworks/eksctl/releases/ \
download/latest_release/eksctl_$(uname -s)_amd64.tar.gz" | tar xz -C /tmp
sudo mv /tmp/eksctl /usr/local/bin
```

Install AWS IAM Authenticator

To keep your Kubernetes cluster secure, you will need to install AWS IAM Authenticator. IAM supports authentication to your cluster using your AWS IAM credentials which were set up earlier.

To install AWS IAM for Kubernetes, use the following curl command:

```
$ curl -o aws-iam-authenticator https://amazon-eks.s3-us-west-2.amazonaws.com \
    /1.13.7/2019-06-11/bin/linux/amd64/aws-iam-authenticator
```

Next, we need to give the authenticator execute permissions. You can use the following command to do this:

```
$ chmod +x ./aws-iam-authenticator
```

Install jq

kubectl output can be overwhelming without the right tools. In order to interpret the output, we will be using jq, a command-line JSON processor. jq will allow us to filter and map output data to find what we are looking for much easier.

To install jq on Linux, use the following command:

```
$ sudo apt-get install jq
```

Using Managed Kubernetes on Amazon EKS

In this section, you will provision and configure your EKS cluster.

Create an EKS Service Role

First, we need to create an IAM role (*https://oreil.ly/SC0By*) for your cluster. The IAM role is used to manage AWS resources. Then click Roles from the menu on the left-hand side of the page, as shown in Figure 6-4.

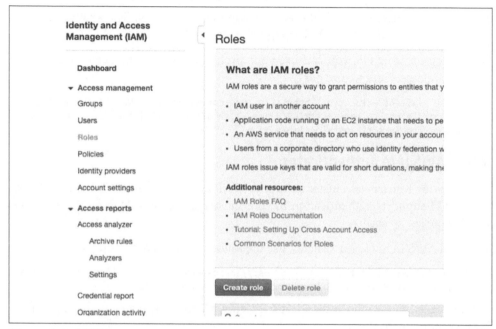

Figure 6-4. AWS account management screen

Next, we need to create a role for your EKS cluster to use. Click the Create Role option in the middle of your screen, and a list of AWS services will be displayed. Select EKS from the list, and click Next Permissions on the righthand bottom corner of the screen. Certain AWS IAM roles have one or more policies associated with it. For EKS, the AmazonEKSClusterPolicy and the AmazonEKSServicePolicy policies are required. These policies give the Amazon Elastic Container Service the permission needed to create and manage AWS resources.

You should see the page shown in Figure 6-5.

Figure 6-5. AWS EKS IAM role policy permissions options

Choose AmazonEKSServicePolicy, which will allow Amazon EKS to manage clusters on your behalf. Then click Next on the righthand bottom corner of your screen to move to the next step. This step allows you to add IAM tags to the role you are creating. IAM tags are simple key-value pairs that allow you to manage, search, and filter through resources. You define what key-values you would like to use for a given AWS resource. These tags can also be used to monitor billing for a given AWS resource or service. To configure IAM tags, enter your key-value pair. Otherwise, you can click Next: Review. This is the last step in the role-creation process.

If you have successfully configured your role, you will see a screen that looks like Figure 6-6.

Figure 6-6. AWS EKS IAM Role policy permissions review

The review step shown here summarizes your new IAM role. The role's description, policies, and permissions boundaries, if set, should be confirmed. Once confirmed, enter a Role Name for your role. This should be a unique name; in our case we use *eksClusterRole*. For more information on role naming conventions, guidelines and restrictions check out this AWS page (*https://oreil.ly/JZcBY*). Click Create Role to finish the role creation process. You should now see a new IAM role that your EKS cluster can assume to manage its resources under Roles in the IAM management console.

Create an AWS VPC

Now, we need to create an Amazon Virtual Private Cloud (VPC) (*https://oreil.ly/Sew9N*) to deploy our EKS cluster into. AWS resources can be deployed within a single VPC as it is dedicated to your account. A VPC provides network control and functionality to your deployment as you would have in your own datacenter. Security groups and access control lists in addition to other security measures can be configured to protect your resources. Public or private subnets, depending on your use case, can be configured within the same VPC. Public subnet traffic is delivered to an internet gateway that communicates with the internet, whereas private subnets are accessed via a virtual private gateway.

To get started creating an AWS Virtual Private Cloud, visit the AWS CloudFormation console (*https://oreil.ly/itkAo*). Before we begin, you need to verify what region the AWS console is set to. The region displayed should be the region where you plan to deploy your EKS cluster. In the upper-right corner of your screen, the region is displayed as a drop-down menu. Once you have confirmed your region, you need to create an AWS CloudFormation stack.

The purpose of a stack is to allow you to configure multiple AWS resources into a single manageable unit (known as a stack). The stack is completely user-defined and allows you to create, manage, and delete sets of resources much more efficiently. Without stacks, you would need to spin up each individual component of your applications one at a time. With stacks, resources can be provisioned and deployed easily as they are needed. Resources that should be included in the stack are defined in a CloudFormation template. The template can be created three separate ways: JSON, YAML, and AWS Designer (which we will talk about later on in this section).

To create a new stack, click the Create Stack button in the middle of the page. In the Prerequisite section of the page, click the first option, "Template is ready," as shown in Figure 6-7.

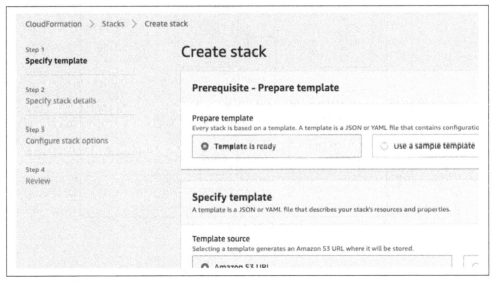

Figure 6-7. The CloudFormation AWS console web page

For the purpose of gaining foundational knowledge of AWS EKS we will be using a pre-existing AWS CloudFormation sample template provided for Amazon. To use this template, choose "Amazon S3 URL" under Template Source. Next, we need to provide a file or URL where our CloudFormation template is filled out.

Enter the following URL[1] in the AWS sample template:

```
https://amazon-eks.s3-us-west-2.amazonaws.com/cloud.../amazon-eks-vpc-sample.yaml
```

This method of supplying the template is extremely common. However, AWS provides a tool called AWS CloudFormation Designer that can be used to create templates in addition to uploading a JSON and YAML file. Designer is a graphical interface tool that creates a template file behind the scenes. It supports editing template files while visualizing the architecture of your system and its components. To see the sample template in Designer, click View in Designer in the bottom-right corner of the Specify Template form. If you are using the sample template, you should see the architecture shown in Figure 6-8.

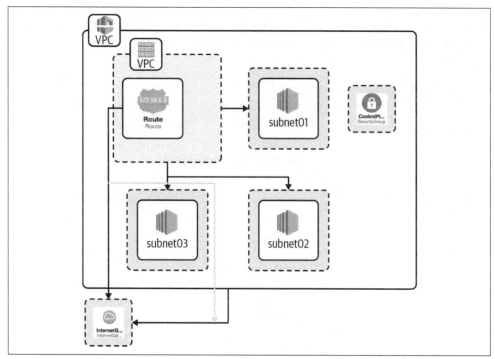

Figure 6-8. The Designer graphical interface tool used to edit stack templates

The stack consists of your VPC configured with a routing table and three subnets, and an internet gateway for public subnets. The AWS Designer web application gives you the ability to edit your template before creating your stack. It is a graphical interface for editing your template.

---

1 This URL has been shortened to fit the page; the full URL is *https://amazon-eks.s3-us-west-2.amazonaws.com/cloudformation/2019-09-17/amazon-eks-vpc-sample.yaml*.

Then click Next to move on. The next step is to specify your stack's details. Enter your stack's name and configure your subnet's Classless Inter-Domain Routing (CIDR). If you are following along with the book, these values should already be filled from information within the template, and you can click Next. In this step we need to configure our stack to use the IAM role we created earlier in this section. In the Permissions section, enter the name of your IAM role that you created earlier and move on to the next step. This step is for review. Confirm your stack's configuration and click Create Stack. This begins the process of instantiating all the resources defined in the CloudFormation stack. Next, we'll walk through the steps to create an EKS cluster.

Creating EKS Clusters

Before we begin this section you should confirm you have successfully installed the AWS CLI and have installed and configured kubectl for AWS EKS. To determine if you installed AWS CLI correctly, execute the following command on your local machine:

```
$ aws --version and kubectl --version
```

You should see output describing the current version of your installation. If you do not have kubectl or AWS CLI installed, follow the instructions at the beginning of this chapter. To begin, head to the cluster management page (*https://oreil.ly/Su6tt*) on your AWS console.

You should see the Amazon Container Service heading at the top left of your screen. To begin creating the EKS cluster, click Create Cluster. First, fill out the General Configuration. This includes the cluster name, Kubernetes version, and your IAM role we created at the beginning of the chapter. Next, choose the default VPC, and click Create Cluster.

This should bring you back to the Amazon Container Services page. Click Clusters in the menu on the left. You should see your EKS cluster in the list of clusters as well as the Kubernetes version it is running and its current status. If you just completed the cluster created process, you should see something similar to Figure 6-9.

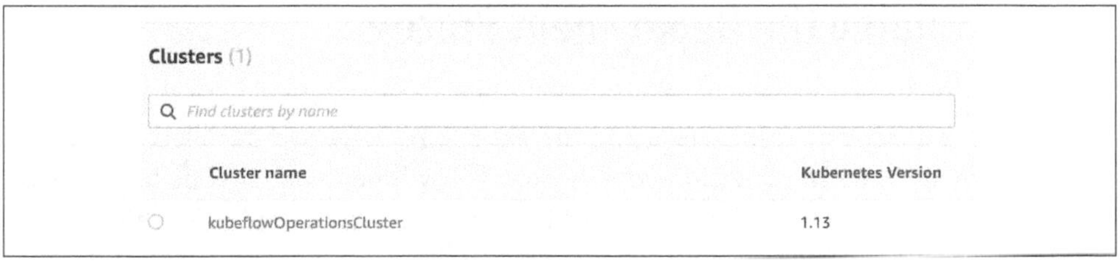

Figure 6-9. EKS cluster management console shows the current status of your EKS cluster

In Figure 6-9, you can see the name of our EKS cluster is "kubeflowOperationsCluster," it is running Kubernetes 1.13, and is currently in the process of being created. To find out more details or make changes to your cluster, choose the cluster within the list. Using this information, we can configure kubectl. kubectl configuration requires the EKS cluster API server endpoint and the certificate authority.

Deploying an EKS Cluster with eksctl

If you prefer to use eksctl over the AWS EKS management console, this section will walk you through the steps to deploy your EKS cluster. The same prerequisite steps hold true whether you deploy your EKS cluster with the management console or eksctl. The installation process is covered previously in this chapter. If you have installed and configured eksctl, you are ready to deploy your cluster.

We will be using the eksctl create command to create our cluster:

```
$ eksctl create cluster \
    --name kubeflowOperationCluster \
    --version 1.14 \
    --nodegroup-name standard-workers \
    --node-type t3.medium \
    --nodes 3 \
    --nodes-min 1 \
    --nodes-max 4
```

The text in bold should be replaced with your desired configuration. First, --name is the desired name of your EKS cluster. Depending on support and compatibility, you may need to use a specific version of Kubernetes, this can be set using the --version argument. Multiple AWS compute instance types can be used within the same EKS cluster. These are defined by distinct node groups. For our cluster, we will only have one node group of one AWS compute type. The --nodegropu-name and --node-type arguments can be used to create node groups within the cluster and the AWS instance type. The last arguments should be self-explanatory. They define the number of nodes and the limits of the cluster.

Understanding the Deployment Process

Now, with our local machine configured, let's discuss the next steps to deploy Kubeflow to our Kubernetes resources using the eksctl package we installed previously. There are many ways to provision your cluster. We will be using eksctl to provision our EKS cluster. Then, we will use the kfctl command-tool to deploy Kubeflow:

1. Create an EKS cluster.
2. Configure an AWS account.

3. Deploy Kubeflow.

We'll start with the Kubeflow configuration process.

Kubeflow Configuration and Deployment

This section assumes you have finished the previous section. In this section, we will install Kubeflow on the EKS cluster deployed in the previous section. First, we will need to download some prerequisites for Kubeflow on our local machine.

Download and configure kfctl

To deploy Kubeflow applications, we need to install kfctl (*https://oreil.ly/XXf25*). kfctl is a command-line interface developed in golang. We will use it to deploy Kubeflow applications to our EKS cluster. After downloading, unpack the file with the following:

```
$ tar -xvf kfctl_<release tag>_<platform>.tar.gz
```

To makes things easier, add kfctl to your local machine's PATH by using:

```
$ export PATH=$PATH:"<path to kfctl>"
```

Now you need to download the kfctl AWS config file. Set a PATH variable and download the file using the following commands. First, set the PATH variable for the EKS configuration file:

```
$ export CONFIG="/tmp/kfctl_aws.yaml"
```

Then, download the YAML file that will be used to install Kubeflow on our existing AWS EKS cluster:

```
$ wget https://raw.githubusercontent.com/kubeflow/kubeflow/ \
v0.6.2/bootstrap/config/kfctl_aws.yaml -O ${CONFIG}
```

Create two new environment variables. The first one will be AWS_CLUSTER_NAME. The value will be your EKS cluster name. This can be done with the following command:

```
$ export AWS_CLUSTER_NAME=<EKS CLUSTER NAME>
```

Next, you need to choose a name for your application directory. We will set our Kubeflow application directory to the name of our EKS cluster. If you wish to do this as well, you can set it using:

```
$ export KF_NAME=${AWS_CLUSTER_NAME}
```

We now have our AWS Kubeflow configuration file we need to configure and deploy Kubeflow on our EKS cluster. Before we do so, you need to update the *kfctl_aws.yaml* file. Open the config file we downloaded in the previous step. If you followed along with us, your file should be located in the */tmp/* directory. In this file, change your

AWS region to the same region as your EKS cluster. Then, add your Amazon EKS IAM role we created earlier on in this chapter and add it to the roles dictionary.

The IAM role is located under the AWS plug-in at the bottom of the file under `spec:roles:{AWS_ROLE_NAME}`. We created our IAM EKS role with its corresponding policies earlier in this chapter. You can retrieve your IAM role name using the `eksctl` we installed earlier using:

```
$ aws iam list-roles \
    | jq -r ".Roles[] \
    | select(.RoleName \
    | startswith(\"eksctl-$AWS_CLUSTER_NAME\")  \
and contains(\"NodeInstanceRole\")) \
    .RoleName"
```

The output of this command is your EKS IAM role name. Use this as the value to the `spec:roles:{AWS_ROLE_NAME}` in the *kfctl_aws.yaml* file.

Deploy Kubeflow to EKS

Now we can deploy Kubeflow to your EKS cluster. First, we need to run `init`. This command is only run one time to initially set up your Kubeflow cluster and its environment. To do this we use the `CONFIG` and `KFAPP` path variables we created in the last section. To perform the one-time instantiation run:

```
$ kfctl init ${KFAPP} --config=${CONFIG} -V
```

This command will generate a new subdirectory specified by the `KFAPP` PATH variable. Now change your working directory to `${KFAPP}` subdirectory. Next, we will use the `generate` command to generate configuration files for our resources. Once in the `${KFAPP}` directory, execute:

```
$ kfctl generate all -V
```

Lastly, the `apply` command will create our resources using these configuration files. This command can also be used to update resources. To deploy the Kubeflow application, run:

```
$ kfctl apply all -V
```

Before moving on, let's discuss the Kubeflow application layout and the files we created using the previous commands. The Kubeflow application directory should now contain the following files generated by the `generate` command. First, the *app.yml* configuration file contains the configuration of your Kubeflow deployment which was set when you executed `kfctl init`. These resources and configurations are a single instance of your application.

Next, the ${KFAPP}/aws_config directory contains configuration files created by the generate command, and describes and defines your EKS cluster configuration. These files will be used in the next section to customize your deployment.

Lastly, the generate command creates the kustomize directory which consists of the Kustomize packages for Kubeflow applications. kustomize can be used to manage your Kubernetes resources.

Confirm EKS Deployment

From here we can confirm that we have successfully created and deployed your Kubeflow cluster. To do this, change to your Kubeflow application directory. If you are following along from the previous section, you may need to allow some time for the resources to be allocated. It can take three to five minutes for your resources to be configured and set up. When ready, you can confirm your deployment by executing the following command in your application directory.

```
$ kubectl -n kubeflow get all
```

Customize the Kubeflow Deployment

In this section, we will walk through resizing, editing authentication configurations, enabling authentication, and deleting an existing cluster. This will provide you with the final steps to ensure you can properly deploy and configure your EKS cluster.

Customize Authentication

Initially, the default configuration of your Kubeflow deployment is not configured with Transport Layer Security (TLS) or authentication. You will first need a domain name. This can be done via a number of providers. Next, you can use the AWS Certificate Manager to create a certificate for your Kubeflow deployment. AWS Certificate Manager is easy to use and allows the provisioning of private and public certificates. Additionally, other AWS services can also utilize AWS Certificate Manager, making it easy to manage large-scale deployments.

Resizing EKS Clusters

In some situations, you may need to scale up or down your EKS cluster. To resize your AWS EKS cluster, execute:

```
eksctl scale nodegroup --cluster=<clusterName> --nodes=<desiredCount> \
--name=<nodegroupName>
```

This will allow you to scale your cluster based on your needs.

Deleting EKS Clusters

When you wish to delete your cluster, you can either use your AWS Management Console or use the command-line tools. In this section, we will walk through the steps for deleting your EKS cluster using both options.

Using the AWS Management Console, log in and then navigate to the AWS EKS console. The EKS console is shown in Figure 6-10.

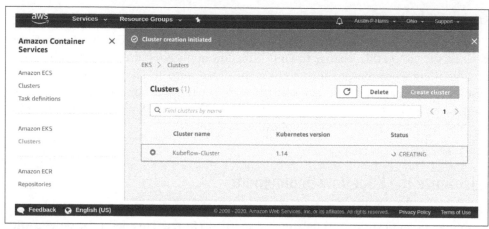

Figure 6-10. AWS EKS console

Then, choose the cluster that you would like to delete while making sure that it is the only selected item in order to ensure you do not accidentally delete the wrong resource. While selected, click the Delete option in the top right of your window. The prompt shown in Figure 6-11 will request that you enter the name of the cluster you would like to delete. Similarly, to delete the VPC CloudFormation stack, open the CloudFormation console we used earlier in this chapter. Select the stack you created for your Kubeflow deployment. Then under Actions, click Delete.

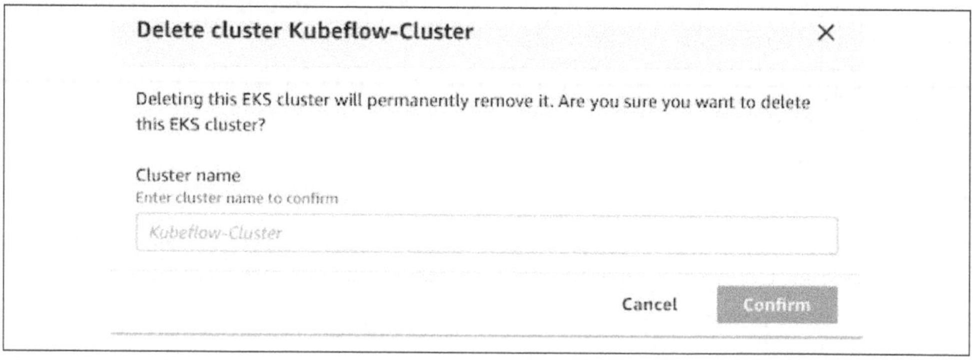

Delete cluster Kubeflow-Cluster ✕

Deleting this EKS cluster will permanently remove it. Are you sure you want to delete this EKS cluster?

Cluster name
Enter cluster name to confirm

> Kubeflow-Cluster

Cancel   Confirm

Figure 6-11. This prompt is the final step to delete your EKS cluster

Adding Logging

AWS CloudWatch is an AWS service that allows you to monitor all of your system's logs and performance in one place. CloudWatch features automated actions, log and performance metric visualizations, notifications, and anomalous behavior on your systems. By default, most AWS services can be easily configured using CloudWatch. CloudWatch supports five main log monitoring components:

API Server
> Logs all API requests

Audit
> Logs cluster access via the Kubernetes API

Authenticator
> Logs all authentification requests

Controller Manager
> Logs providing state information on cluster controllers

Scheduler
> Logs created from configured scheduling decisions

To enable logging, in the Create Cluster configuration view, scroll down to the logging section and enable your desired level of log components. The log configuration section should look like Figure 6-12.

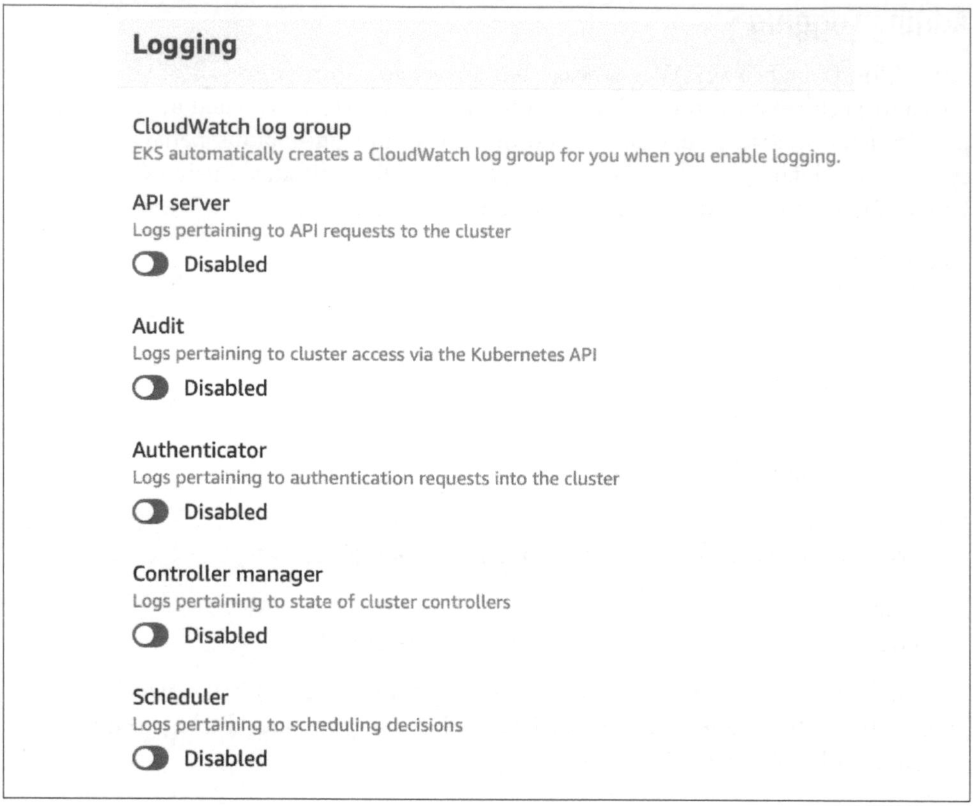

Logging

CloudWatch log group
EKS automatically creates a CloudWatch log group for you when you enable logging.

API server
Logs pertaining to API requests to the cluster
Disabled

Audit
Logs pertaining to cluster access via the Kubernetes API
Disabled

Authenticator
Logs pertaining to authentication requests into the cluster
Disabled

Controller manager
Logs pertaining to state of cluster controllers
Disabled

Scheduler
Logs pertaining to scheduling decisions
Disabled

Figure 6-12. CloudWatch configuration section for AWS EKS

Once you have enabled logging and deployed your EKS cluster, you can visit Cloud-Watch (*https://oreil.ly/zQQUX*) to see your logs. From the CloudWatch console, you can view logs, view visualization dashboards, set rules for automated actions, and set notification alarms.

Troubleshooting Deployments

In this section, we will walk through some of the most common issues when deploying Kubeflow on EKS. If you are looking for troubleshooting support for a specific issue, the following is a list of the issues addressed in this section:

- Environment File Not Found
- KFAPP Already Exists
- Incompatible eksctl Version

The Environment File Not Found error is commonly caused when you have executed generate or apply while not within your KFAPP directory.

If you receive the `KFAPP Already Exists` error, try deleting your KFAPP directory and try again. Usually, this is caused by a simple typing mistake.

The last issue, `Incompatible eksctl Version`, is commonly experienced when executing the `apply` command. In your cluster configuration file, the variable `eksctl.io` must match the `eksctl` version you are using. If not, install the latest version and try again.

Summary

This chapter has many similarities to the previous chapter. However, there are many subtle cloud integration differences you need to consider for deployment specifically on AWS. As you move through the next chapter, you'll further see more aspects of the Azure Kubeflow deployment that are tailored to its specific cloud infrastructure.

## CHAPTER 7

Running Kubeflow on Azure

The Azure Cloud Platform is Microsoft's entry into the public cloud market. Azure lets us build, deploy, and manage applications and services across a network of datacenters around the world.

Overview of the Azure Cloud Platform

We'll start off with a review of relevant components of the Azure Cloud Platform. Most public clouds have the concept of a "region" within their datacenters, and Azure follows this pattern as well. The Azure platform defines a region as a "set of datacenters deployed within a latency-defined perimeter and connected through a dedicated regional low-latency network." The Azure platform offers 46 regions around the world, with each region grouped into a *geography*.

Each geography generally contains two or more regions, and regions support distinct markets. Each market typically has its own compliance boundaries and rules for data residency (e.g., GDPR (*https://eugdpr.org*)). Certain customers will be under specific data-residency rules so they need guarantees around where the data will actually live. In Figure 7-1 we can see how availability zones are arranged inside regions that are in turn arranged in data-residency boundaries.

Availability zones are one or more datacenters independent from one another, making up physically separate locations inside each Azure region. Let's now move on to the key services offered on Azure.

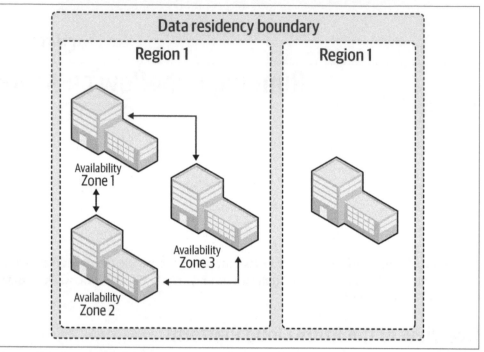

Figure 7-1. Azure global infrastructure and regions (source: Azure Geographies page (https://oreil.ly/2dJct))

Key Azure Components

Most clouds offer similar data storage and compute products, but there are unique aspects to each one. Some of the Azure products relevant to Kubeflow include:

- Multiple types of storage
- Virtual machines for running various clusters
- Azure Kubernetes Services (AKS)
- Standard SQL databases
- Cosmos DB
- App Service

This list is obviously not exhaustive as to all the products available on Azure. Azure also has ways to run containers easily without managing a server, a container registry, and fully managed Red Hat OpenShift cluster instances.

Storage on Azure

The major types of storage on Azure are:

- File (*https://oreil.ly/1v71k*)
- Disk (HDDs/SSDs) (*https://oreil.ly/6OHVk*)
- Blob (*https://oreil.ly/IAxED*)
- Data Lake Storage (Gen2) (*https://oreil.ly/23Y3m*)
- Archive (*https://oreil.ly/lgajo*)
- Avere vFXT (*https://oreil.ly/IpJBl*)

Each storage option has common use cases and its own pricing model.

> **Azure Storage Pricing**
>
> Pricing for Azure storage options has a lot of variables to consider. For more information on how to forecast what your storage project would cost, check out the Azure Storage Overview pricing guide (*https://oreil.ly/4dE7f*).

Now let's get into the properties of each storage type, and determine when to choose each of them.

File storage

File storage on Azure is a simple and inexpensive distributed filesystem that will work cross-platform. It provides an easy way to sync local files securely and is encrypted both at rest and in transit. Files stored in Azure File Storage are accessible via the Server Message Block (SMB) protocol. The same files are also accessible via the REST interface or the storage client libraries.

Use cases include caching configuration files for use by multiple VMs, and sharing utilities/tools between multiple developers in a group. The file storage option lacks Active Directory-based authentication and access control lists (ACLs) at this time. Another scenario where we'd choose to use the Azure File Storage option is if we want to "lift and shift" an application to the cloud which already uses native filesystem APIs to share data.

Disk storage

The disk storage option gives us enterprise-grade durability with low latency and high throughput. This option is typically used for production workloads as it gives us consistent performance at disk sizes up to 64 TiB. Data stored on these disks is encrypted by default using Storage Service Encryption and is controlled with RBAC.

VM workloads typically opt for this type of storage. Options inside this storage class include, from most basic to fastest:

Standard HDD
    Lowest cost disk storage in Azure

Standard SSD
    Cost-effective VM disks

Premium SSD
    Lower latency and higher throughput than Standard SSD

Ultra SSD
    For the most demanding workloads requiring submillisecond latency

Standard HDDs are typically used for backup and archiving applications. Standard SSDs are typically used for diverse workloads such as web servers and development/testing situations. Premium SSDs are a good storage option for production workloads such as SQL Server, Oracle databases, MySQL, Cassandra, or MongoDB. Finally, the Ultra SSD option is selected for workloads that are latency sensitive such as transaction heavy workloads, complex analytical modeling, gaming, rendering, and certain types of message queues.

Lift and shift scenarios are common use cases for Azure Disk Storage, along with situations where the data is not required to be accessed from outside the virtual machine to which the disk is mounted.

Blob Storage

Blob Storage is most cost-effective when we're dealing with large amounts of data where the data is typically unstructured (e.g., text documents, video, audio, web pages, raw log files, etc.).

Blob storage gives us four tiers to choose from, and we base our choice of tier on how often we plan on accessing the data. The Azure Blob Storage option offers a strong consistency model which is key when we're doing large-scale parallel processing with analytical systems such as Apache Spark with a dataset that may be replicated across multiple machines. The Blob Storage option also offers object mutability and multiple Blob types, some of which allow you the option of appending data to a Blob.

We'd choose Azure Blob Storage (*https://oreil.ly/VK6M5*) in situations such as where we need to serve images or documents directly to a web browser or stream video/audio. Stored objects in Blob Storage are also accessible via HTTP/HTTPS using:

- URLs
- Azure Storage REST API
- Azure CLI
- PowerShell
- Azure Storage client library (language support includes: Python, Java, .NET, etc.)

An example of a REST endpoint would be a URL that looks similar to:

```
http://myaccount.blob.core.windows.net/mycontainer/myblob
```

Beyond the Blob Storage option, we see that Azure offers further capabilities around data lake processing.

Azure Data Lake Storage Gen2

Azure Data Lake Storage Gen2 (*https://oreil.ly/YhcK4*) (ADLS Gen2) extends Blob Storage to be specialized for analytical workloads. The "Gen2" moniker comes from the result of combining the capabilities of the Azure Blob Storage offering and the original ADLS Gen1 offering. Properties retained from ADLS Gen1 include:

- Filesystem semantics
- Directory and file-level security
- Scale

Properties from Azure Blog Storage:

- Low cost
- Tiered storage
- High availability
- Disaster recovery capabilities

The primary use case for Data Lake Storage is enterprise big data analytics workloads. Data Lake Storage scales into the Petabytes and is focused on running big data analytics on Azure. Key features of ADLS Gen2 include:

- Hadoop-compatible access (via the ABFS driver (*https://oreil.ly/qE6oh*), works with Hadoop tooling)
- Superset of POSIX permissions (ACL and POSIX permissions, extra granularity specific to ADLS Gen2)
- Cost effectiveness: low-cost storage capacity

ADLS Gen2 (*https://oreil.ly/2XrGm*) is organized as a filesystem at the top level and uses directories for lower-level data organization. The primary data container is a file, and the storage system is focused on supporting analytics. Supported platforms for ADLS Gen2 include:

- HDInsight
- Apache Hadoop
- Cloudera
- Azure Databricks

For more information on how ADLS Gen2 is used, check out the Azure documentation (*https://oreil.ly/f8_YZ*).

Archive storage

The Azure Archive Storage tier is their lowest-priced storage tier and is typically where we stick data we won't access often. Data is encrypted at rest automatically. A primary use case for this storage class is long-term backup retention and magnetic tape replacement. For the purposes of this book, we won't focus on this storage option much.

Avere vFXT

This storage option on Azure is for file-based workloads that are compute-intensive. We see this storage option being used for workloads such as translational medicine in genomics research, and quantitative and risk analytics for financial services.

The Azure Security Model

The Azure platform offers an identity security model similar to the other clouds that supports methods such as:

- Authentication
- Authorization
- Role-based access control (RBAC)

When working with AKS, we'll primarily focus on using RBAC to grant users or groups access to the specific resources we dictate. There is also the option to enhance the security and permissions structure of AKS by using Azure Active Directory.

Authentication and authorization

We can grant users or groups access to Kubernetes within a namespace with Azure Active Directory-integrated AKS clusters.

The integrated approach (based on openID connect and OAuth 2.0 (*https://oreil.ly/014E-*)) provides a single sign-on for `kubectl` users and allows us to effectively manage user accounts and password credentials.

Microsoft's documentation has best practices (*https://oreil.ly/hswsi*) for practitioners who plan on deploying entirely on Azure:

- Authenticate AKS cluster users with Azure Active Directory.
- Control access to resources with RBAC.
- Use a managed identity to authenticate with other services.

Using an Active Directory implementation such as Azure Active Directory will centralize identity management for your Kubeflow platform as Kubernetes does not have a concept of user accounts. Figure 7-2 shows step by step how resource access control is accomplished with Azure Active Directory.

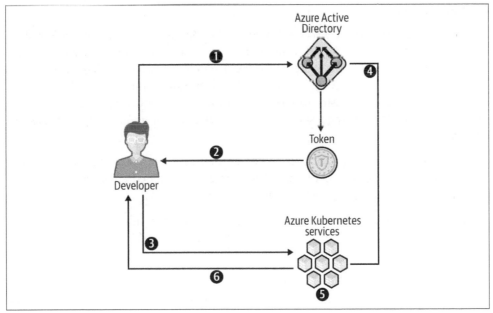

Figure 7-2. Azure Active Directory integration (source: Microsoft Azure documentation (https://oreil.ly/7fU3E))

We can see the following steps in this figure:

1. The user (developer) authenticates with Azure AD.
2. The access token is issued by the Azure AD token issuance endpoint.
3. A user action (e.g., `kubectl create pod`) is performed using the Azure AD token.
4. The user's group memberships are retrieved, and Kubernetes validates the token with Azure Active Directory.
5. Cluster policies are applied along with RBAC.
6. Our user's request is deemed successful or not based on previous confirmation by the Active Directory system of:
   a. AD group membership
   b. RBAC and policies

There are other situations where the organization may want to integrate AKS with its existing on-premise enterprise Active Directory system.

Service Accounts

Kubernetes uses both service accounts managed by Kubernetes and that we'd consider a normal user account. Service accounts are users that are managed by the Kubernetes API bound to specific namespaces and are tied to a set of credentials stored as secrets (*https://oreil.ly/OKXze*). These secrets are mounted into pods, allowing processes in a Kubernetes cluster to talk to the Kubernetes API. Kubernetes uses these service accounts for API requests between pods that are communicating with the API server.

Kubernetes does not have an internal representation of normal user accounts and cannot add them through API calls. Kubernetes is designed such that an outside independent system manages normal user accounts.

When dealing with AKS clusters, the outside independent identity solution inside Azure would be Azure Active Directory (*https://oreil.ly/Ct0mY*).

Resources and Resource Groups

A *resource* on the Azure platform is a manageable item we can use such as a virtual machine, a storage account, or a web application. A *resource group* on Azure is an association that binds related resources together for a particular Azure solution. Sometimes we want to think about how to apply policies to a related set of resources so we can manage these resources with an Azure resource group.

Resource groups on Azure are controlled by the Azure Resource Manager (see Figure 7-3). The Azure Resource Manager gives us a consistent management layer to create, update, and delete resources in our applications on the Azure platform.

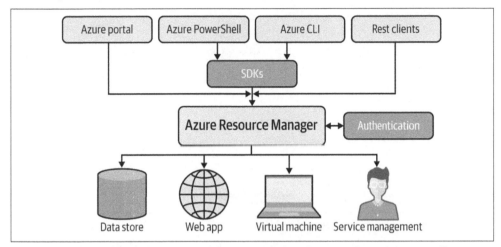

Figure 7-3. Azure Resource Manager (source: Microsoft Azure documentation (https:// oreil.ly/sOOXM))

Azure Virtual Machines

The Azure platform allows us to run VMs for both Linux and Windows images on hardware up to 128 vCPUs and 6 TB of memory. Azure VMs (*http:// portal.azure.com*) run on an Azure hypervisor that is designed specifically for their platform and is not accessible to the public (see Figure 7-4).

Each physical machine is divided into a number of guest VMs by a hypervisor running on the physical machine. Each VM has the Windows Firewall enabled, and we can configure which ports are open and addressable internally or externally. The hypervisor mediates all traffic and access to the disk and network on the machine and root operating system. Each host is running Windows Server with only the base components needed to run the VMs.

Each datacenter is divided into clusters, and a software system known as the fabric controller (FC) manages the VMs in clusters of around 1000 physical servers. The fabric controller manages life cycles of applications in the cluster and keeps VM instances running if a server fails.

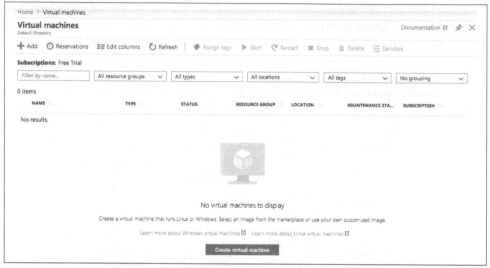

Figure 7-4. The Azure virtual machine UI

Containers and Managed Azure Kubernetes Services

As mentioned previously in this chapter, Azure offers its own container registry, ways to run containers without managing a server, and fully managed Red Hat OpenShift cluster instances. The Kubeflow installer can deploy Kubeflow and a Kubernetes cluster all at once on AKS or it can install Kubeflow on a pre-existing AKS cluster. For the purposes of this section, we'll review the basics of using the AKS system. In Figure 7-5 we can see the main web portal page for the AKS system.

Figure 7-5. The Azure Kubernetes services main web portal

From this page we can deploy and manage multiple AKS clusters for our Kubeflow projects. We can also monitor the health of each cluster, change the number of nodes, or delete the cluster.

The Azure CLI

The Azure command-line tools are similar to those of the other major clouds in terms of functionality and role. While there is a web portal UI for almost every function we need to do on Azure, the CLI is the method of preference for many administrators out there.

Installing the Azure CLI

For instructions on installing the Azure CLI on most major platforms, see the Azure documentation (*https://oreil.ly/2xhq5*).

Next, we'll highlight the install commands for some of common platforms.

macOS install

For macOS users, the install process is simple if they are using Homebrew:

```
brew update && brew install azure-cli
```

Windows install

For Windows, we can just download the MSI Installer from the Microsoft documentation (*https://oreil.ly/bVcrK*).

Debian and Ubuntu (x86_64)

There are two ways to install based on the instructions (*https://oreil.ly/fJ1mP*) for Debian/Ubuntu. The first is to use a single command:

```
curl -sL https://aka.ms/InstallAzureCLIDeb | sudo bash
```

For the extended manual instructions, check out the link.

Once we have the Azure CLI tools installed locally, we can move on to the Kubeflow installation process.

Installing Kubeflow on Azure Kubernetes

In this section we'll walk you through the core steps for deploying Kubeflow 1.0 on a new Azure account. Let's start out with getting our Azure account set up so that our command-line tools can interact with the Azure AKS system.

Azure Login and Configuration

You'll need to authenticate your local Azure client with the Azure cloud services. To do this, you will type the following command into your shell or command prompt:

```
az login
```

After you type this command, a browser window will pop up, as seen in Figure 7-6.

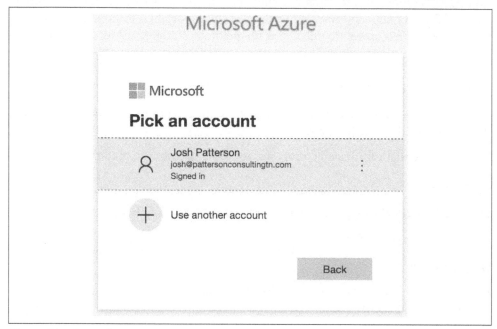

Figure 7-6. Azure login screen

Once you select an account, the command line will output text similar to what you see in Example 7-1.

Example 7-1. Azure post-login console output

```
You have logged in. Now let us find all the subscriptions to which you have access...
[
  {
    "cloudName": "AzureCloud",
    "homeTenantId": "0befce41-7982-4144-foo9-5fd4ebar7ecb",
    "id": "9de60f00-0cbe-4063-92bd-barf074b6e56",
    "isDefault": true,
    "managedByTenants": [],
    "name": "Pay-As-You-Go",
    "state": "Enabled",
    "tenantId": "0bef0040-7980-4154-add9-bar4e8ae7ecb",
    "user": {
```

```
      "name": "josh@pattersonconsultingtn.com",
      "type": "user"
    }
  }
]
```

You'll Need an Azure Subscription

You can either sign up for the free account on Azure or set up a paid subscription.

When you log in, if you see the message `No subscriptions found`, this means the system has not found a valid subscription and you'll have to go online and set one up.

Now that we have an authenticated client for Azure, let's move on to setting up our local machine for deploying Kubeflow 1.0 on Azure.

Create an AKS Cluster for Kubeflow

In this section, we'll use the Azure command-line tool `az` to create a resource group and an Azure Kubernetes Services cluster to use for our Kubeflow deployment.

Creating AKS Clusters

While it's possible to use an existing AKS cluster to install Kubeflow 1.0, we'll take you through the required steps in this chapter to create a new AKS Kubernetes cluster in the event that you do not already have one.

Creating an Azure resource group

Before we can create our AKS Kubernetes cluster for our Kubeflow deployment, we'll need to create a resource group for this cluster to live in. We can create a resource group on Azure with the following command:

```
az group create -n <RESOURCE_GROUP_NAME> -l <LOCATION>
```

We'll need to provide two variables for this command:

- `RESOURCE_GROUP_NAME`
- `LOCATION`

For this example, we'll use:

- RESOURCE_GROUP_NAME: KubeflowAzureTestGroup
- LOCATION: eastus

In this example case, our command would look like:

```
az group create -n KubeflowAzureTestGroup -l eastus
```

When we choose our variables and run this command, the output should look similar to Example 7-2.

Example 7-2. Create a resource group on Azure output on CLI

```
{
  "id": "/subscriptions/9de60f0.../resourceGroups/KubeflowAzureTestGroup",
  "location": "eastus",
  "managedBy": null,
  "name": "KubeflowAzureTestGroup",
  "properties": {
    "provisioningState": "Succeeded"
  },
  "tags": null,
  "type": "Microsoft.Resources/resourceGroups"
}
```

If you check your Azure UI console and go to the resource groups page, you'll see a new resource group was created, as in Figure 7-7.

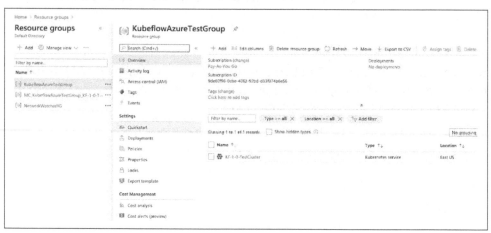

Figure 7-7. Azure Resource groups detail page

Let's move on to actually creating the AKS cluster for our Kubeflow deployment.

Creating an AKS cluster for Kubeflow

Now we'll create a specifically defined cluster with the `az` command with the following pattern:

```
az aks create -g <RESOURCE_GROUP_NAME> -n <NAME> -s <AGENT_SIZE> -c \
    <AGENT_COUNT> -l <LOCATION> --generate-ssh-keys
```

You can plug in your own variables for this command, but for our example we use the following variables:

- `NAME=KFTestCluster`
- `AGENT_SIZE=Standard_D4s_v3`
- `AGENT_COUNT=2`

We need to use the same resource group name and location from when we created our resource group.

Once you've run this `az aks create ...` command, you can check the Azure UI to confirm that the AKS cluster was created. In Figure 7-8, we can see a cluster was created in AKS.

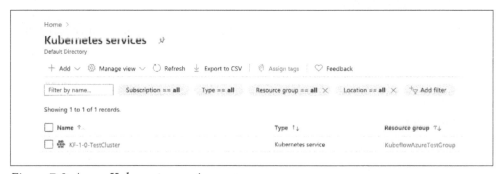

Figure 7-8. Azure Kubernetes services screen

If you click the cluster name in the Azure UI, you'll see the cluster detail, as shown in Figure 7-9.

Figure 7-9. Azure Kubernetes cluster detail screen

As you can confirm from Figure 7-9, our AKS-managed Kubernetes cluster was created successfully.

Now let's set up `kfctl` and install Kubeflow on our new AKS cluster.

Kubeflow Installation

To install Kubeflow on our Azure AKS Kubernetes cluster, we have to complete the following steps:

1. Get our Azure user credentials.
2. Create environment variables.
3. Set up `kfctl`.
4. Run `kfctl` comands.
5. Confirm deployment.

Let's now work through each of these high-level steps in detail.

Get Azure credentials

We need to get the credentials for our resource group name on Azure. To do this from the command line, use the following command.

```
az aks get-credentials -n <NAME> -g <RESOURCE_GROUP_NAME>
```

The output on the command line should look like this:

```
Merged "KF-1-0-TestCluster" as current context in /Users/josh/.kube/config
```

Now that we have our credentials for Azure set up locally so that `kubectl` can access it, let's move on and set up `kfctl`.

Download, install, and configure kfctl

We need to download and set up the `kfctl` tool before we can continue our Kubeflow installation. `kfctl` is similar to `kubectl` but specialized for Kubeflow.

First, download the kfctl v1.0.2 release from the Kubeflow releases page (*https://oreil.ly/1VUVy*).

Then unpack the downloaded tarball for the release with the command:

```
tar -xvf kfctl_<release tag>_<platform>.tar.gz
```

Optionally, we can add `kfctl` location to our path, which is recommended unless we want to use the full path for `kfctl` each time we use it:

```
export PATH=$PATH:<path to kfctl in your Kubeflow installation>
```

Now when we type the `kfctl` command from anywhere, we should see what appears in Example 7-3.

Example 7-3. kfctl command default output

```
A client CLI to create Kubeflow applications for specific platforms or 'on-prem'...

Usage:
  kfctl [command]

Available Commands:
  alpha       Alpha kfctl features.
  apply       deploys a Kubeflow application.
  build       Builds a KF App from a config file
  completion  Generate shell completions
  delete      Delete a Kubeflow application.
  generate    'kfctl generate' has been replaced by 'kfctl build'
Please switch to new semantics.
To build a KFAPP run -> kfctl build -f ${CONFIG}
Then to install -> kfctl apply
For more information, run 'kfctl build -h' or read the docs at www.kubeflow.org.
  help        Help about any command
  init        'kfctl init' has been removed.
Please switch to new semantics.
To install run -> kfctl apply -f ${CONFIG}
For more information, run 'kfctl apply -h' or read the docs at www.kubeflow.org.
  version     Print the version of kfctl.

Flags:
  -h, --help   help for kfctl

Use "kfctl [command] --help" for more information about a command.
```

We're now ready to configure `kfctl` for our specific environment.

Set up environment variables for kfctl

We need to set up the following environment variables for use with `kfctl`:

- KF_NAME
- BASE_DIR
- KF_DIR
- CONFIG_URI

The first environment variable we need is the zone in which we want to deploy our GKE cluster and Kubeflow installation.

Setting the CONFIG environment variable. Next, we'll specify a configuration file during the `init` phase of the Kubeflow install. First, we need to set our CONFIG environment variable to point to the Kubeflow deployment configuration:

```
export CONFIG_URI=<url of your configuration file for init>
```

Kubeflow deployment configuration files are YAML files for specific ways to deploy Kubeflow. In this case, we'll use the standard Kubernetes with Istio deployment configuration:[1]

```
export CONFIG_URI="https://raw.githubusercontent...kfctl_k8s_istio.v1.0.2.yaml"
```

Setting the Kubeflow deployment environment variables. Now we need to set the environmental variable for the name of the directory where we want Kubeflow configurations to be stored. We do this with the following three environment variables:

- $KF_NAME
- $BASE_DIR
- $KF_DIR

Use the following export command:

```
export KF_NAME=<your choice of application directory name>
```

Building on this environment variable, we further define:

```
export BASE_DIR=<path to a base directory>
export KF_DIR=${BASE_DIR}/${KF_NAME}
```

This gives us a full directory path to our new Kubeflow deployment subdirectory.

---

1 This URL has been shortened to fit the space; the full URL is *https://raw.githubusercontent.com/kubeflow/manifests/v1.0-branch/kfdef/kfctl_k8s_istio.v1.0.2.yaml*.

Once we have these environment variables set, we can use `kfctl` to deploy Kubeflow on Azure.

Kubeflow deployment with kfctl

Kubeflow deployment on Azure with `kfctl` at this point requires only the following commands now that we have our variables set up:

```
mkdir -p ${KF_DIR}
cd ${KF_DIR}
kfctl apply -V -f ${CONFIG_URI}
```

When we run this command we should see output similar to Example 7-4.

Example 7-4. Sample output of kctl apply -V -f ${CONFIG_URI}

```
...

INFO[0125] Successfully applied application profiles      filename="kustomize...
INFO[0125] Deploying application seldon-core-operator     filename="kustomize...
customresourcedefinition.apiextensions.k8s.io/seldondeployments.machine...
mutatingwebhookconfiguration.admissionregistration.k8s.io/seldon-mutating...
role.rbac.authorization.k8s.io/seldon-leader-election-role created
role.rbac.authorization.k8s.io/seldon-manager-cm-role created
clusterrole.rbac.authorization.k8s.io/seldon-manager-role-kubeflow created
clusterrole.rbac.authorization.k8s.io/seldon-manager-sas-role-kubeflow created
rolebinding.rbac.authorization.k8s.io/seldon-leader-election-rolebinding...
rolebinding.rbac.authorization.k8s.io/seldon-manager-cm-rolebinding created
clusterrolebinding.rbac.authorization.k8s.io/seldon-manager-rolebinding...
clusterrolebinding.rbac.authorization.k8s.io/seldon-manager-sas-rolebinding...
configmap/seldon-config created
service/seldon-webhook-service created
deployment.apps/seldon-controller-manager created
application.app.k8s.io/seldon-core-operator created
certificate.cert-manager.io/seldon-serving-cert created
issuer.cert-manager.io/seldon-selfsigned-issuer created
validatingwebhookconfiguration.admissionregistration.k8s.io/seldon-validating...
INFO[0127] Successfully applied application seldon-core-operator  filename=...
INFO[0127] Applied the configuration Successfully!       filename="cmd/apply.go:72"
```

The Kubeflow application should now be deployed on Azure. It may take a few minutes to show up as deployed in the Azure console, but from the administrator's end of things, you are done with deployment commands.

Confirm Kubeflow deployment

If we want to confirm that we successfully deployed Kubeflow, we can use the command:

```
kubectl -n kubeflow get  all
```

The output for this should look like Example 7-5.

Example 7-5. kubectl -n kubeflow get all sample output

```
NAME                                   READY   STATUS             RESTARTS   AGE
pod/admission-webhook-bootstrap....    1/1     Running            0          55s
pod/admission-webhook-deployment....   0/1     ContainerCreating  0          10s
pod/application-controller...          1/1     Running            0          114s
pod/argo-ui-7ffb9b6577-fcbwq           1/1     Running            0          58s
pod/centraldashboard-659bd78c-875qx    1/1     Running            0          56s
pod/jupyter-web-app-deployment...      0/1     ContainerCreating  0          52s
pod/katib-controller-7f58569f7d-mrjng  0/1     ContainerCreating  0          29s
pod/katib-db-manager-54b66f9f9d-9dr5x  0/1     ContainerCreating  0          29s
pod/katib-mysql-dcf7dcbd5-t6nlk        0/1     ContainerCreating  0          29s
pod/katib-ui-6f97756598-xd78z          0/1     ContainerCreating  0          29s
pod/kfserving-controller-manager-0     0/2     ContainerCreating  0          35s
pod/metacontroller-0                   1/1     Running            0          59s
pod/metadata-db-65fb5b695d-dm5p6       0/1     ContainerCreating  0          49s
pod/metadata-deployment...             0/1     ContainerCreating  0          49s
pod/metadata-envoy-deployment...       1/1     Running            0          48s
pod/metadata-grpc-deployment....       0/1     ContainerCreating  0          48s
pod/metadata-ui-7c85545947-jq7xd       1/1     Running            0          48s
pod/minio-6b67f98977-w2fwd             0/1     ContainerCreating  0          27s
pod/ml-pipeline-6cf777c7bc-cngzq       0/1     ContainerCreating  0          27s
pod/ml-pipeline-ml-pipeline...         0/1     ContainerCreating  0          21s
pod/ml-pipeline-persistenceagent...    0/1     ContainerCreating  0          25s
pod/ml-pipeline-scheduledworkflow...   0/1     ContainerCreating  0          21s
pod/ml-pipeline-ui-549b5b6744-4s4hp    0/1     ContainerCreating  0          24s
pod/ml-pipeline-viewer...              0/1     ContainerCreating  0          22s
pod/mysql-85bc64f5c4-x5666             0/1     ContainerCreating  0          26s
pod/notebook-controller-deployment...  0/1     ContainerCreating  0          46s
pod/profiles-deployment...             0/2     ContainerCreating  0          20s
pod/pytorch-operator-cf8c5c497-v6qn7   1/1     Running            0          45s
pod/seldon-controller-manager...       0/1     ContainerCreating  0          17s
pod/spark-operatorcrd-cleanup-xmsqb    0/2     ContainerCreating  0          50s
pod/spark-operatorsparkoperator...     0/1     ContainerCreating  0          51s
pod/spartakus-volunteer...             0/1     ContainerCreating  0          34s
pod/tensorboard-5f685f9d79-6l8x4       0/1     ContainerCreating  0          34s
pod/tf-job-operator-5fb85c5fb7-dzdpf   0/1     ContainerCreating  0          32s
pod/workflow-controller...             1/1     Running            0          58s

NAME                        TYPE       CLUSTER-IP     EXTERNAL-IP  PORT(S)        AGE
service/admission...        ClusterIP  10.0.218.52    <none>       443/TCP        54s
service/application...      ClusterIP  10.0.189.152   <none>       443/TCP        114s
service/argo-ui            NodePort   10.0.12.53     <none>       80:32051/TCP   58s
service/centraldashboard    ClusterIP  10.0.67.222    <none>       80/TCP         56s
service/jupyter-web-app...  ClusterIP  10.0.44.255    <none>       80/TCP         52s
service/katib-controller    ClusterIP  10.0.131.36    <none>       443/TCP,...    30s
service/katib-db-manager    ClusterIP  10.0.175.154   <none>       6789/TCP       30s
service/katib-mysql         ClusterIP  10.0.122.93    <none>       3306/TCP       29s
service/katib-ui            ClusterIP  10.0.206.223   <none>       80/TCP         29s
```

```
service/kfserving...          ClusterIP   10.0.188.73    <none>   8443/TCP        35s
service/kfserving...          ClusterIP   10.0.17.232    <none>   443/TCP         35s
service/metadata-db           ClusterIP   10.0.32.198    <none>   3306/TCP        49s
service/metadata-envoy...     ClusterIP   10.0.225.15    <none>   9090/TCP        49s
service/metadata-grpc...      ClusterIP   10.0.189.179   <none>   8080/TCP        49s
service/metadata-service      ClusterIP   10.0.23.231    <none>   8080/TCP        49s
service/metadata-ui           ClusterIP   10.0.195.153   <none>   80/TCP          49s
service/minio-service         ClusterIP   10.0.151.45    <none>   9000/TCP        27s
service/ml-pipeline           ClusterIP   10.0.188.75    <none>   8888/TCP,...    28s
service/ml-pipeline-ml...     ClusterIP   10.0.158.115   <none>   8888/TCP        21s
service/ml-pipeline...        ClusterIP   10.0.33.171    <none>   80/TCP          24s
service/ml-pipeline-ui        ClusterIP   10.0.133.49    <none>   80/TCP          24s
service/mysql                 ClusterIP   10.0.0.108     <none>   3306/TCP        26s
service/notebook...           ClusterIP   10.0.242.145   <none>   443/TCP         46s
service/profiles-kfam         ClusterIP   10.0.20.131    <none>   8081/TCP        20s
service/pytorch-operator      ClusterIP   10.0.118.141   <none>   8443/TCP        45s
service/seldon-webhook...     ClusterIP   10.0.64.30     <none>   443/TCP         17s
service/tensorboard           ClusterIP   10.0.12.52     <none>   9000/TCP        34s
service/tf-job-operator       ClusterIP   10.0.245.121   <none>   8443/TCP        32s
```

NAME	READY	UP-TO-DATE	AVAILABLE	AGE
deployment.apps/admission-webhook...	0/1	1	0	54s
deployment.apps/argo-ui	1/1	1	1	58s
deployment.apps/centraldashboard	1/1	1	1	56s
deployment.apps/jupyter-web-app-deployment	0/1	1	0	52s
deployment.apps/katib-controller	0/1	1	0	29s
deployment.apps/katib-db-manager	0/1	1	0	29s
deployment.apps/katib-mysql	0/1	1	0	29s
deployment.apps/katib-ui	0/1	1	0	29s
deployment.apps/metadata-db	0/1	1	0	49s
deployment.apps/metadata-deployment	0/1	1	0	49s
deployment.apps/metadata-envoy-deployment	1/1	1	1	48s
deployment.apps/metadata-grpc-deployment	0/1	1	0	48s
deployment.apps/metadata-ui	1/1	1	1	48s
deployment.apps/minio	0/1	1	0	27s
deployment.apps/ml-pipeline	0/1	1	0	27s
deployment.apps/ml-pipeline-ml-pipeline...	0/1	1	0	21s
deployment.apps/ml-pipeline-persistenceagent	0/1	1	0	25s
deployment.apps/ml-pipeline-scheduledworkflow	0/1	1	0	21s
deployment.apps/ml-pipeline-ui	0/1	1	0	24s
deployment.apps/ml-pipeline-viewer....	0/1	1	0	22s
deployment.apps/mysql	0/1	1	0	26s
deployment.apps/notebook-controller...	0/1	1	0	46s
deployment.apps/profiles-deployment	0/1	1	0	20s
deployment.apps/pytorch-operator	1/1	1	1	45s
deployment.apps/seldon-controller-manager	0/1	1	0	17s
deployment.apps/spark-operatorsparkoperator	0/1	1	0	51s
deployment.apps/spartakus-volunteer	0/1	1	0	34s
deployment.apps/tensorboard	0/1	1	0	34s
deployment.apps/tf-job-operator	0/1	1	0	32s
deployment.apps/workflow-controller	1/1	1	1	58s

```
NAME                                                DESIRED CURRENT READY AGE
replicaset.apps/admission-webhook-deployment...     1       1       0     54s
replicaset.apps/argo-ui-7ffb9b6577                  1       1       1     58s
replicaset.apps/centraldashboard-659bd78c           1       1       1     56s
replicaset.apps/jupyter-web-app-deployment...       1       1       0     52s
replicaset.apps/katib-controller-7f58569f7d         1       1       0     29s
replicaset.apps/katib-db-manager-54b66f9f9d         1       1       0     29s
replicaset.apps/katib-mysql-dcf7dcbd5               1       1       0     29s
replicaset.apps/katib-ui-6f97756598                 1       1       0     29s
replicaset.apps/metadata-db-65fb5b695d              1       1       0     49s
replicaset.apps/metadata-deployment-65ccddfd4c      1       1       0     49s
replicaset.apps/metadata-envoy-deployment...        1       1       1     48s
replicaset.apps/metadata-grpc-deployment-5c6db9749  1       1       0     48s
replicaset.apps/metadata-ui-7c85545947              1       1       1     48s
replicaset.apps/minio-6b67f98977                    1       1       0     27s
replicaset.apps/ml-pipeline-6cf777c7bc              1       1       0     27s
replicaset.apps/ml-pipeline-ml-pipeline...          1       1       0     21s
replicaset.apps/ml-pipeline-persistenceagent...     1       1       0     25s
replicaset.apps/ml-pipeline-scheduledworkflow...    1       1       0     21s
replicaset.apps/ml-pipeline-ui-549b5b6744           1       1       0     24s
replicaset.apps/ml-pipeline-viewer-controller...    1       1       0     22s
replicaset.apps/mysql-85bc64f5c4                    1       1       0     26s
replicaset.apps/notebook-controller-deployment...   1       1       0     46s
replicaset.apps/profiles-deployment-c775584c7       1       1       0     20s
replicaset.apps/pytorch-operator-cf8c5c497          1       1       1     45s
replicaset.apps/seldon-controller-manager...        1       1       0     17s
replicaset.apps/spark-operatorsparkoperator...      1       1       0     51s
replicaset.apps/spartakus-volunteer-5dc96f4447      1       1       0     34s
replicaset.apps/tensorboard-5f685f9d79              1       1       0     34s
replicaset.apps/tf-job-operator-5fb85c5fb7          1       1       0     32s
replicaset.apps/workflow-controller-689d6c8846      1       1       1     58s

NAME                                                        READY   AGE
statefulset.apps/admission-webhook-bootstrap-stateful-set   1/1     55s
statefulset.apps/application-controller-stateful-set        1/1     114s
statefulset.apps/kfserving-controller-manager               0/1     35s
statefulset.apps/metacontroller                             1/1     59s

NAME                             COMPLETIONS   DURATION   AGE
job.batch/spark-operatorcrd-cleanup   0/1      50s        50s
```

Now we have confirmed that Kubeflow deployed on GKE, let's take a look at the main user interface and check out the Kubeflow application.

Authorizing Network Access to Deployment

In Chapter 2, we discussed the fundamentals of how Istio controls access to endpoints in Kubeflow. Kubeflow on Azure uses the Istio ingress gateway as its ingress point.

However, the default install does not create an external endpoint, so we'll need to set up port-forwarding to test out our new Kubeflow deployment on Azure with the command:

```
kubectl port-forward svc/istio-ingressgateway -n istio-system 8080:80
```

Once we've done this locally on the command line, we can visit this address in the browser: `http://localhost:8080`.

Exposing Kubeflow on Azure to the Public

We want to set up network access to prevent unauthorized access before we open the Kubeflow Dashboard as a public IP.

Summary

At this point, you have covered how to install Kubeflow on-premise and in the cloud. We'll now move into the final topic of the book, understanding model deployment in Kubeflow with KFServing.

## CHAPTER 8

Model Serving and Integration

Machine learning in practice is largely focused on the training of machine learning models. Many theory books, however, do not address issues surrounding how to integrate a model into a production application and manage the life cycle of the model. Kubeflow as a platform covers all phases of model development and deployment.

In this chapter we build up your understanding of machine learning operational concepts, and then show how these concepts are executed with KFServing on Kubernetes in practice. Let's start out learning about the core concepts in model management.

Basic Concepts of Model Management

You need to understand the following core concepts related to machine learning operations:

- Model training versus model inference
- Inference latencies
- The high-level components of operationalizing a model in production
- Batch versus transactional operation latencies
- Transforming raw data into vectors
- Hard-wiring a single model versus model management
- Knowing when to retrain a model
- Model rollbacks
- Security models for model management
- Scaling a model in production
- Monitoring performance of a model

- Model explainability
- Detecting input outliers

The challenge is compounded when the machine learning operations practitioner has to execute the preceding concepts in the context of the following technologies:

- Model serialization
- Model servers
- Protocol standards, HTTP/GRPC
- Dealing with multiple machine learning frameworks
- Containerization (*https://oreil.ly/KyW2I*)
- GitOps
- Kubernetes (*https://kubernetes.io/*)
- Deployments, services
- HPAs, VPAs, KPAs
- Readiness/liveness probes
- Persistent volumes (*https://oreil.ly/JnJoq*)
- Service meshes (*https://oreil.ly/Bq6nu*)
- Cloud events
- GPUs

There is a strong industry trend toward standardizing infrastructure deployment on Kubernetes (scalability, reliability, etc.), so we can see many of the technologies here linked to its ecosystem. This chapter focuses on the core concepts you should know in model management, and then how they can be accomplished with KFServing.

Let's start off by looking at the fundamental differences between training a machine learning model and producing inference from a saved machine learning model.

Understanding Training Models Versus Model Inference

Machine learning model training is the process of making multiple passes over an input training dataset, where we change our model parameters until we fit the dataset for a model's goal criteria. Input for machine learning model training is:

- An input training dataset
- Associated labels for the training dataset (if this is supervised learning)
- Hyperparameters

In machine learning, modeling a single pass over a dataset is called an *epoch*, and this training pass can take anywhere from seconds to days. Given the latency of this operation, and the need to make multiple passes over the dataset, we consider model training to be a batch-class operation. A batch-class operation is similar in latency to how we process data to produce analytical data output. This batch operation can be sped up with special hardware such as GPUs, but even with GPUs, more complex models may take hours or days to train.

Machine learning model inference is different from training. It is the process of taking an existing trained model and using new data as input to produce model output such as a classification (e.g., "label"), or a continuous real-valued number from a regression model (e.g., "house price"). The input to a model for output is:

- 1 or N input records (the features should match the features from the training dataset)
- The input record features need to be transformed in the same way as during training

Model inference is typically a low-latency operation. The latency is measured in milliseconds (ms) most of the time, but can get up into the low second range for larger models.[1] We consider the model inference process to be transactional in nature and should be thought of more similarly to a transactional database query (e.g., "select * from [table] where ROWID = 100;"). We make this comparison to a transactional database as in the case of model inference where we seek to get a single statistical inference based on a global population of data (e.g., the training data) with respect to specific input features.

Historically in computer science we've seen request/response systems (e.g., web servers, databases) use metrics such as requests per second or queries per second (QPS). Given that we intend to serve inferences to remote applications in a request/response pattern in a similar fashion, we could think of our model hosting servers in the same framing. Based on that context, we could say we seek to hit a certain inferences per second (IPS) rating for our scaled-out model in production. We'll talk more about this later in this chapter.

---

1 For more details, see the computer vision model inference latencies over at TensorFlow's GitHub repository (*https://oreil.ly/cVaxC*).

Machine Learning Models as Materialized Views of Training Data

If we continue to the database references further from this section, we can describe machine learning models as materialized views of training data. In the same way that we might run a transform against an input table (or multiple tables) and produce a materialized view that may be saved as a table, we could consider the machine learning training process here to produce a new materialized view of the input training data. The machine learning model is then used to serve new information about the original training data.

Now that we have a better idea of the differences between model creation and model inference, let's build an intuition for ways we can integrate a model with an application.

Building an Intuition for Model Integration

Integration for machine learning models has two variants:

- A scenario where we copy a model locally and load it into memory
- A scenario where we access the model across a network

This chapter primarily focuses on the second scenario where we remotely access a deployed model across a network. We focus on this second scenario because the first scenario typically is not a practical DevOps practice for operations, as we'll see in this chapter. In this network-accessible scenario, we consider the distinct stages of executing model inference:

1. Client encodes model input for network transport.
2. Client transmits encoded model input across network to model server.
3. Model server receives and decodes the input data payload.
4. Model server uses the input data to produce an inference output.
5. Model server encodes the inference result for network transport.
6. Model server transmits the encoded inference result across the network back to the client.

We can see the general flow described here in Figure 8-1.

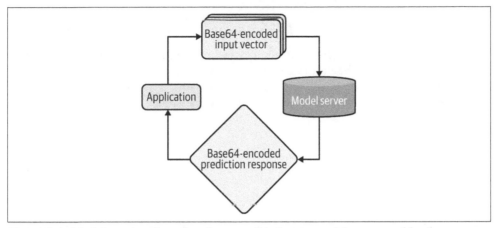

Figure 8-1. Model serving data flow from application to model server and back

A fundamental component of the client-server inference transaction is the use of REST APIs (*https://restfulapi.net/*).

Kubeflow and REST APIs

Most Kubeflow model-serving systems use RESTful APIs as they provide a large degree of flexibility. With a RESTful API, data is not tied to methods or resources so REST can:

- Expose many types of function calls
- Return different data formats (XML, JSON, YAML, etc.)
- Work with clients of different implementations

Another aspect is that most web developers find that REST is easy to understand and develop for. REST APIs provide a well-known building block on which to base a model-serving infrastructure. An example of a REST API endpoint follows:

```
http://<ambassadorEndpoint>/seldon/<deploymentName>/api/v0.1/predictions
```

Exposing our model as a REST API, we can now access the model from across a network, independently. A physical model is mapped to this specific version of the endpoint. This allows our DevOps teams to provide an endpoint representing the "latest" version of the production model, and then allows client applications to consume this endpoint. At any time, the DevOps team can update the model behind this endpoint while not breaking the integration with the consuming application. This aspect sets up our mechanics for model management, which we'll cover in a later section of this chapter.

API Gateways

API Management (APIM) has been the key technology used to implement modern API use cases. Across the past decade we've seen API gateway technology evolve to support larger and more elaborate use cases, culminating in what the industry terms "full life cycle API management." Topics in this arena include:

- Testing
- Documentation
- Monetization
- Monitoring

In the context of Kubeflow and model serving, we see technologies such as Istio driving certain key parts of the API management, such as routing traffic to the model and exposing the model through the Istio gateway.

Once we've decided on using REST, we now need to send our input data (or input *vector*) from our application to the model server over the network. We'll need to encode our model input data in a representation appropriate for transfer via HTTP (*https://restfulapi.net/http-methods*). The HTTP method we'll likely use here is a POST method and we'll need to encode our model input data in such a way that it can be represented as a string for embedding inside the POST HTTP call. We also need to keep in mind how the exposed API endpoint expects to receive the data on the server side. Later in this chapter we'll look at specific implementation samples of these aspects of REST-based model inference.

The server side will receive the HTTP POST-call, and then map the call to the appropriate implementation locally. The server will then decode the base64-encoded body payload to extract the model input. If the model deployment is configured to do any input data pre-processing, it will now apply the transforms to the input data. Once the transforms are complete, the deployment will then use the input data as input to the machine learning model to produce the model inference.

Some deployments will perform post-processing on the raw model inference, but this does not always happen. Once the output inference of the model is complete, this output will be re-encoded to be sent back via HTTP to the client application.

Now that we've discussed the life cycle of a model inference request/response cycle, let's move on and look at how model inference throughput can be scaled.

Scaling Model Inference Throughput

As usage of deployed production machine learning models increases, some models will become more accessed than others. This is similar to how specific tables in a database are more frequently accessed than others. In both cases we may have to look at ways to serve more transactions to a growing user base.

Just as with query cost and relational database tables, each machine learning model requires a specific computational cost to produce the desired model inference output.

For instance, a small model (e.g., simple multilayer perceptron with five parameters) can return inference responses on CPU hardware in under 10 ms or less. However, larger (1 GB) models (e.g., R-CNN image classification models (*https://oreil.ly/cVaxC*)) can take 7 seconds or longer to return a single inference on CPU.

Typically, our users require a responsive application, and they will not want to wait more than 500 ms for responsiveness on application interaction. At this point in developing a scalable deployment strategy, we need to consider:

- The expectations of the user-facing application with respect to response latency (e.g., how fast do we need an answer?)
- How many users we need to serve during peak hours of usage

To do this we will develop an inference-per-second (IPS) forecast. Inferences per second should be thought of similarly to queries per second, as previously mentioned in this chapter. Inferences per second is the average number of inferences our model serving system needs to produce each second to sustain our application at its peak period.

We can calculate IPS by determining:

1. Peak usage time period (e.g., hour) of the day
2. Total number of inferences required to power the application during the peak time period
3. Dividing the total inferences in time period by the time period to get inferences per second

Beyond pure inference latency, we need to consider the other parts of the inference transaction, especially as we deal with larger models. The stages of inference transaction are:

1. Client data encode
2. Client data transmission to model server

3. Model server data payload decode

4. Model server: inference

5. Model server: inference result encode

6. Model server to client transmission

Our server-side IPS calculations won't be affected by client data encoding and transmission.

Overhead of Base64 Decoding Input Data

The full life cycle of an inference call involves more than just getting an inference result from a model. Some models will have large input data (e.g., image data), and base64 decoding may impact model server performance. Application designers should be aware of the full inference life cycle when designing their systems.

Sometimes post-processing is done on the output of the inference pass as well, so that may need to be considered. Application designers should be aware of the pure model inference latency along with the deployed model latency with transaction overhead.

In the next subsection we put this method into practice through some scenarios.

Developing example inference-per-second forecasts

In this section we walk through a few sample scenarios to show how we'd develop a rough inference-per-second forecast.

Let's say we are starting out and only need to average one inference per minute (something simple to show how the numbers work). For this example we'll pretend our model is a simple multilayer perceptron with a few parameters, and inference on CPU only takes 5 ms.

In this case our forecast is only (1 inference/60 seconds) 0.016 inferences per second (e.g., a single inference per minute). Given these requirements, we could start out with a single server on a CPU and just deal with the application latency (5 ms). This is obviously a simple toy forecast, so let's now look at something a bit more realistic.

For this forecast scenario, let's say we are building an application that needs to detect objects within an image. We have chosen `ssd_inception_v2_coco` from the model zoo (*https://oreil.ly/cVaxC*) that produces inferences with a 42-ms latency on a Titan X GPU card.

Thinking About CPU Versus GPU for Model Serving

Many computer vision models in the TensorFlow model zoo take more than 1 second to produce inference output. Many apps expect to be consistently responsive to user actions, so having a response blocked on a 5- to 10-second (or more) latency with CPU-based inference will be a nonstarter for those applications.

Therefore, in most cases for computer vision models, CPUs will not be performant enough to serve computer vision model inferences at meaningful latencies. Most computer vision production applications will require GPUs to accelerate the inference latency to the desired thresholds.

In this scenario, let's say our application has 1100 users at the peak of our daily usage. On average, each application makes 3 inferences per minute, so this gives us (3 x 1100) 3300 inferences per minute, or 55 inferences per second.

If we cannot batch the inferences (and here with a transactional system we cannot), then we must consider the inference requests to be processed linearly in a queue.

So if we need to sustain 55 inferences per second, and each inference takes 42 ms, this is (55 inferences x 42 ms) 2310 ms of processing time. Unfortunately a single machine only has 1000 ms of inference processing time and can only server roughly 24 inferences per second.

Wall Clock Versus Compute Time and IPS

For this rough IPS forecast we're ignoring the reality of the other things on the host that may eat up compute time, such as operating system overhead. If the user runs a single inference N times and then takes the average, some of the background overhead will likely get picked up in the average.

We can serve more inferences if we use more model servers. This technique, in distributed systems, is called "scale out." We'll have to deploy 3 model servers (3 servers x 24 IPS = 72 IPS) which is greater than our requirement of 55 IPS, so we should be OK.

Calculations such as these are good for getting a "back of the envelope" number for the peak IPS that our system may need. Cloud-based systems allow us to scale out resources on demand, but on-premise Kubeflow installations will need to do hardware allocation, and management will expect a team to give them a forecast on how much hardware they'll need to sustain the inference load.

Later in this chapter we'll see how KFServing handles scaling out for model serving, and also autoscaling of model serving containers as demand changes.

Model Management

It's easy to work with a single model at a time as a data scientist. However, similar to a database of many individual tables, operationalizing many teams' models can be a challenge.

Early iterations of machine learning applications will often load a saved machine learning model from the local disk into memory for the consumer application to use. This tends to work well with local notebooks and development applications, but scales poorly when we start needing to support a group of users or serve inferences to a web-scale application. Certainly, any DevOps team will seek to make production machine learning model rollout as manageable as possible.

We can further illustrate this challenge with a scenario. If we had 20 different machine learning pipelines, each producing a new model once a month over the course of a year, we would have (12 x 20 = 240) different versions of model files sitting around on different hard drives in our division. This quickly creates resource management issues such as:

- Updating a deployed machine learning model
- Rolling back and replacing an existing production model
- Managing secure access to the model

Any DevOps team would want to step in and introduce basic controls for:

- Current best model
- Previous best model (for model rollbacks)
- Integration method for serving inferences (API REST bridge)

All of these issues exist with any basic modeling workflow, yet they get progressively harder to manage as more teams create more models.

If we follow the database parallels we established in the previous section, we could also note that early pre-database concepts (*https://oreil.ly/b57aJ*) involved copying around flat files to local machines much in the same manner. Over time, we saw databases evolve into centralized servers with access mechanisms such as JDBC and ODBC.

Further complicating model tracking is the issue of *concept drift* (*https://oreil.ly/iIawo*). Machine learning models "age" as the distribution of the training data drifts (*https://oreil.ly/Boy9H*) from what the full population of the data becomes over time. When this happens, our model is no longer going to be able to produce as good inferences as it could if it were retrained on new data. Tracking concept drift allows us to be alerted when a model may need to be retrained.

As machine learning production methods mature, we will see the sector mature much in the same way. This chapter is focused on communicating methods for model management that are evolving toward more pragmatic approaches.[2]

Introduction to KFServing

In this section, we introduce KFServing, the core model management component of Kubeflow. KFServing's core value can be expressed as:

- Helping to standardize model serving across orgs with unified data plane and pre-built model servers
- A single way to deploy, monitor inference services/server, and scale inference workload
- Dramatically shortening time for data scientists to deploy models to production

Kubeflow offers two open source multiframework serving options (*https://oreil.ly/ JksGC*):

- KFServing
- Seldon Core

KFServing is part of the Kubeflow project ecosystem. However, Seldon Core is an external project supported by Kubeflow components.

Of course, the user always has the option with open source systems to use a standalone model-serving system of their choice. The list of frameworks supported by both KFServing and Seldon Core is as follows:

- TensorFlow
- XGBoost
- scikit-learn
- Nvidia Triton Inference Server
- ONNX
- PyTorch

However, using one of these supported options allows a Kubeflow user to leverage all of the integrated features to make model management that much easier.

---

2 It's been a long hill to climb to get this far into the book. Before you take that last mile to the top of the mountain, take a break and check out RJD2's latest album *The Fun Ones* (*https://oreil.ly/_FYW6*).

The major components KFServing uses are shown in Figure 8-2.

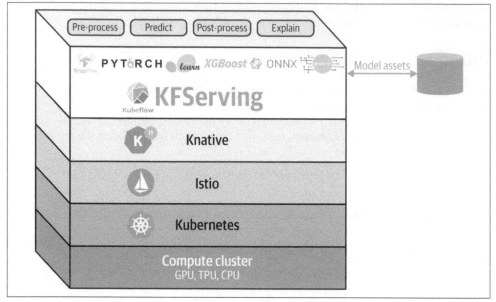

Figure 8-2. Major components of KFServing (source: KFServing GitHub repository (https://oreil.ly/oCAEC))

These components include

- Knative
- Istio
- Kubernetes

These foundational components allow KFServing to execute on a compute cluster involving different types of hardware (GPU, TPU, CPU).

Other considerations when evaluating model serving options include:

- Graph support
- Analytics on model serving
- Scaling inferences
- Rollout options

Graph support is important in a production situation because we rarely "just get a model inference." Typically we see raw data coming over the wire as a request (e.g., base64-encoded image pixel data) and it may need to be converted into the appropriate feature structure that the machine learning model expects.

Let's now look further into the advantages of using a multiframework system such as KFServing.

Advantages of Using KFServing

KFServing was designed so that model serving could be operated in a standardized way across frameworks, right out of the box. There was a need for a model serving system that could easily run on existing Kubernetes and Istio stacks, and also provide model explainability, inference graph operations, and other model management functions. Kubeflow needed a way to allow both data scientists and DevOps/MLOps teams to collaborate from model production to modern production model deployment.

Two key aspects today of KFServing are the included pre-built model servers, along with the ability to autoscale the model deployments. Further, by building on components such as Istio and Knative, KFServing offers basic metrics such as latency and RPC counts for monitoring and operational management. The deployment system needs to be intuitive and consistent while offering power features, such as canary roll-outs and GPU autoscaling, for later in development.

The concept of a model server has existed for a while now, yet many popular model servers (e.g., TFServing, ONNX, etc.) all communicate using similar yet noninteroperable HTTP/gRPC protocols. KFServing was designed to provide abstraction interfaces and a standardized prediction workflow for common machine learning frameworks such as TensorFlow, XGBoost, and PyTorch.

Building on this standardized prediction workflow gives us a simple and pluggable machine learning serving story for tasks such as:

- Prediction
- Pre-processing
- Post-processing
- Explainability

To better understand how KFServing standardizes these tasks (and more), let's dig further into the core concepts of KFServing and model serving.

Core Concepts in KFServing

In Figure 8-3 we show the KFServing InferenceService data plane architecture.

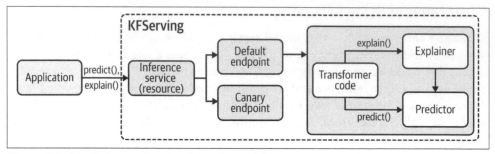

Figure 8-3. The InferenceService data plane architecture

KFServing's data plane has a standardized prediction workflow across all model frameworks.

The core concepts shown in Figure 8-3 are:

- InferenceService
- Endpoint
- Component
- Predictor
- Explainer
- Transformer

In the following sections we give further details on each of these concepts.

InferenceService

An InferenceService is the core object in KFServing that represents all of the parts of a deployed machine learning model. InferenceService manages the life cycle of models via the KFServing system. When we want to get an inference from a model hosted on KFServing, we will make a call to an instance of an InferenceService process running on KFServing.

Each InferenceService is represented by two different endpoints:

- Default endpoint
- Canary endpoint

There are two exposed API methods for every InferenceService endpoint:

- Predict[3]
- Explain

As we can see in Figure 8-3, an application can make a network request to KFServing against one of the API methods to access the functionality for the given deployed model. Istio is running as part of the KFServing system and provides any dynamic routing needed for moving traffic between the default endpoint and the canary endpoint.

To best understand the InferenceService object and how it sits within the overall KFServing context, let's jump right into how a model is deployed as an InferenceService with KFServing. To deploy a model as an InferenceService on KFServing, we have two methods:

1. Using `kubectl` and apply a YAML file to a Kubernetes cluster with KFServing installed.
2. Using the Python KFServing SDK to deploy to a Kubernetes cluster with KFServing installed.

KFServing maintains these two methods of model management to cater to both data scientists and MLOps Engineers.

DevOps and MLOps engineers tend to prefer a method that is command-line tool based and declarative (to gain advantages such as the ability to roll back state). To deploy a model by using a YAML file and `kubectl`, we'd need to create an Inference-Service (*https://oreil.ly/1z8Qr*) spec in a *YAML* file for our specific model deployment based on the InferenceService specification, as shown in Example 8-1.

Example 8-1. YAML InferenceService example

```
apiVersion: "serving.kubeflow.org/v1alpha2"
kind: "InferenceService"
metadata:
  name: "flowers-sample"
spec:
  default:
    predictor:
      tensorflow:
        storageUri: "gs://kfserving-samples/models/tensorflow/flowers"
```

---

3 All InferenceServices speak the TensorFlow V1 HTTP API (*https://oreil.ly/alhUC*).

Once we have our YAML file saved locally (*tf_flowers.yaml* in this case), we can deploy the model as an InferenceService by applying a YAMLfile from the command line, as seen in this code snippet:

```
kubectl apply -f tf_flowers.yaml
```

The data science crowd, however, may prefer methods that allow them to deploy and manage their models directly from Python code. In this case we'd use the KFServing Python SDK and the KFServingClient (*https://oreil.ly/g6C2s*) class from our Python code. An example of deploying the same TensorFlow model with the Python KFServingClient class is shown in Example 8-2.

Example 8-2. Basic usage of KFServingClient in Python

```
from kubernetes import client

from kfserving import KFServingClient
from kfserving import constants
from kfserving import V1alpha2EndpointSpec
from kfserving import V1alpha2PredictorSpec
from kfserving import V1alpha2TensorflowSpec
from kfserving import V1alpha2InferenceServiceSpec
from kfserving import V1alpha2InferenceService


default_model_spec = V1alpha2EndpointSpec(predictor=V1alpha2PredictorSpec \
    (tensorflow=V1alpha2TensorflowSpec(
    storage_uri='gs://kfserving-samples/models/tensorflow/flowers')))

isvc = V1alpha2InferenceService(api_version=constants.KFSERVING_GROUP + '/' + \
    constants.KFSERVING_VERSION,
                        kind=constants.KFSERVING_KIND,
                        metadata=client.V1ObjectMeta(name='flower-sample', \
                          namespace='kubeflow'),
                        spec=V1alpha2InferenceServiceSpec \
                          (default=default_model_spec))


KFServing = KFServingClient()
KFServing.create(isvc)
```

To run this code we'd execute the Python file or the notebook that contains the preceding code. Assuming we have a cluster with KFServing installed and our Kubernetes credentials locally accessible to our Python code, this code would deploy our model as an InferenceService on our Kubernetes cluster.

Treating Models as Infrastructure

Currently, KFServing operationally treats model deployment as infrastructure deployment. We contrast this to how Kubeflow treats Jupyter Notebook deployment as a user land function. As Kubeflow and KFServing continue to evolve in the future, there is a good chance that we will see model deployment in KFServing look more like Jupyter Notebook deployment in Kubeflow (e.g., as a user land operation).

Once our model is deployed as an InferenceService, we can access its inference output (e.g., prediction) API via one of the exposed endpoints.

Endpoint

A KFServing InferenceServer endpoint is a server-side web API that is accessed via a URI with HTTP requests.

Endpoints and Web APIs

An HTTP endpoint specifies where resources are located that can be accessed by a third-party application or user. Generally, access to the endpoint is via a URI to which HTTP requests are posted. The entity making the request to the endpoint will expect a response as well.

In KFServing, every InferenceServer instance is divided into two endpoints:

- Default
- Canary

Most traffic will (at least initially) travel through the "default" endpoint. The canary endpoint is optionally used to test out new revisions of the model. In canary development, only a small part of the user base is exposed to a new feature via this canary endpoint, as we'll cover later in this chapter. In a standard blue-green deployment we can simply deploy on the "default" endpoint.

Blue-Green Deployments

A model deployment strategy of note is a *blue-green* deployment. Blue-green deployment is a technique where a team runs two identical production environments called "blue" and "green." Only one of the deployments is live at any given time, with this live deployment getting all of the production traffic. This technique is considered a strategy to mitigate risk and reduce downtime in production deployments.

Each endpoint is made up of multiple components:

- Predictor
- Explainer
- Transformer

The predictor is the only required component as it is the core of the endpoint.

Future Supported Components

The KFServing project plans on supporting more upcoming components, such as outlier detection.

Predictor

Deployed models on a model server are represented by the predictor component of the InferenceService. The models hosted on the model server are represented by the exposed network endpoint.

To access the predictor API (for the v1 data plane) on the endpoint, we'd send a POST verb via HTTP to the *predict* endpoint at the path:

```
/v1/models/<model_name>:predict
```

The payload returned via the HTTP response would resemble:

```
Request:{"instances": [ ... ]} Response:{"predictions": [ ... ]}
```

Predict and the TensorFlow v1 HTTP API

At this point, all InferenceServices are able to communicate via the TensorFlow v1 HTTP API. However, only TensorFlow models support the specific fields signature_name and inputs.

Explainer

When we call the explainer API for an endpoint, we can access an alternate data plane that provides a model explanation along with the prediction. The explainer API data plane adds an extra stage in the prediction execution to production information about how the model arrived at its answer based on the input.

KFServing provides an out-of-the-box explainer called Alibi (*https://oreil.ly/vjTwx*) for common use cases.

> **KFServing, Seldon Core, and Alibi**
>
> KFServing and Seldon Core share some technical features, such as Alibi, for explainability in the Kubeflow 1.0 release. KFServing is officially part of the Kubeflow project ecosystem, and Seldon Core is an external separate project that has integration with Kubeflow.
>
> Alibi is a Python library intended to help provide model inspection and interpretation. Alibi is open source and is focused initially on black-box instance-based model explanations. To know more, check out the KFServing income prediction example (*https:// oreil.ly/rkZsF*) for Alibi.

A KFServer user may define their own explanation container, that is then used in the explainer data plane. Explainability in a data plane helps when we want to communicate things about a model's behavior, such as "is input an outlier?" This is helpful in situations where law (e.g., GDPR) mandates that the data subject be able to access meaningful information about the logic involved in producing the prediction with the model.

Any InferenceService deployed with explainer supports a standardized explanation API. This interface is similar to the TensorFlow v1 HTTP API with the difference being the additional `explain` verb.

To access the explainer API (for the v1 data plane) on the endpoint, we'd send an `explain` POST verb via HTTP to the endpoint at the path:

```
/v1/models/<model_name>:explain
```

The payload returned via the HTTP response would resemble:

```
Request:{"instances": [ ... ]} Response:{"predictions": [ ... ], \
    "explanations": [ ... ]}
```

Let's now move on to how we can customize deployed predictors and explainers with transformers.

Transformers

Transformers in KFServing allow a user to define pre- and post-processing steps to manipulate the data before the prediction phase of model inference.

Machine learning models expect tensors as input and will not work with raw data (e.g., a raw string). In our machine learning workflows, we typically vectorize data before we input it as a tensor into a saved model for inference.

In the context of models managed by a model server such as KFServing, each time we deploy a model we have to make decisions around where we'll execute the vectorization code:

- Do we leave it to the client to vectorize their own input data?
- Do we let the client send data across the network, and then do we do the vectorization in a transformer pre-process function?

An example (*https://oreil.ly/gUYlO*) would be a transformer that pre-processes image data before running the inference prediction. We'll see an example of this later in the chapter.

Scaling Transforms and Predictions Separately

Note that transformers and predictors can be scaled differently. A DevOps team, for example, may have one of them on CPU and the other on GPU.

Let's now take a look at how we can control deploying new models with canarying and KFServing.

Don't Confuse KFServing Transformers and Deep Learning Transformers

Given that we're talking about machine learning models in this context, it is easy to confuse KFServing transformers as a concept with the overloaded term in deep learning, *transformer*.[4]

Transformers in attention-based deep learning models help improve the performance of neural translation applications. Similar to an LSTM model, a transformer is an architecture for transforming one sequence into another one in the context of executing as part of the deep learning model itself.

However, transformers in KFServing are an API construct to allow your model to express code to run before and after the prediction models phase. This KFServing kind of transformer is external to the machine learning model and is a construct to manage components of code to convert data. Similarly named items, yet different purposes.

---

4 A. Vaswani et al., "Attention Is All You Need," June 12, 2017, *https://arxiv.org/abs/1706.03762*.

Leveraging canarying with KFServing

In canary development, only a small part of the user base is exposed to a new feature, and this fraction of user base (unwittingly) plays the role of the "canary in the coal mine." Canary releases are commonly short-lived, and used to validate the quality of a release, and to see if it hits the success criteria set for the feature or release.

In practice, canarying is done by splitting incoming traffic to two different endpoints:

- Default endpoint
- Canary endpoint

Generally, the idea is to deploy a production change to a small subset of users/servers with canarying, see how it performs, and then expand the new model rollout to the remaining users.

Canarying is a useful tool to let us safely roll out and roll back a new model into a live production environment, as we'll see toward the end of this chapter.

The Canary in the Coal Mine

The phrase "canary in the coal mine" is related to the concept of canarying in DevOps.

Coal mines often contained carbon and other gases that are lethal for the miners at certain levels. Canaries, being more sensitive to airborne toxins than humans, would be brought down into the mines to serve as a gas-level sensor in the mine. The bird would often fall victim to the gas before the miners, and this would trigger a mine evacuation to save human lives.

Outlier detection

The Seldon Core project has contributed code (KFServing CIFAR10 Model with Alibi:Detect VAE Outlier Detector (*https://oreil.ly/tXzBk*)) to KFServing to detect outlier input data. Outlier detection is important as it allows a user to recognize when their model is seeing input data outside of the training data distribution. The user can then evaluate how much they trust the prediction of the model given the new information about the input data.

Concept drift

Previously in this chapter, we wrote about how some models may "age" over time, because the distribution of the training data may shift over time (e.g., bad actors might change their intrusion strategies). In other cases, production data distribution may not be the same as the training data distribution, and in that case, we need to detect it.

The Seldon Core project has contributed code for detecting model drift with their CIFAR10 drift detector example (*https://oreil.ly/oNgq6*).

Supported Pre-Built Model Servers

Currently KFServing v0.3.0 has support for the following pre-built model servers:

- TensorFlow
- XGBoost
- scikit-learn
- Nvidia TensorRT Inference Server
- ONNX
- PyTorch

A version of each of these model servers already exists as part of the KFServing system and can be configured by the KFServing YAML configuration at deployment time.

Pre-Built Model Servers and Dependency Versions

Just because a model server exists for your preferred framework, it does not mean your model will always be able to run on a model server. Sometimes a model will be built with dependency versions that are incompatible with the dependency versions the model server was built with; so, for now, you will have to manually check the model server dependency versions (for example, SKLearn (*https://oreil.ly/U4-LL*)).

Every InferenceService object deployed in KFServing has two endpoints:

- Default
- Canary

Each of these endpoints can be the same language/type of model server or they can be different (e.g., "default as TensorFlow" and "canary as Pytorch"). We define the model server type in the YAML for the InferenceService object creation.

Specifics for Interacting with Pre-Built Model Servers

Each model server may have different semantics for the file format it expects of the saved model, and how it passes the deserialized model parameters (for example, xgbserver (*https://oreil.ly/Hw9HD*) versus sklearnserver (*https://oreil.ly/SV8Bb*)).

For example, to use the pre-built SKLearn model server, SKLearn-based models in KFServing v0.3.0 will need to support:

```
"scikit-learn == 0.20.3",
"argparse >= 1.4.0",
"numpy >= 1.8.2",
"joblib >= 0.13.0"
```

Be advised that some trial and error may be needed when getting used to wiring up models for deployment.

The storageUri will further tell KFServing where to get the serialized model we wish to deploy with this type of pre-built model server. We show two example YAML files in Example 8-3 to illustrate the concept.

Example 8-3. InferenceService resource deployment YAML example for a PyTorch model

```
apiVersion: "serving.kubeflow.org/v1alpha2"
kind: "InferenceService"
metadata:
  name: "pytorch-cifar10"
spec:
  default:
    predictor:
      pytorch:
        storageUri: "gs://kfserving-samples/models/pytorch/cifar10/"
        modelClassName: "Net"
```

And in Example 8-4, we can see how a Sklearn model deployment look different.

Example 8-4. InferenceService resource deployment YAML example for a SKLearn model

```
apiVersion: "serving.kubeflow.org/v1alpha2"
kind: "InferenceService"
metadata:
  name: "sklearn-iris"
spec:
  default:
    predictor:
      sklearn:
        storageUri: "gs://kfserving-samples/models/sklearn/iris"
```

When kubectl calls the Kubernetes API and sends the YAML (such as the preceding examples) for the requested InferenceService object to be created, Kubernetes and KFServing look up a pre-build model server based on the nested model server name.

KFS has a container specifically built for each of the supported model types, and KFServing will launch code on the container to handle the specific model wire-up functionality. Finally, the model is loaded under the hood with a model wrapper and passed to the KFServer process (for example, pytorchserver (*https://oreil.ly/cvwPb*)).

The preceding two YAML files will produce two different model deployments with different pre-built model servers, but will be served from HTTP endpoints with the same exposed API signature.

This allows the DevOps team to create a consistent experience no matter which machine learning framework each team wants to use.

InferenceService and storage provider support

KFServing currently has support for the following storage providers:

1. Google Cloud Storage (prefix: "`gs://`)
2. S3 compatible (AWS, MinIO) object storage (prefix: "`s3://`")
3. Azure Blob Storage
4. Local container filesystem (prefix: "`file://`)
5. Persistent volume claim (PVC) (format: "`pvc://{$pvcname}/[path]`)

In the following subsections, we list quick notes about usage for each of these storage options.

Google Cloud Storage. The default for Google Cloud Storage is for KFServing to use the `GOOGLE_APPLICATION_CREDENTIALS` environment variable for user authentication. If this environment variable is not provided, then the anonymous client will attempt to be used to download the model artifacts.

S3-compatible object storage. The default strategy for KFServing when using S3-compatible object storage is to look for the following environment variables during container execution:

- `S3_ENDPOINT`
- `AWS_ACCESS_KEY_ID`
- `AWS_SECRET_ACCESS_KEY`

To set up these environment variables, we need to create a Kubernetes `Secret` object and a `ServiceAccount` on our cluster. We can see an example of this in the sample YAML in Example 8-5.

Example 8-5. YAML file to create both a Secret and ServiceAccount

```
apiVersion: v1
kind: Secret
metadata:
  name: mysecret
  annotations:
    serving.kubeflow.org/s3-endpoint: s3.amazonaws.com # replace with s3 endpoint
    serving.kubeflow.org/s3-usehttps: "1" # by default 1, for testing with minio...
type: Opaque
stringData:
  awsAccessKeyID: AAABBBCCCFOOFOO
  awsSecretAccessKey: isuG9fAAAAA+dtOBdArBBBBBaDht+u/pFOO
---
apiVersion: v1
kind: ServiceAccount
metadata:
  name: sa
secrets:
  - name: mysecret
```

We would then associate this `ServiceAccount` with our `InferenceService` during deployment in the object creation YAML, as we can see in Example 8-6.

Example 8-6. Example InferenceService object creation with ServiceAccount in YAML

```
apiVersion: "serving.kubeflow.org/v1alpha2"
kind: "InferenceService"
metadata:
  name: "aws-sklearn-model"
spec:
  default:
    predictor:
      serviceAccountName: sa
      minReplicas: 1
      sklearn:
        storageUri: "s3://pattersonconsulting/kubeflow/kfserving/models/sklearn"
```

The `serviceAccountName` field links to our specific `ServiceAccount` that has access to our AWS account `Secret`. By setting the preceding object fields, the container can then pull the appropriate S3-compliant credentials for the storage system to use.

Azure Blob Storage.   Azure Blob Storage currently supports the format:

```
"https://{$STORAGE_ACCOUNT_NAME}.blob.core.windows.net/{$CONTAINER}/{$PATH}"
```

The default mode for the Azure storage system is to use the client in anonymous mode to download the model artifacts.

Local container filesystem. KFServing also supports storing model artifacts on the local container filesystem with both absolute (`/absolute/path`) and relative paths (`relative/path`).

Persistent volume claim. We can also express a model artifact location with a persistent volume claim (PVC) in Kubernetes in the format `"pvc://{$pvcname}/[path]"`, where the `$pvcname` is the name of the PCV containing the model, and `[path]` is the relative path on the PVC.

KFServing Security Model

Like many other cluster-based platforms, Kubeflow operates as a group of services, tools, and frameworks that are deployed together on a Kubernetes cluster to support machine learning applications.

The majority of these components are open source projects in their own right and were developed independently by different groups of people. Combining these components into a new system is a challenge in that we need all the parts to work as a seamless whole. Istio plays a critical role in allowing all of these components to interoperate.

In Kubeflow we see Istio used to do things such as:

- Securing the control plane
- Providing endpoint security
- Managing access to Kubeflow applications
- Enabling end-to-end authentication and access control

Kubeflow uses Istio specifically to secure service-to-service communication in a Kubeflow deployment via identity-based authentication and authorization. Istio allows for encryption of service communication (with Istio, this is the default) and also for enforced policies across diverse runtimes and protocols.

Istio is considered to be foundational in multitenancy support for Kubeflow. As of Kubeflow version 0.6, Istio is core to options and Kubeflow can't operate without it.

KFServing InferenceServices can be secured with Istio policies to control which users have access to which models.

Managing Models with KFServing

We spend the last portion of this chapter looking at how to put the deployment concepts we've covered here into practice with real examples on KFServing. In this section, we cover methods for:

- Installing standalone KFServing with Minikube
- Deploying a model as an InferenceService
- Managing InferenceService traffic with canarying
- Deploying a custom transformer
- Performing model rollback
- Removing a deployed model

Let's start out with looking at our options for deploying KFServing.

Installing KFServing on a Kubernetes Cluster

KFServing (v0.2.2) installs by default with the full Kubeflow 1.0 install on Kubernetes. Other install options for KFServing are:

- Install standalone with manual Istio and Knative installations
- Install standalone "quick install" (installs Istio and Knative for us)
- Customized install
- Build from source and install

The full Kubeflow install was covered earlier in this book, so in this section we'll focus on installing KFServing locally on Minikube. This allows you to more quickly work with KFServing in a working session.

Installing KFServing standalone on Minikube

To install KFServing standalone on Minikube, you'll first need to install the dependencies kubectl (*https://oreil.ly/0GZjP*), kustomize v3.5.4+ (*https://oreil.ly/6Xs7k*), and helm 3 (*https://oreil.ly/sWAaD*). Once you have these dependencies installed, you can follow the Minikube install instructions (*https://oreil.ly/Wdu8w*).

Customizing Minikube for Kubernetes and Kubeflow

Kubeflow will deploy a lot of pods on our local Kubernetes cluster in Minikube, and your machine may experience some sluggishness. Two ways to help avoid Minikube sluggishness are to adjust memory and RAM for the hypervisor. Suggested settings to update before you start your Minikube cluster are:

```
minikube config set memory 12288
minikube config set cpus 4
```

Not all desktop or laptop machines will have this many resources available, so you will have to adjust accordingly. There is always the option of spinning up a single VM instance on a cloud provider and deploying Minikube in that context.

Once we have Minikube installed and configured, we can start up our local Kubernetes development node with the command:

```
minikube start
```

This will start up the local Kubernetes cluster, and some provisioning and container image downloads.

Make Sure You Have a Good Internet Connection During Kubernetes Deployments

A full Kubeflow install will download at least 10 GB of container images. A KFServing install will download fewer images, but it's still a good idea to make sure you have a consistently good internet connection during the KFServing install process. Bad internet connections can create long, delayed install processes.

Now that we have our cluster operationally, we can confirm the state of the cluster at any time with the following command:

```
minikube status
```

If our cluster is healthy, we should see the following output:

```
host: Running
kubelet: Running
apiserver: Running
kubeconfig: Configured
```

The Minikube install will automatically configure our local install of kubectl such that it can interact with our Minikube Kubernetes cluster. Now that we have Minikube installed and operational, let's move on and install KFServing standalone on our Minikube Kubernetes cluster.

First, we need to get a copy of the KFServing repository on our local system. Assuming you have Git installed, we can do this with the following `git clone` command:

```
git clone git@github.com:kubeflow/kfserving.git
```

The KFServing installer will install Istio (lean version), Knative Serving, and KFServing all with the same install script. This install takes around 30-60 seconds, depending on your system. Let's change into the cloned KFServing repository directly and execute the *quick_install.sh* script:

```
cd kfserving
./hack/quick_install.sh
```

Sometimes Quick Install Hangs

The quick installer sometimes will exit without completing the full install. Some components are dependent on other components to fully deploy before they can install, and the quick installer does not have "backoff logic" in it currently. If you hit this issue, just wait 10-20 seconds and run the quick installer again.

Once our install is complete, we can confirm that the KFServing install is working on our Minikube cluster with the command:

```
kubectl get po -n kfserving-system
```

This command should give us console output that looks like the following:

```
NAME                              READY   STATUS    RESTARTS   AGE
kfserving-controller-manager-0    2/2     Running   2          13m
```

If your output looks like this, then your install finished successfully. To interact with deployed models on KFServing under Minikube, we'll need to set up port-forwarding (*https://oreil.ly/go4T0*) with `kubectl` so that we can make `curl` commands via Istio (as we'll see after we do a model deployment). We do this with this command:

```
kubectl port-forward --namespace istio-system $(kubectl get pod --namespace \
    istio-system --selector="app=istio-ingressgateway" \
    --output jsonpath='{.items[0].metadata.name}') 8080:80
```

With this command we mapped our local port 8080 to port 80 in the `istio-ingressgateway`.

Let's now move on and deploy a model on our new KFServing installation.

Deploying a Model on KFServing

There are two main ways to deploy a model as an InferenceService on KFServing:

1. Deploy the saved model with a pre-built model server on a pre-existing image.
2. Deploy a saved model already wrapped in a pre-existing container as a custom.

Most of the time we want to deploy on a pre-built model server as this will create the least amount of work for our engineering team. However, if the pre-built model server has incompatible dependencies, or our model requires special "wiring" for inferences that does not line up with the stock model server images, then we'll have to build our own model server to deploy as an InferenceService. We cover both methods in this section.

Advanced Model Deployment Strategies

Certain advanced model deployment strategies such as A/B testing, multi-armed bandits, and ensembling should use multiple InferenceServices deployed together. However, these topics are outside the scope of this book.

Deploying a Python TensorFlow model as an InferenceService

To deploy a model as an InferenceService on KFServing, we need to create a YAML file to describe the custom object to deploy. Given that KFServing treats models as infrastructure, we deploy a model on KFServing (*https://oreil.ly/1MS93*) with a YAML file to describe the Kubernetes model resource (e.g., InferenceService) as a custom object.

We need to set four parameters to uniquely identify the model, such as:

```
apiVersion: "serving.kubeflow.org/v1alpha2"
kind: "InferenceService"
metadata.name: the model's unique name inside the namespace
metadata.namespace
the namespace your model will live in
```

A YAML file (*tf_flowers.yaml*) to deploy our TensorFlow model as an InferenceService custom object is shown in Example 8-7.

Example 8-7. Example TensorFlow model InferenceService deployment in YAML

```
apiVersion: "serving.kubeflow.org/v1alpha2"
kind: "InferenceService"
metadata:
  name: "my-tf-flowers-model"
spec:
  default:
    predictor:
      tensorflow:
        storageUri: "gs://kfserving-samples/models/tensorflow/flowers-2"
```

The first two levels of the hierarchy of the InferenceService subobjects are listed in the following tree:

- default (*required*)
  - explainer
  - predictor (*required*)
  - transformer
- canary
  - explainer
  - predictor (*required*)
  - transformer
- canaryTrafficPercent

This allows us to configure a default endpoint along with an optional canary endpoint in the same YAML file. The predictor field defines the model serving spec (and is required for both default and canary). A predictor has a number of options for the custom model server it will represent, and this is configured with the predictor-type label on the next line. Our built-in model server options are as follows:

- TensorFlow
- Sklearn
- PyTorch
- ONNX
- TensorRT
- XGBoost

As we can see in Example 8-7, this example has the TensorFlow model server configured with a `storageUri` field containing the following value:

```
storageUri: "gs://kfserving-samples/models/tensorflow/flowers-2"
```

The `storageUri` for a model tells KFServing where to look to download the model to wire up with the pre-built model server image to serve predictions.

Google Cloud Storage, kfserving-samples, and the flowers-2 Model

The TensorFlow flowers-2 model is not located in a directory in the KFServing repository. The `storageUri: ""` points us to a public bucket on the Google Cloud Storage system (*https://oreil.ly/12m1t*).

This is a model used by multiple Google examples and is publicly accessible with no security credentials or logins required.

As we've noted, this example isn't included in the KFServing repository and is located on a public Google Cloud Storage bucket. If we want to access a model that is not public, we'll have to (securely) add credential information to our Kubernetes cluster to be used by our InferenceService to download the model.

More Options for Configuring a Predictor

Beyond those fields, we have other fields for our predictor object that don't represent built-in model servers:

- `serviceAccountName`
- `parallelism`
- `minReplicas`
- `maxReplicas`
- `logger`
- `custom`

Now that we have our model configured and available on a public cloud storage system, we can stand up our InferenceService on our Minikube cluster with this `kubectl` command:

```
kubectl apply -f tf_flowers.yaml
```

Once this command runs, we can check the status of our model with this:

```
kubectl get inferenceservices
```

This will search for all the deployed InferenceService objects on our cluster, and will produce console output similar to the following:

```
NAME                    URL                           READY  DEFAULT TRAFFIC  AGE
my-tf-flowers-model     http://my-tf-flowers-model    True   100              129s
```

Initially, the model will report READY to be False. But if there are no issues, once the model is downloaded and the container executes, when we rerun the kubectl command, the READY field will change to True.

To check our deployed model (remember that we've already set up port-forwarding with kubectl during install), we can use the curl command from the command line with some pre-built input (file here (*https://oreil.ly/OGWoy*), save as *tf_flowers_input.json* locally):

```
curl -v -H "Host: my-tf-flowers-model.default.example.com" \
    http://localhost:8080/v1/models/my-tf-flowers-model:predict \
    -d @./tf_flowers_input.json
```

This should result in output similar to the following:

```
*   Trying ::1:8080...
* Connected to localhost (::1) port 8080 (#0)
> POST /v1/models/my-tf-flowers-model:predict HTTP/1.1
> Host: my-tf-flowers-model.default.example.com
> User-Agent: curl/7.69.1
> Accept: */*
> Content-Length: 16201
> Content-Type: application/x-www-form-urlencoded
>
* upload completely sent off: 16201 out of 16201 bytes
* Mark bundle as not supporting multiuse
< HTTP/1.1 200 OK
< content-length: 220
< content-type: application/json
< date: Tue, 19 May 2020 18:20:41 GMT
< x-envoy-upstream-service-time: 850
< server: istio-envoy
<
{
    "predictions": [
        {
            "scores": [0.999114931, 9.2098875e-05, 0.000136786344...,
            "prediction": 0,
            "key": "   1"
        }
    ]
* Connection #0 to host localhost left intact
}%
```

Let's now look at some ways to build custom model servers for KFServing.

Deploy InferenceService with custom model serving strategy

There are many pre-built model servers included with KFServing out of the box, but sometimes we'll have a model that will not wire up correctly with the pre-built images. The reasons this could happen include:

- The model was built with different dependency versions than the model server.
- The model was not saved in a file format model that the server expects.
- The model was built with a new/custom framework not yet supported by KFServing.
- The model is in a container image that has a REST interface that is different than the TensorFlow V1 HTTP API (*https://oreil.ly/DrCZy*) that KFServing expects.

For any of the preceding cases, we have three options (*https://oreil.ly/H6Erc*) for deploying our model:

- Wrap our custom model in our own container where our container runs its own web server to expose the model endpoint (*https://oreil.ly/y4wbl*).
- Use the KFServing KFServer as the web server (*https://oreil.ly/F_1og*) (with its standard TensorFlow V1 API) and then overload the load() and predict() methods.
- Deploy a pre-built container image with a custom REST API, bypassing InferenceService (*https://oreil.ly/PlJ9J*) and send the HTTP request directly to the predictor.

Of the three options, using KFServer as the mode server and just doing custom over-loads will likely be the most popular route for folks just wanting to deploy a custom model. In this case, we need to do two key tasks:

- Create a new Python class that inherits from KFModel (*https://oreil.ly/-e0pZ*), with custom methods for load() (*https://oreil.ly/87_DD*) and predict() (*https://oreil.ly/nXXn6*).
- Build a custom container image and then store it in a container repository.

We can see a custom KFServer model server (*https://oreil.ly/2wXrr*) in Example 8-8.

Example 8-8. Custom KFServer model server loading AlexNet in Python

```
class KFServingSampleModel(kfserving.KFModel):
    def __init__(self, name: str):
        super().__init__(name)
        self.name = name
        self.ready = False
```

```
    def load(self):
        f = open('imagenet_classes.txt')
        self.classes = [line.strip() for line in f.readlines()]

        model = models.alexnet(pretrained=True)
        model.eval()
        self.model = model

        self.ready = True

    def predict(self, request: Dict) -> Dict:
        inputs = request["instances"]

        # Input follows the TensorFlow V1 HTTP API for binary values
        # https://www.tensorflow.org/tfx/serving/api_rest#encoding_binary_values
        data = inputs[0]["image"]["b64"]

        raw_img_data = base64.b64decode(data)
        input_image = Image.open(io.BytesIO(raw_img_data))

        preprocess = transforms.Compose([
            transforms.Resize(256),
            transforms.CenterCrop(224),
            transforms.ToTensor(),
            transforms.Normalize(mean=[0.405, 0.456, 0.406],
                                 std=[0.229, 0.224, 0.225]),
        ])

        input_tensor = preprocess(input_image)
        input_batch = input_tensor.unsqueeze(0)

        output = self.model(input_batch)

        scores = torch.nn.functional.softmax(output, dim=1)[0]

        _, top_5 = torch.topk(output, 5)

        results = {}
        for idx in top_5[0]:
            results[self.classes[idx]] = scores[idx].item()

        return {"predictions": results}


if __name__ == "__main__":
    model = KFServingSampleModel("kfserving-custom-model")
    model.load()
    kfserving.KFServer(workers=1).start([model])
```

Once this model serving code is saved locally, we'll build a new Docker container image with the code packaged inside. We can see examples of the container `build` command and the container repository `store` command (here, Docker Hub) in the following:

```
# Build the container on your local machine
docker build -t {username}/kfserving-custom-model ./model-server

# Push the container to docker registry
docker push {username}/kfserving-custom-model
```

With our custom container image in the repository, we can then create a YAML file (*https://oreil.ly/BCp-x*) to create our custom model server on our KFServing cluster. See Example 8-9.

Example 8-9. Hello World in Python

```
apiVersion: serving.kubeflow.org/v1alpha2
kind: InferenceService
metadata:
  labels:
    controller-tools.k8s.io: "1.0"
  name: kfserving-custom-model
spec:
  default:
    predictor:
      custom:
        container:
          image: {username}/kfserving-custom-model
```

And finally, just like with a pre-built InferenceService, we can create the Kubernetes object with `kubectl` as follows:

```
kubectl apply -f custom.yaml
```

Deploying a custom model on KFServing is not as easy as using a pre-built model server, but it's not terribly difficult. The steps in the preceding should give most DevOps teams a good start on how to wire up whatever the data science team throws at them.

Managing Model Traffic with Canarying

With canarying and model deployment, we want to deploy a production change to a small subset of users/servers with canarying. We'll watch how the new model performs on the subset of traffic and then expand the new model rollout to the remaining users as warranted.

To deploy a model with canarying, we change the InferenceService custom object YAML. In our YAML we add a field for `canary` in the spec allowing us to specify an alternative model for a certain percentage of incoming traffic to access; see Example 8-10.

Example 8-10. Example canary InferenceService in YAML

```yaml
apiVersion: "serving.kubeflow.org/v1alpha2"
kind: "InferenceService"
metadata:
  name: "my-tf-canary-model"
spec:
  default:
    predictor:
      # 90% of traffic is sent to this model
      tensorflow:
        storageUri: "gs://kfserving-samples/models/tensorflow/flowers"
  canaryTrafficPercent: 10
  canary:
    predictor:
      # 10% of traffic is sent to this model
      tensorflow:
        storageUri: "gs://kfserving-samples/models/tensorflow/flowers-2"
```

We control this percentage of traffic with the `canaryTrafficPercent` field in the spec, as seen in the preceding example.

We can deploy the model with canarying enabled as an InferenceService by applying the YAML file from the command line, as in this code snippet:

```
kubectl apply -f tf_flowers.yaml
```

You may notice that we deploy canarying the same way as we deploy a stock model in KFServing; we just add more fields to the spec to define the canary parameters.

If we decided that we wanted to shut down the canary version of the model (but keep it as part of our resource for now), we'd create a new YAML file and update the following line:

```
canaryTrafficPercent: 0
```

Once we updated the running Kubernetes resource with `kubectl`, we essentially would be rolling back the canary version of the model.

Alternatively, we may decide that the canary version of the model is the version we want for all traffic. In this case, we'd "promote" the canary model by updating our YAML file. The new YAML file might look like Example 8-11.

Example 8-11. Example canary promotion in YAML

```yaml
apiVersion: "serving.kubeflow.org/v1alpha2"
kind: "InferenceService"
metadata:
  name: "my-model"
spec:
  # this is now the promoted / default model
  default:
    predictor:
      tensorflow:
        storageUri: "gs://kfserving-samples/models/tensorflow/flowers-2"
```

Note that this process is still based around the DevOps engineer tracking the default, previous, and current canary models all by hand.

Deploying a Custom Transformer

The general steps in building a custom transformer are:

1. Extend KFModel (*https://oreil.ly/PSJnf*) and implement pre-/post-processing functions (Python).
2. Build a Docker image with the extended KFModel code.
3. Deploy the new Docker image as an InferenceService.

In Example 8-12 (from the KFServing GitHub repository (*https://oreil.ly/Wx1DL*)), we can see an example of how the KFServing.KFModel base class could be extended.

Example 8-12. A custom KFServing transformer in Python

```python
import kfserving
from typing import List, Dict
from PIL import Image
import torchvision.transforms as transforms
import logging
import io
import numpy as np
import base64

logging.basicConfig(level=kfserving.constants.KFSERVING_LOGLEVEL)

transform = transforms.Compose(
        [transforms.ToTensor(),
         transforms.Normalize((0.5, 0.5, 0.5), (0.5, 0.5, 0.5))])


def image_transform(instance):
```

```python
        byte_array = base64.b64decode(instance['image_bytes']['b64'])
        image = Image.open(io.BytesIO(byte_array))
        a = np.asarray(image)
        im = Image.fromarray(a)
        res = transform(im)
        logging.info(res)
        return res.tolist()


class ImageTransformer(kfserving.KFModel):
    def __init__(self, name: str, predictor_host: str):
        super().__init__(name)
        self.predictor_host = predictor_host

    def preprocess(self, inputs: Dict) -> Dict:
        return {'instances': [image_transform(instance) for instance \
            in inputs['instances']]}

    def postprocess(self, inputs: List) -> List:
        return inputs
```

In Example 8-12, we can see how the Python code extends the KFModel base class and then extends both the preprocess and the postprocess methods to provide custom implementations.

Once we have our Python code ready, we'll need to build a new container image to serve the custom Python code. We see an example of this in the following Docker command:

```
docker build -t gcr.io/kubeflow-ci/kfserving/image-transformer:latest -f \
    transformer.Dockerfile .
```

After we build our new container image, we'll need to use custom YAML to deploy it. Example 8-13 shows how we'd deploy our custom transformer code inside our Docker container as part of our InferenceService.

Example 8-13. Image transformer in YAML

```yaml
apiVersion: serving.kubeflow.org/v1alpha2
kind: InferenceService
metadata:
  name: transformer-cifar10
spec:
  default:
    predictor:
      pytorch:
        modelClassName: Net
        resources:
          limits:
            cpu: 100m
```

```
          memory: 1Gi
        requests:
          cpu: 100m
          memory: 1Gi
      storageUri: gs://kfserving-samples/models/pytorch/cifar10
  transformer:
    custom:
      container:
        image: gcr.io/kubeflow-ci/kfserving/image-transformer:latest
        name: user-container
        resources:
          limits:
            cpu: 100m
            memory: 1Gi
          requests:
            cpu: 100m
            memory: 1Gi
```

Now we can use `kubectl` to deploy the `InferenceService`, as shown in the following command:

```
kubectl apply -f image_transformer.yaml
```

When we run this command we should see output similar to the following console log:

```
$ inferenceservice.serving.kubeflow.org/transformer-cifar10 created
```

Let's now look at methods of managing existing model deployments.

Roll Back a Deployed Model

Given that KFServing currently treats deploying a model as if deploying a Kubernetes resource, to roll back a model we can just update the InferenceService resource associated with the YAML fields:

```
apiVersion: "serving.kubeflow.org/v1alpha2"
kind: "InferenceService"
metadata:
  name: my-model-name-here
metadata:
  namespace: my-namespace-here
```

To roll back a model, we would create a file in YAML (similar to how we did with the preceding canarying examples) and just update the resource corresponding to the preceding values with the location of a model we had previously deployed. We can see an example of this in Example 8-14.

Example 8-14. Example model update InferenceService in YAML

```
apiVersion: "serving.kubeflow.org/v1alpha2"
kind: "InferenceService"
metadata:
  name: "my-model"
spec:
  # this is now the promoted/default model
  default:
    predictor:
      tensorflow:
        storageUri: "gs://kfserving-samples/models/tensorflow/flowers-1"
```

Model Revision Tracking

The current version of KFServing in Kubeflow 1.0 does not have functionality to track lineage of a model, so we need to manage this manually for now.

Removing a Deployed Model

To remove a deployed model on KFServing, we'll use a command of the following form:

```
kubectl delete inferenceservice [metadata.name] -n [namespace]
```

Here is a specific example:

```
kubectl delete inferenceservice my-tf-flowers-model -n kubeflow
```

The console output should be similar to this:

```
inferenceservice.serving.kubeflow.org "my-tf-flowers-model" deleted
```

Confirm the model is no longer running on KFServing by using this command:

```
kubectl get inferenceservices
```

The output of the command should no longer show our deleted TensorFlow model.

Summary

In this chapter we reviewed some of the concepts of model deployment. We also had a deep dive into KFServing and looked at the different ways we can deploy a model to production and then manage the model. KFServing still has a ways to go in terms of developing out key features and improving usability, but it remains a key component in the Kubeflow suite of tools to deploy models to production.

We hope you have enjoyed the book. The remainder of the book has appendixes on infrastructure concepts, Kubernetes, and Istio.

Infrastructure Concepts

In this appendix we'll review some topics about the components used in building the security architecture of many types of distributed systems. The veteran reader may already be familiar with the items discussed here, but most any reader can use the section as a quick review on these key topics in security. This appendix progressively builds on the concepts introduced earlier, so if you are newer to DevOps security, you may not want to skip any sections. The more seasoned DevOps professional might want to jump on down to the Istio or multitenancy sections, however.

Public Key Infrastructure

The function of a *public key infrastructure* (*https://oreil.ly/l35lf*) (PKI) is to enable the secure electronic transfer of information for network traffic. These secure transactions enable use cases such as:

- Ecommerce
- Internet banking
- Identity management
- Secure email

PKI is a group of roles, policies, hardware, software, and methods required to together create, distribute, use, store, and manage digital certificates. These techniques also manage public key encryption, which is a foundational component of PKI.

Sometimes we need a more rigorous methodology to confirm the identity of the parties involved in communications. We also may want to validate the information being transferred, and PKI is the foundation to enable these secure electronic transfers of information.

Authentication

Authentication is the method of validating a person or entity's identity. *End-user authentication* is a process that allows a device to verify the identify of someone who connects to a network resource.

An authentication protocol may also communicate to an application more about a user such as a unique identifier or an email address when the user is authenticated.

Distributed applications are built on the foundation of the different components being able to validate a user across the system. Internet-scale authentication protocols have to be able to validate users across network and security boundaries.

Kubeflow and Authentication

The initial version of Kubeflow added a few operators to Kubernetes to build its core APIs (CRDs). With this design we could use kubectl at the command line with the Kubernetes API server handling authentication and authorization, making things relatively straightforward.

Later versions of Kubeflow introduced web applications in addition to the core APIs to build out the UI system for Kubeflow. At this point, the authentication and authorization story became more complex as it now was based at the application tier and not at the Kubernetes API level. We cover more details later in this appendix.

Authorization

Authorization is a way to define access policies, or specify access rights for users. We can then set up a system to utilize these policies to allow or deny access to resources for the requesting user or service account. A system or application will constantly check what permissions a user or service account has each time an action is requested by the user or service account.

Authorization and Role-Based Access Control

Many times, systems match a principal with a set of actions they have permission (or not) to access and define this as a role. RBAC has been implemented in multiple forms on many different systems for a while now.

Once a system has defined a role, we can then assign permissions to the role. Then when we give a user a defined role, that user will inherit all of the permissions previously assigned to that role. A user may have multiple roles in some cases as well.

There are multiple platforms to deploy Kubeflow (e.g., on-premise, AWS, GCP, etc.). Each system has its own RBAC/IAM system, and Kubeflow will use this RBAC system. For example, Kubeflow manages Kubernetes resources with Kubernetes RBAC. Separately, Kubeflow manages network endpoints and resources with Istio RBAC. In the cloud, Kubeflow uses GCP/Azure/AWS IAM for cloud resources.

Authorization/RBAC in Kubernetes is based around answering the question: Can IDENTITY perform ACTION on RESOURCE in NAMESPACE?

Lightweight Directory Access Protocol

The *Lightweight Access Directory Protocol* (LDAP) is a lightweight client-server protocol for accessing directory services (specifically X.500-based directory services). LDAP is defined in RFC 2251 (*ftp://ftp.isi.edu/in-notes/rfc2251.txt*) *The Lightweight Directory Access Protocol (v3)* and runs over TCP/IP (or other connection-oriented transfer services).

LDAP data stores typically are used to store user information that is infrequently updated and queried often. The size of the data per user is typically small and the common practice is for the system to hold user-lookup information (e.g., contact details, login, password, permissions) as well as organizational structure information.

Kerberos

Kerberos is a network security solution that defines a network authentication protocol. Kerberos was created by the Massachusetts Institute of Technology (MIT) as a way to provide strong authentication for client/server applications by using secret-key cryptography.

Kerberos allows us to authenticate users with strong cryptography over the network and secure our information systems across the enterprise. The Kerberos protocol uses strong cryptography that allows a client to prove its identity to a server (and vice versa) over an insecure network. A client and server can encrypt further communications once they have proven their identity with Kerberos to ensure privacy and data integrity.

MIT offers a free implementation, along with the commercial versions such as the one Microsoft offers.

Transport Layer Security

Transport layer security (TLS) is a cryptographic protocol designed to provide secure communications over a network.

 TLS and SSL

TLS's predecessor was called Secure Sockets Layer (SSL).

We see TLS used in applications such as:

- Email
- Instant messaging
- Web browsing
- Voice over IP

Often we see web browsers secure communications with a website via TLS. There are several versions in use today, but TLS was first defined in 1999 by an Internet Engineering Task Force (*https://oreil.ly/Mimx0*) (IETF) standard (*https://oreil.ly/Z9g_f*). The current version of TLS is version 1.3 defined by RFC (*https://oreil.ly/1mXda*) (August 2018).

X.509 Cert

X.509 certificates are used for different internet protocols (e.g., TLS; TLS is the foundation of HTTPS, enabling secure web browsing). A public key and an identity (hostname, organization, or an individual) are both contained in an X.509 certificate, and it is either self-signed or signed by a certificate authority (*https://oreil.ly/TmtqH*).

Someone holding the certificate can rely on its contained public key to provide secure communications when a certificate is signed by a trusted certificate authority (or validated by other trusted means).

Webhook

Authentication in Kubeflow can be set up to use webhooks with the Kubernetes API Server. A webhook is a user-defined HTTP callback that is triggered by some event. When the event occurs, the source application makes an HTTP request to the URL designated for the webhook. The format of a webhook is usually JSON, and the request is executed as an HTTP POST request.

Active Directory

Active Directory (AD) is an umbrella title for a wide range of directory-based identity-related services. Initially, AD was only in charge of centralized domain management. Active Directory was developed by Microsoft for Windows domain networks and is included in most Windows Server operating systems.

A domain controller in Active Directory is a server running Active Directory Domain Service (AD DS). For a Windows domain type network, this server authenticates and authorizes all users and computers. It assigns and enforces security policies for all computers under its control.

LDAP is the protocol used to talk to Active Directory sitting on top of the TCP/IP stack. Active Directory uses DNS (*https://oreil.ly/BLOyo*), (Microsoft's version of) Kerberos, and LDAP (versions 2 and 3).

Identity Providers

A system that creates, maintains, and manages identity information for principals, while backing authentication services to reliant applications, is an identity provider. This identity system may be operating within a federation or distributed network.

The primary role of an identity provider is to offer user authentication as a service. Web applications or other relying party applications may outsource the user authentication step to a trusted identity provider. In the event that an application is relying on an outside entity to provide user authentication as a service, it is said to be federated because it leverages federated identity.

With distributed systems composed of different separate components, such as Kubeflow, there is a need for an identity provider to facilitate connections between resources and users, decreasing the need for reauthentication.

There are two major types of identity providers:

- SAML identity provider
- OpenID provider

SAML stands for Security Assertion Markup Language and is a set of profiles for managing the exchange of authentication and authorization data between security domains.

OpenID Connect is an identity layer on top of OAuth, both of which are covered in more detail later in this section.

Identity-Aware Proxy (IAP)

An identity-aware proxy (IAP) is a zero trust approach (*https://oreil.ly/mcVVy*) for identity and access at the application layer, as opposed to the network layer. This zero trust approach is commonly implemented in the cloud.

> **Zero Trust Security Models**
>
> A security model based on the concept of not trusting anyone by default (even entities already inside the network perimeter) and maintaining strict access controls is called a zero trust security model.
>
> The core concept in zero trust security models is that trust should never be based on where the user is located in a network. Every request to access a network resource must be authenticated and authorized in this model.

The IAP architecture gives access to applications via a cloud-based proxy. Identity and authorization reside in the cloud, centrally in the IAP model, and are based on the "need to know" least access principles. A proxy layer provides authenticated and authorized secure access to specific applications in the IAP architecture. Applications are then accessed via the HTTPS (*https://oreil.ly/-PGV5*) standard protocol at the application layer (Layer 7).

Benefits of the proxy strategy are that users are verified along with how application requests can be terminated, examined, and authorized. Application-level access controls are relied on by IAP, as opposed to firewall rules. This allows for configured policies to reflect user and application intent, as opposed to only ports and IPs. The IAP strategy can shield the applications and other components behind a firewall, or in the cloud, and allows for client-less operations for web applications.

The IAP architecture is shown in Figure A-1.

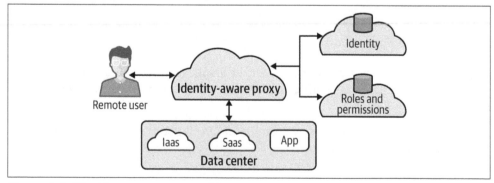

Figure A-1. Identity-aware proxy architecture

As we see in this figure, a trusted identity source is used to validate who users and devices are (authentication). This identity source also authorizes what they are allowed to access.

We can implement an identity source with a corporate directory (Active Directory) or a cloud-based identity provider.

IAP and Google Cloud Platform

One example of how a public cloud manages access to applications is how Google Cloud uses IAP. For GCP-hosted applications running in Google Cloud's App Engine standard environment, Compute Engine, and GKE, we need to use the Cloud IAP.

IAP will attach a signed JSON Web Token (JWT) to the request. Kubeflow services use this JWT to:

- Identify the user (e.g., to create custom views of resources specific to the user)
- Perform fine-grained authorization

As we mentioned in Chapter 5:

> Kubeflow uses Istio to provide fine-grained access control to individual services within a Kubeflow cluster. For example, Kubeflow relies on Istio to ensure Alice can only access her notebooks, and not notebooks owned by Bob.
>
> A major advantage of IAP over traditional VPN solutions is that access can be restricted based on a user's context. For example, we may want to allow Alice access to Kubeflow but only if she is running on a trusted corporate device that has all of the latest security patches, and not from untrusted devices (e.g., a hotel's business center).

Arguably, Cloud IAP isn't the only way to securely access web services running on GCP, but it is highly recommended.

First-Party Services Access Versus Third-Party Services Access

There are multiple ways to access components of GCP, so we want you to note that gcloud auth login is used to provide credentials for accessing first-party services (e.g., Google-owned services like GCE). IAP is used to access third-party services (e.g., services not run by Google). This means that, by design, gcloud credentials can't be used with IAP protected services. gcloud auth login gets you a credential for first-party services, not third-party services.

Also note that Kubeflow on GKE is considered a third-party service.

We are able to use an application-level access control model as Cloud IAP establishes a central authorization layer for applications such as Kubeflow that are accessed by HTTPS. This allows us an alternative to using network-level firewalls.

We want to use Cloud IAP when we want to keep our users using access control policies for applications and resources. This means we can set up a group policy for members of one group to access the system, such as our data scientists, and then another group policy for engineers working on another system such that they cannot use Kubeflow. In Chapter 5, we saw how Cloud IAP manages the authentication and authorization flow.

OAuth

OAuth (*https://oauth.net/*) is an open standard that permits users to share information about their accounts (e.g., access delegation) with third-party websites or applications. OAuth is commonly used for allowing internet users to grant an application or website to access their information on another website on their behalf without the user sharing their password. You see OAuth used by major websites such as Google, Facebook, Twitter, and Amazon.

In the context of a collection of distributed system components with APIs, OAuth lets application developers get access to certain user data without the user sharing their password.

OpenID Connect

OpenID Connect 1.0 is an identity layer on top of the OAuth 2.0 protocol that allows clients to verify the identity of an end user. This verification is based on the authentication executed by an authorization server. The verification process can also obtain profile information about the end user via a REST-like operation.

OpenID Connect is different from OpenID 2.0 in that OpenID Connect provides much of the same functionality as OpenID 2.0 but does it in a manner that is API friendly. This makes OpenID Connect more usable by mobile and native applications. OpenID Connect is built on other technologies such as OAuth 2.0 and JWT.

End-User Authentication with JWT

JSON Web Tokens (JTW) are an open industry standard (RFC 7519 (*https://oreil.ly/Q4l49*)) method for representing claims securely between two parties.

These tokens are signed, either with a private secret or a public/private key pair. An example of a generated token would be a token that has the claim "logged in as admin" and then give that to a client application. These claims are held as JSON payloads in a JWT.

JWT and OpenID Connect ID Tokens

In a previous section we mentioned the OpenID Connect ID token; this token is a signed JWT that a client gets in addition to the normal OAuth access token.

This ID token carries a set of claims about the authentication section with information that includes:

sub
> Identifier for the user

iss
> Identifier for the identity provider who issued the token

aud
> Identifier of the client for whom this token was created

Simple and Protected GSS_API Negotiation Mechanism

The Simple and Protected GSS_API Negotiation Mechanism (SPNEGO) is a "pseudo mechanism" used by client-server software to negotiate which security technology is used. SPNEGO extends a Kerberos-based single sign-on (SSO) environment for use with web applications.

An application requests a service ticket from the Kerberos Key Distribution Center (KDC) and once the ticket is received, the application sends the ticket (wrapped in a SPNEGO format) to a web application via the browser for authentication. If the ticket authenticates successfully, the user is granted access.

Dex: A Federated OpenID Connect Provider

Dex is an identity service that drives authentication for other applications using OpenID Connect (*https://openid.net/connect/*).

Dev uses the concept of connectors (*https://oreil.ly/OtSBI*) for authenticating a user against another identity provider. The client application only needs to implement the OpenID Connect protocol to interact with Dex, as we can see in Figure A-2.

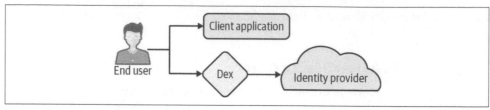

Figure A-2. Dex authentication flow

Dex handles further protocol interactions via connectors with other user-management systems such as:

- LDAP
- GitHub
- GitLab
- SAML 2.0
- Google
- LinkedIn
- Microsoft

Dex runs natively on Kubernetes and can use the OpenID Connect plug-in to drive API server authentication. Tools such as kubectl can act on a user's behalf once the user has logged in to the cluster via an identity provider Dex supports.

A primary feature with Dex is ID Tokens. ID Tokens were introduced by the OpenID Connect project (as an OAuth2 extension) and are JWT signed by Dex. These JWTs are returned as part of the OAuth2 response and represent the users' validated identity. Following is an example of a JWT:

```
eyJhbGciOiJSUzI1NiIsImtpACI6IjlkNDQ3NDFmNzczYjkzOYNmNjVkZDM...
```

Dex is a federated OpenID service and provides an OpenID Connect (OIDC) token and authority, *but it doesn't actually authenticate the user*. It provides a spot where a user can enter a username and password, and then sends that request somewhere else, like LDAP, SAML, etc.—hence the term federated. It delegates the actual authority of the authentication somewhere upstream of itself.

The issue is that it doesn't support Kerberos as an upstream authentication provider.

Kerberos uses its own tokens once a user authenticates, and those tokens can be passed around as needed.

Dex and Kerberos

The intersection of Kerberos and Dex is somewhat interesting, as they both strive to provide the same service: single sign-on. Dex (via OIDC) does it in a disconnect manner via OIDC/PKI, etc., where a user only requires connectivity to obtain their token (and to refresh their tokens). Tokens can be authenticated/validated offline, so long as there's a copy of the signer's public key. Kerberos requires connectivity to things like the KDC (if you can't reach the KDC, you might not be able to authenticate), and though it too uses the notion of tokens, there's a greater need to maintain connectivity to be authenticated. The amount of connectivity varies, depending on whether you reconnect to the same service, or attempt to authenticate to a new service.

Given that they both strive to achieve the same goal, Kerberos is often considered as "legacy," and OIDC is the new kid on the block.

The Staying Power of Kerberos

In a way, OIDC (and thus Dex) does have greater flexibility (as a result of its ability to function in a disconnected or offline way), but the reality is that a lot of organizations still use Kerberos as their main security implementation.

Kerberos and AD are very often bundled together as one, and when someone says authenticate against Active Directory, they might be including Kerberos as an implicit requirement. Though, technically, AD is a conglomerate of things, one of them being Kerberos, it also provides LDAP. When some systems say they "integrate with AD," they might mean Kerberos authentication, or LDAP authentication—by the LDAP servers that are provided by Active Directory.

Watch Out for Language Around Active Directory

When a product says it can authenticate against AD, it doesn't always mean it integrates with Kerberos.

Having said that, and even though Kerberos and OIDC (and thus Dex) can be viewed as "competing" (for lack of a better word) implementations of the same goal, they can still be easily used together. OIDC typically uses an HTTP flow, and Kerberos has its own HTTP implementation, namely SPNEGO. If a service provides a SPNEGO endpoint, Kerberos can be used, and tied neatly into the Dex and OIDC flow.

Service Accounts

Sometimes we want an account to represent an application on a platform as opposed to a user on the platform. For this purpose we use *service accounts*. These service accounts allow our application to access other APIs on our behalf.

Kubernetes (since version 1.12) has support for `ProjectedServiceAccountToken` which contains the service account identity and is an OIDC JSON Web Token. It also supports a configurable audience.

Kubernetes and Service Accounts

Service accounts have been used for a while as Kubernetes' own internal identity system.

The Kubernetes API server can authenticate with pods using an auto-mounted token. This token is a non-OIDC JWT and only can be validated by the Kubernetes API server. These legacy tokens do not expire and it is difficult to rotate the signing key.

The Control Plane

A control plane is responsible for receiving instructions from users and acting upon them. At a high level, there are two levels of actions: a user submits a request to the control plane, and the control plane acts upon the request. For purposes of security, the control plane is required to authenticate and authorize a request prior to acting upon it.

The Control Plane, Kubernetes, and Istio

While in some contexts you may see the term control plane used in conjunction with Kubernetes, as we'll see over the course of this appendix, Kubeflow lets Istio manage the control plane for its components on top of Kubernetes.

For the purposes of this book, the control plane refers to traffic that involves control and configuration messages sent between Istio components to configure the operations of the service mesh.

End users (and systems interacting with the control plane) do so by communicating with the Kubernetes API server. Typically, this is done either by using tools such as `kubectl`, or the associated API. Authentication and authorization are decoupled at the control plane, authorization is typically handled by RBAC, and authentication is "pluggable."

RBAC, Kubernetes, Istio, and the Cloud

Kubernetes, Istio, and public clouds all have their own separate RBAC systems. Kubeflow uses each of these RBAC systems, depending on deployment.

What is important is that authorization defines what a user is able to do at the control plane level (e.g., launch pods, use volumes, etc.). But it makes no assumption as to how authentication occurred.

As mentioned, authentication is "pluggable," which simply means there are a variety of built-in methods that can be used to authorize a user. There are a number of methods: X509 clients, tokens, username/password, OIDC, and webhooks.

Some quick terminology:

Tokens
Refers to static tokens.

Username/password
Refers to static username/passwords.

Webhooks
Simply pass on any tokens received to a third-party webhook for processing.

For the purposes of practical security, only X509 and OIDC will be further discussed.

Of the two possibilities for authentication, X509 client certificates is one option, having clients present a signed trusted certificate. The username is determined from the subject, and membership is determined from the OU fields within the certificate. Open ID Connect (OIDC) is another option, whereby users present a signed JWT token, issued by a trusted authority, with all the required claims present in the token. Kubernetes itself simply verifies the validity of the token and does no further OIDC processing or interactions.

Example OIDC Authentication Scenario with Kerberos

We'll consider the case where a Kubernetes cluster backing the Kubeflow installation has been configured with OIDC authentication. Users obtain an OIDC token, based on their local Kerberos ticket, which is then authenticated by Kubernetes. Authorization happens as described elsewhere, via Kubernetes RBAC roles.

This could support `kubectl` interactions, using a custom client-go credential plug-in. This plug-in is invoked prior to contacting the API server and would be responsible for facilitating the Kerberos/ OIDC token interaction. Once an OIDC token has been acquired, `kubectl` uses that token when communicating with the API server.

Options for Securing the Control Plane

As described above, the control plane security is an area that is well addressed. It is the Kubeflow and other deployed applications that require additional effort. To provide the desired level of security for deployed applications, one or more of the following is required:

Limit which containers can be deployed
> This effectively eliminates a large surface area of risk, but is highly restrictive to users.

Disallow users to expose ingresses of their own
> Allow users to deploy what they need, and expose any service *within* the cluster, but disallow any outside access, or intra-namespace access.

Allow users to deploy ingresses, but deploy an authenticating proxy or system
> This allows users to deploy what they need; allows them to expose service to the outside world, but is fronted by an authenticating proxy or service (such as Istio).

A hybrid of the above
> For example, create a finite list of services that are exposed, secure them, and disallow any other ingress into the cluster.

> **On-Premise Clusters and Securing the Control Plane**
>
> Most on-premise installations will have to make some situation-dependent decisions based on the above paths.

An Overview of Kubernetes

This appendix is meant as a further introduction on core concepts in Kubernetes. We don't have the space in Chapter 1 to touch on all of the concepts in this appendix and we didn't want to just point to scattered links, so we've collected just enough core concepts in this appendix to keep you going.

Core Kubernetes Concepts

For the newer practitioner, we want to cover a few basic Kubernetes concepts in this section as not every reader will be a battle hardened DevOps engineer. In Figure B-1 we can see the core processes involved in operating a Kubernetes cluster.

We use the Kubernetes API to describe a cluster's desired state (what are we trying to run? what components and resources do they need?). We set the desired state through creating (and/or modifying) objects via the Kubernetes API. To work with the Kubernetes API (e.g., the kube-api-server in Figure B-1), we typically use the command-line interface kubectl. There are also ways to use the Kubernetes API directly from your code via SDKs.

Kubernetes provides an API via HTTP that is a resource-based (RESTful) programmatic interface. This RESTful API supports the standard HTTP verbs (POST, PUT, PATCH, DELETE, GET) for retrieving, creating, updating, and deleting primary resources. Kubernetes also allows fine-grained authorization (e.g., binding a pod to a node). We can use the Kubernetes API to read and write Kubernetes resource objects via a Kubernetes API endpoint.

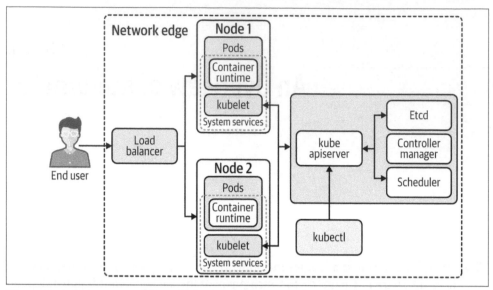

Figure B-1. Core processes in a Kubernetes cluster

Objects are the primary Kubernetes API resource type as they represent a concrete instance of a concept (e.g., pod or namespace) on a cluster. Another Kubernetes resource type is a virtual resource type (e.g., SubjectAccessReview), but they are less common than the object resource types. Kubernetes gives us *idempotent* create and retrieval for objects through the use of unique names. However, virtual resource types may not have unique names in some situations.

Some RESTful terminology commonly used by Kubernetes:

Resource type
     The name used in the URL

Kind
     The object schema representation in JSON

Collection
     List of instances of a resource type

Resource
     A single instance of the resource type

A Kubernetes resource (*https://oreil.ly/JL0rA*) is an endpoint in the Kubernetes API that stores a group of API objects of a certain kind.

Demystifying Kubernetes Endpoints

The term *endpoint* in Kubernetes can sound abstract, but in practice it is the IP address and port that represent the object in Kubernetes. Each resource exposed via an HTTP API is addressable as a service-oriented architecture component in Kubernetes. While we tend to not manipulate the endpoint of a Kubernetes object directly, it is the URI we use to access the component.

Once we've set our desired state, the Kubernetes control plane will continuously work to make the cluster's current state match the described intended state. Some of the ways the control plane does this include scaling the number of replicas of a given application or restarting containers.

In Figure B-1 the Kubernetes Master ("Control Plane" box) is a collection of processes that run on a master node in the Kubernetes cluster. Each individual non-master node in the cluster runs two processes:

kubelet
> Communicates with the master

kube-proxy
> Network proxy that reflects Kubernetes networking services on each node

In the sections below we look further at more components of Kubernetes.

Pod

A pod (as in "a pod of whales") in Kubernetes is defined as the smallest unit of computing we can deploy that can be created and managed in Kubernetes. Further defined, a pod is a group of one or more containers with shared storage/network, combined with a specification on how to run the containers. The contents of a pod always co-located and co-scheduled to run in a shared context.

For more details, you can check out the official reference for Kubernetes pods (*https://oreil.ly/SgJxJ*).

A pod is the smallest deployable unit in Kubernetes and it has one or more containers. Multiple containers within a pod share:

- The network stack
- The filesystem
- The pod "life cycle"

Some notes on pods versus jobs: whereas pods are the smallest deployable units in Kubernetes, and can be scheduled to execute on their own, they are typically scheduled in more higher-level objects within Kubernetes, such as as part of deployment, a StatefulSet, a job, etc. A job within Kubernetes would be the first higher-level deployable unit above a pod. Some of the key differences between a pod and job include:

- When a "bare pod" is running on a node that reboots or fails, it will not be rescheduled.
- A job is similar to a "bare pod"; however, Kubernetes will attempt to reschedule terminated jobs.
- A job provides additional semantics compared to "bare pods."

Object Spec and Status

Nearly every Kubernetes objects includes two nested fields that control the object's configuration:

- spec
- status

Objects that have a spec field need to have the field set when we create the object so that we can provide a description of the characteristics we want the resource to have. We refer to these characteristics as the *desired state* of our object on our Kubernetes cluster.

Get Used to Defining the Spec Field

Every time we want to create a resource on a Kubernetes cluster using kubectl, we will be providing information via the spec field. In Example B-1, you can see an example of this (from Chapter 8) where we are defining how we want to deploy a machine learning model on KFServing.

Example B-1. InferenceService resource config example in YAML

```
apiVersion: "serving.kubeflow.org/v1alpha2"
kind: "InferenceService"
metadata:
  name: "flowers-sample"
spec:
  default:
    predictor:
      tensorflow:
        storageUri: "gs://kfserving-samples/models/tensorflow/flowers"
```

We'll use the spec field over and over for Kubernetes and Kubeflow.

Every Kubernetes object defines a different format of the object spec and may contain nested fields for subobjects of that object.

The status field documents the current state of the object as the Kubernetes cluster sees it. A Kubernetes cluster's control plane is continually trying to make each object's actual state match the desired state specified in the CRD for the object.

Describing a Kubernetes Object

To create an object in Kubernetes we must provide the object spec that describes its desired state. Beyond the object spec, we need to provide other basic information about the object (e.g., "name"). An API request must include this information as JSON in the request body when we use the Kubernetes API to create the object through using kubectl or another method.

The most common way to provide information for the request is to save it in a YAML file before issuing the request. kubectl will convert the information in the YAML file to JSON for us when making the API request.

Submitting Containers to Kubernetes

Containers are submitted as part of a pod, and not standalone. Pods are defined using YAML syntax, as we can see in Example B-2. Kubernetes doesn't actually accept a container as a first-class object, rather it accepts a "pod definition." It then attempts to schedule the pod, and pulls the containers defined within the pod.

Typically, pods are submitted via the kubectl CLI. An example YAML file definition for a pod is shown in Example B-2.

Example B-2. A sample YAML file definition for a Kubernetes pod

```
apiVersion: v1
kind: Pod
metadata:
  name: myapp-pod
  labels:
    app: myapp
spec:
  containers:
  - name: myapp-container
    image: busybox
    command: ['sh', '-c', 'echo Hello Kubernetes! && sleep 3600']
```

Kubernetes Resource Model

Resources in Kubernetes are instances of Kubernetes objects (deployment, services, and namespaces). Resources that run containers are called workloads. Specific examples of workloads:

- Deployments
- StatefulSets
- Jobs
- CronJobs
- DaemonSets

A user works with a Resource API by declaring it in a file (a "Resource Config", aka "CRD") that is then applied to a Kubernetes cluster. Using a tool such as kubectl, we can make declarative (create, update, delete) changes to a cluster. These changes are then actuated by a controller.

Kubernetes uniquely identifies a resource by the Resource Config fields:

apiVersion
>API type group and verison

kind
>API type name

metadata.namespace
>Instance namespace

metadata.name
>Instance name

The apiVersion was "serving.kubeflow.org/v1alpha2," the kind field was "Inference-Service," and metadata.name was defined as "flowers-sample."

Beyond the standard resources in Kubernetes, we can further extend the cluster with custom resources.

Custom Resources, Controllers, and Operators

A custom resource (*https://oreil.ly/F0ViT*) is a Kubernetes API extension that is specific to a cluster once installed. Custom resources can be created, updated, and deleted on a running cluster through dynamic registration. Once we have installed a custom resource, we can control it with the kubectl tool just like we would built-in resources (e.g., "pods," etc.).

By themselves custom resources allow us to store and retrieve structured data. When we combine custom resources with controllers, then they become a true declarative API.

Controllers are tasked with actuating Kubernetes APIs as they watch the state of the system, and look for changes to either the desired state of resources or the system. The controllers then work to make changes to bring the cluster back in line with the intent specified by the user or automation system.

The controller interprets the structured data as a record of the user's desired state. The controller continually takes action to get to this state.

Custom controllers are especially effective when combined with custom resources (but they can work with any kind of resource). One example of this combination (custom controller and custom resource) is the *operator pattern*. The operator pattern allows us to encode domain knowledge for specific applications into an extension of the Kubernetes API.

Custom Controllers

Custom resources let us store and retrieve structured data. They also need to be combined with a controller to be considered a *declarative API*. Being a declarative API means they allow us to declare/specify the desired state of our resource

Kubernetes is constantly trying to match the desired state with an actual state. The controller interprets the structured data as the user's intent for the state and attempts to achieve and maintain this desired state inside the Kubernetes cluster.

A custom controller is a controller that can be deployed by a user and be updated independent from the cluster's own life cycle. Custom controllers can work with any kind of resource, and are most effective when paired with a custom resource.

Custom Resource Definition

When we want to define our own custom resource we write a custom resource definition (CRD). Once we have the CRD set up in Kubernetes, we can use it like any other native Kubernetes object (leveraging other features such as CLI, security, API services, RBAC, etc.).

Istio Operations and Kubeflow

This appendix provides material around the basic functionality of Istio and how that relates to managing the service mesh for Kubeflow components. It is meant as background and reference information for the rest of the book, and Chapter 2 specifically.

Service Mesh Management with Istio

Modern infrastructure is often composed of many microservices where each microservice defines its own APIs, and the services interact with one another using these APIs in order to serve end-user requests.

The distributed microservices architecture is foundational to most modern applications. We create complex systems by combining multiple microservices where each microservice defines its own APIs. These separate services interact with each other via these APIs to serve end-user requests.

A service mesh is a network of microservices that make up applications and the interactions between the microservices. As a service mesh grows larger and more complex, it naturally becomes more difficult to manage and operate. Challenges in service mesh operations include:

- Discovery
- Load balancing
- Failure recovery
- Metrics
- Monitoring

There are also more complex operations, such as:

- A/B testing
- Canary rollouts
- Rate limiting
- Access control
- End-to-end authentication

Istio (*https://oreil.ly/giPuC*) is an open source service mesh that transparently layers onto existing distributed applications. Istio supports operations in the distributed microservice architectures that are progressively being adopted on cloud platforms. Developers are keenly focused on architectures requiring portability, and operators increasingly are working with distributed deployments that span on-premises, cloud, and hybrid platforms. Istio lets us manage microservice deployments more efficiently by providing a consistent way to connect, monitor, and secure microservices.

Istio support gives applications features such as:

- Automatic load balancing for HTTP, gRPC, TCP, and WebSocket traffic
- Fine-grained control of traffic behavior via fault injection, failovers, retries, and rich routing rules
- Pluggable policy layer and configuration API allowing for rate limits, quotas, and access controls
- Automatic traces, logs, and metrics for all traffic inside a cluster that includes ingress and egress
- Secure intra-cluster service-to-service communication with strong identity-based authentication and authorization

Like many other cluster-based platforms, Kubeflow operates as a group of services, tools, and frameworks that are deployed together on a Kubernetes cluster to support machine learning applications.

The majority of these components are open source projects in their own right, and were developed independently by different groups of people. Combining these components into a new system is a challenge, in that we need all parts to work as a seamless whole. Istio plays a critical role in allowing all of these components to interoperate.

Istio is considered to be foundational in multitenancy support for Kubeflow. As of version 0.6 of Kubeflow, Istio is core to options, and Kubeflow cannot operate without it. The use of Istio by Kubeflow provides end-to-end authentication and access control, making Istio a core part of Kubeflow's internal operations.

Kubeflow Versions and Istio Versions

The base on-premise install of Kubeflow 1.0.2 uses Istio 1.1.6. However, the Kubeflow 1.0.2 install for GCP installs with Istio 1.3. The latest version listed for Istio during the final stages of writing this book is Istio 1.6. The diagrams in this chapter for Istio are based on the 1.1.6 version of Istio.

Istio core features are:

- Traffic management (*https://oreil.ly/nWyok*)
- Security
- Observability

Istio traffic management gives us A/B testing, canary rollouts, and staged rollouts with percentage-based traffic splits. It also gives us gateways for controlling inbound and outbound traffic for our service mesh.

Istio security provides the underlying secure communication channel and manages authentication and authorization for our service mesh. It also provides encryption of service communication (with Istio, this is the default) and allows for enforced policies across diverse runtimes and protocols.

Istio observability gives our service mesh metrics for latency, traffic, errors, and saturation. It also provides distributed traces that span each service. Further, it generates a full record of each traffic flow request, enabling auditing.

What Is Tracing?

Distributed systems and microservers interactions can involve many machines and many request/response transactions. It can be a challenge to understand what happened inside a system once the logs start flying.

(Distributed) tracing allows us to capture requests and build a view of the entire chain of calls made from the user requests to the interactions between different services.

Tracing also allows us to:

- Enable instrumentation of application latency (e.g., how long each request takes)
- Identify performance issues
- Track the life cycle of network calls (e.g., HTTP, RPC, etc.)

In an environment where there are a lot of moving parts, tracing is a key DevOps debugging tool.

In Kubeflow we see Istio used to do things such as:

- Securing the control plane
- Providing endpoint security
- Managing access to Kubeflow applications
- Enabling end-to-end authentication and access control

Let's now dig deeper into the architecture of Istio to better understand how Istio provides this functionality.

Istio Architecture

Istio logically splits a service mesh into a control plane and a data plane, as shown in Figure C-1.

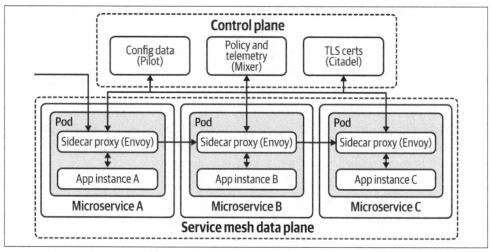

Figure C-1. Istio service mesh architecture

In this figure we can see how the data plane and the control plane separate the components in Istio. The control plane refers to traffic that involves control and configuration messages sent between Istio components to configure the operations of the service mesh. The data plane involves data traffic for business logic sent from and to workload components.

Let's dig into how the control plane differs from the data plane and then what components are managed by each respective plane.

Control plane

The Istio control plane configures and manages the proxies in the data plane used to route network traffic. The control plane additionally configures Mixers to collect telemetry data and enforce policies.

The components we can see in Figure C-1 in the control plane are:

Pilot
> Config data

Mixer
> Policy and telemetry

Citadel
> TLS certs

Pilot gives your service mesh service resiliency (e.g., retries, circuit breakers, timeouts, etc.), traffic management (e.g., canary rollouts, A/B testing), and discovery for the Envoy sidecars. Pilot is the core traffic management component in Istio and programs the Envoy proxies. Pilot is responsible for load balancing, routing, and service discovery.

> **The Role of Envoy Sidecars**
>
> Part of the foundation of Istio is the usage of an extended version of the Envoy (*https://oreil.ly/IJGXk*) proxy to mediate all inbound and outbound traffic for all services in the service mesh.
>
> Envoy proxies are deployed as "sidecars" inside a Kubernetes pod for a relevant service. The sidecar proxy, as its name implies, is meant to run alongside the pod application without rewriting the application code.
>
> Istio support is added to services via a special sidecar (*https://oreil.ly/wnAE7*) proxy throughout the environment that intercepts all network communications between the microservices in your system. Istio allows us to perform these operations with few or no code changes in the service code.

Mixer collects telemetry data from the Envoy proxy (plus other services) and enforces access control and usage policies across the service mesh. Mixer evaluates the request-level attributes extracted by Envoy proxies.

Citadel can be used to encrypt traffic in the service mesh. Citadel provides string service-to-service and end-user authentication via built-in credential and identity management. We'd use Citadel to enforce policies based on service identity for Istio.

API Gateway Versus Service Mesh

You may notice that ingress for a system may sometimes be handled by an API gateway (e.g., Ambassador) and other times handled by a service mesh such as Istio.

There are two types of traffic management we focus on:

- North/south traffic: data into/out of your datacenter
- East/west traffic: traffic between services in your datacenter

The difference is that with north/south traffic you don't control the edge (client), and we will manage each type of traffic with different types of control planes.

Istio (service mesh) handles east/west traffic, where API gateways focus on north/south traffic.

Most of the time an organization will start with an API gateway as it doesn't yet need a service mesh. Over time it may add a service mesh, and at that point it may choose to begin managing ingress with the service mesh as well. For reference, Istio uses the gateway abstraction to support managing ingress.

Data plane

Istio's data plane uses sidecar proxies (Envoy) to control and manage traffic that a service mesh sends and receives. The data plane controls the communication between workload components in a service mesh. Having Istio manage this traffic via sidecar proxies makes it easier to direct and control traffic around your service mesh.

The only Istio components that handle data plane traffic are Envoy proxies. Configurations and traffic rules are enforced by Envoy proxies as the proxies route data plane traffic across the service mesh. While this is happening, the service components in the service mesh do not have to be aware of this routing by the proxies.

Traffic Management

One of the critical functions Istio plays in Kubeflow is traffic management between components. Istio uses a service registry to track endpoints and services in a service mesh in order to direct traffic within the mesh. Kubeflow runs on a Kubernetes cluster, and this allows Istio to automatically detect the services and endpoints in that type of cluster.

In this next section, we lightly cover a few of the traffic management API resources used by Kubeflow.

Virtual services

We configure how requests are routed to a service in Istio with a *virtual service*, allowing for more advanced discovery and connectivity provided by Istio. Virtual services are a key building block of Istio's traffic routing strategy in addition to destination rules (covered in the next section).

A virtual service in Istio is made up of a set of routing rules that are evaluated in an ordered sequence. This lets Istio match each request to the virtual service for a specific real destination inside the service mesh. There may be zero or many virtual services in your service mesh.

Virtual services strongly decouple where clients send their requests from the destination components that actually do the processing work. Inside this decoupling, this allows Istio to provide a way to specify different traffic routing rules for how the traffic actually gets to those processing components inside our mesh.

Functionality in Kubeflow, such as A/B testing, is implemented with Istio's virtual services. Here virtual services are used to configure traffic routes based on percentages across different model versions (in KFServing) or other variations of traffic shaping.

Destination rules

Beyond virtual services, we have Istio's destination rules, which are another key part of Istio's traffic routing strategy. If virtual services tell our service mesh how to route the traffic for a given destination, then we'd use destination rules to specify what happens to the traffic for that destination.

Destination rules are only applied after the virtual service routing rules have been applied. This makes destination rules apply to the traffic's "true" destination.

Gateways

Ingress and egress in a service mesh is managed by a gateway (*https://oreil.ly/apeye*) to control what traffic can enter or leave our service mesh. Gateway proxies differ from normal Istio sidecar proxies in that they are standalone Envoy proxies that run at the edge of the service mesh.

Istio Gateways Versus Kubernetes Ingress APIs

Given that Kubeflow runs on Kubernetes and uses Istio, it's worth noting the difference between Istio gateways used for gateways versus Kubernetes ingress APIs, as both can be used for Kubeflow.

Istio gateways are different in that they let you use the more powerful features for traffic routing than the normal Kubernetes ingress APIs, such as configuring layers 4-6 load-balancing properties (e.g., ports to expose), TLS settings, etc.

Further, we can bind an Istio virtual service to our gateway (as opposed to adding application-layer traffic routing to the same API resource), and this allows us to manage gateway traffic similar to other data plane traffic in our Istio service mesh.

Ingress traffic management is the primary use case for Istio gateways, but you can also set up egress gateways. An egress dedicated exit node allows us to limit which services can (or should) access external networks. It also allows us to add security to our mesh by enabling secure control of egress traffic (*https://oreil.ly/dZS31*), for example.

Two preconfigured gateway proxy deployments that Istio provides out of the box are `istio-ingressgateway` and `istio-egressgateway`. You can apply your own gateway configurations for each of these to customize how Istio and Kubeflow work.

Istio Security Architecture

In this section we provide a light overview of the Istio security architecture. For a more in-depth review of the topic, check out the Istio page for security (*https://oreil.ly/5Mn6W*).

We can see the Istio security architecture in Figure C-2.

We note that microservices have specific security needs such as:

- Auditing tools to track who did what and when
- Mutual TLS and fine-grained access policies for flexible service access control
- Traffic encryption to defend against man-in-the-middle attacks

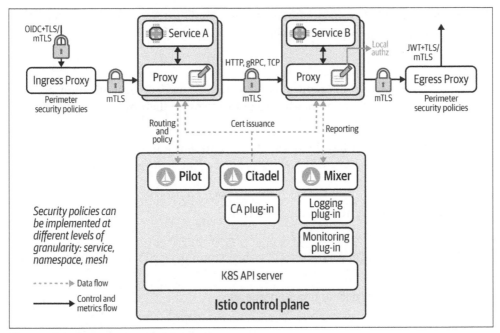

Figure C-2. Istio security architecture

To accomplish the above security needs (and more), Istio's security goals are operating with a zero-trust network mentality, providing security by default, and setting up multiple layers of defense for depth.

Istio security involves the Citadel, sidecar and perimeter proxies, Pilot, and Mixer components. We've covered most of these previously, so here we'll just give an overview of Citadel.

The Citadel component is used for key and certificate management. Istio uses sidecar and perimeter proxies to allow for secure communication between clients and servers. The Pilot component is used to distribute secure naming information and authentication policies to the proxies, and the mixer is used to manage auditing and authorization.

Policies

You can create custom policies for your application to enforce runtime rules such as:

- Header redirects and rewrites
- Whitelists, blacklists, and denials to restrict access to services
- Dynamically limit the traffic to a service with rate limiting

Another feature of Istio is that you can add your own custom authorization functionality by adding your own policy adapters.

Istio identity

The Istio identity model allows it to control access based on authorization policies, track usage for users, reject users who are not current on their bill, and audit who did what at what time.

The Istio identity model has the flexibility to represent a human user, an individual service, or a group of services. Following is a list of the Istio service identities on different platforms:

- AWS IAM user/role account for AWS
- CGP service account on GCP
- GCP service account on GKE/GCE (when running as a Google Kubernetes cluster)
- Kubernetes service account on Kubernetes

Istio authentication

There are two types of authentication provided by Istio:

- Origin authentication
- Transport authentication

Origin authentication (also known as end-user authentication) verifies the client making the request as a device or end user. This authentication type is enabled with JWT validation.

Transport authentication (also referred to as service-to-service authentication) uses strong identity and secures service-to-service communication along with end-user-to-service communication. Transport authentication in Istio also provides a key management system to automate certificate and key generation, rotation, and distribution.

Where to Find Authentication Policies

Istio authentication policies are stored in `Istio config store` via a custom Kubernetes API.

Each authentication policy (along with keys) is kept up to date for each proxy by the Pilot service in Istio. Let's now move into how authorization is handled in Istio.

Istio Authorization and Role-Based Access Control

Authorization in Istio is also called RBAC. Authorization/RBAC in Istio gives our service mesh namespace-level, service-level, and method-level access control for services in our service mesh.

Istio authorization has role-based semantics, and provides authorization for end-user-to-service and service-to-service security requirements. In Figure C-3, we can see the Istio authorization architecture (*https://oreil.ly/ajVGR*).

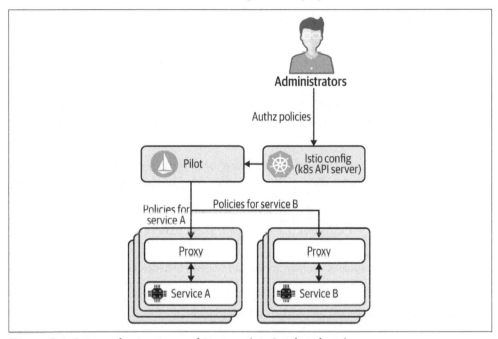

Figure C-3. Istio authorization architecture (via Istio's website)

In Figure C-3 we can see how Istio operators specify Istio authorization policies based on YAML files. The policies created by the YAML files are then stored in the `Istio Config Store`. As changes are made to the collection of Istio authorization policies, Pilot will pick up the changes and distribute the changes to the Envoy proxies that are co-located with the service instances.

Runtime requests are authorized by each Envoy proxy by its local authorization engine. Each incoming request to the proxy is evaluated against the current authorization policies, and an `ALLOW` or `DENY` result is returned per request.

You enable Istio authorization on a service mesh with the `ClusterRbacConfig` object.

> **There Can Only Be One ClusterRbacConfig**
>
> Each service mesh can only have a single `ClusterRbacConfig` object as it is a cluster-scoped singleton with a fixed name value of `default`.

Let's now look at more specifics around creating authorization policies in Istio.

Authorization policies

The two key concepts for an Istio authorization policy are:

- `ServiceRole`
- `ServiceRoleBinding`

`ServiceRole` specifies a group of permissions in a policy for access to services. You can grant a `ServiceRole` to particular subjects, such as user, group, or service, with a `ServiceRoleBinding`.

The combination of `ServiceRole` and `ServiceRoleBinding` creates an Istio authorization policy. This authorization policy specifies *who* is allowed to do *what* under *which* conditions.

We can further define this as:

Who
> Defined by the `subjects` section in the `ServiceRoleBinding` definition

What
> Defined by the `permissions` section in `ServiceRole`

Which
> Defined by the `conditions` section in either `ServiceRole` or `ServiceRoleBind ings`

Let's now dig into more specifics about both `ServiceRole` and `ServiceRoleBinding`.

ServiceRole

A `ServiceRole` contains a list of rules that each have the following fields:

- `Services`
- `Methods`
- `Paths`

Services is a list of service names, or we can set the value to * to include all services in a specific namespace. Methods are a list of permissible HTTP methods for the ServiceRole, and the * wildcard here works as well. The HTTP list of paths is set by the paths field. The paths field can also define gRPC methods.

We specify a namespace in the metadata section, and our ServiceRole only applies to this namespace. Example C-1 shows a ServiceRole creation for the hypothetical kf-admin role via a YAML file.

Example C-1. ServiceRole creation example in YAML

```
apiVersion: "rbac.istio.io/v1alpha1"
kind: ServiceRole
metadata:
  name: kf-test
  namespace: default
spec:
  rules:
  - services: ["*"]
```

In this simplistic example, the kf-admin role would have full access to all services in the default namespace.

Deploying Istio Policies

You would use kubectl to deploy a policy in Istio.

We can further define specific services and methods (e.g., GET, HEAD) in the rules section of the spec.

Istio and Kubernetes Service DNS Naming Conventions

The Services field in the ServiceRole spec mentions Kubernetes service names. "Normal" services in Kubernetes are assigned a DNS A record (*https://oreil.ly/iGFhf*) for a name of the form:

```
my-svc.my-namespace.svc.cluster.local
```

In Kubernetes, DNS resolutions are done on a per service basis in the format of <serviceName>.<namespaceName>.svc.cluster.local

Kubernetes uses this domain name to resolve to the IP address of the service. For more details on this topic, check out the Kubernetes documentation (*https://oreil.ly/aIzfl*) on DNS.

ServiceRoleBinding

The ServiceRoleBinding contains a list of subjects assigned to the role and then a roleRef. The roleRef field configures that associated ServiceRole (in the same namespace). We can see an example of a ServiceRoleBinding in Example C-2.

Example C-2. ServiceRoleBinding YAML code

```
apiVersion: "rbac.istio.io/v1alpha1"
kind: ServiceRoleBinding
metadata:
  name: test-kf-role-binding
  namespace: default
spec:
  subjects:
  - user: "service-account-a"
  - user: "istio-ingress-service-account"
    properties:
      request.auth.claims[email]: "josh@pattersonconsultingtn.com"
  roleRef:
    kind: ServiceRole
    name: "kf-test"
```

As you can see in this example, you can set a subject field with a user or with a set of properties.

Index

A

A/B testing, 220, 256, 261
Active Directory (AD), 99, 237, 243
Active Directory Domain Serice (AD DS), 237
ADLS Gen2, 172
AI Platform Training & Prediction API, 123
Alibi, 209
Amazon Auto Scaling, 143
Amazon AWS CloudFormation console, 154
Amazon AWS CloudWatch, 163
Amazon CloudFront, 143
Amazon EC2, 143, 146
Amazon ECS, 146
Amazon Elastic Beanstalk, 143
Amazon Elastic Block Store, 144
Amazon Elastic File System, 144
Amazon Elastic Kubernetes Service (EKS)
    about, 6, 146
    creating clusters, 157
    creating service role, 152-154
    deleting clusters, 162
    deploying clusters with eksctl, 158
    installing eksctl CLI for, 151
    resizing clusters, 161
    using managed Kubernetes on, 152-158
Amazon ElastiCache, 143
Amazon Fargate, 146
Amazon FSx for Lustre, 144
Amazon FSx for Windows File Server, 144
Amazon Glacier, 144
Amazon Kubernetes Engine (AKE), 38
Amazon Lambda, 143, 146
Amazon Lightsail, 146
Amazon RDS, 143

Amazon Simple Storage Service (S3), 144, 214
Amazon SNS, 143
Amazon Virtual Cloud (VPC), 143
Amazon Virtual Private Cloud (VPC), 154-158
Amazon Web Service (AWS)
    about, 4, 37, 81, 86, 143
    Amazon Cloud security, 145
    compute services, 145
    configuring CLI, 148
    creating Amazon Virtual Private Cloud
        (VPC), 154-158
    installing CLI, 147
    installing IAM Authenticator, 151
    Kubeflow on, 150
    managed Kubernetes on EKS, 146
    Management Console, 147
    pricing, 145
    running Kubeflow on, 143-165
    signing up for, 146
    storage, 144
Anaconda, 19
Apache Hadoop, 3, 5, 172
API Gateways, 196, 260
API Server (AWS CloudWatch), 163
APIs
    enabling for projects, 123-125
    Web, 207
apiVersion field, 252
applications
    as components of Kubeflow, 28-35
    deploying models to production for inte-
        grating, 23
    GCO projects for deployments of, 118
    Kubeflow and deployed, 68

architecture
  about, 41
  Istio, 258-260
  Kubeflow Pipelines, 56
  multitenancy, 48-52
  multiuser, 49
  notebook, 53-56
Archive storage (Azure), 169, 172
Argo, 28, 42
Argo Workflow Controller, 56
Aronchick, David, 16
Artifact Storage systems, 57
Artifactory, 83, 95, 103
artifacts
  about, 31
  container management and, 103
  defined, 45
  storing, 45
artificial intelligence (AI), 2
Audit (AWS CloudWatch), 163
authenticated entity, 49
authentication
  Azure Cloud Platform, 173
  customizing, 161
  end-user, 240
  Google Cloud Identity-Aware and, 112
  in Google Cloud Platform (GCP), 116
  infrastructure and, 234
  Istio, 264
  password-only, 126
Authenticator (AWS CloudWatch), 163
authorization
  Azure Cloud Platform, 173
  Google Cloud Identity-Aware and, 112
  in Google Cloud Platform (GCP), 117
  infrastructure and, 234
  Istio, 265-268
  network access to deployment, 189
Authorized redirect URI, 131
autoscaling, 83, 199, 203
Availability Zones, in Amazon Web Service
  (AWS), 143
Avere vFXT (Azure), 169, 172
AWS Access Key, 148
AWS command-line interface (AWS CLI)
  Azure Cloud Platform, 177
  deploying Kubeflow using, 131-141
  installing AWS, 147

running machine learning jobs on Kubeflow
  using, 44
AWS Storage Gateway, 144
Azure Active Directory, 174
Azure Blob Storage, 169, 170, 214
Azure Cloud Platform
  about, 37, 167
  CLI, 177
  components of, 168
  containers, 176
  creating AKS cluster for Kubeflow, 179-182
  credentials, 182
  login and configuration, 178
  managed Azure Kubernetes services, 176
  pricing, 169
  resource groups, 174
  resources, 174
  running Kubeflow on, 167-189
  security model, 172-174
  service accounts, 174
  storage, 169-172
  subscription, 179
  virtual machines (VMs), 175
Azure Databricks, 172
Azure Kubernetes Services (AKS), 6, 38
Azure Resource Manager, 175

B

$BASE_DIR environment variable, 137
batch workloads, 74
BentoML, 35
best practices, for Kubeflow, 57-63
big-cloud vendor, 5
Blob, 169, 170, 214
block storage, object storage versus, 112
blue-green deployment, 207
bq tool, 120
build command, 96

C

canary, 204, 211
canary rollouts, 203, 256, 259
canarying, managing model traffic with,
  226-228
certificate authority, 158, 236
Chainer, 26, 66
Cisco Flexpod, 102
Citadel component, 259, 263
Cloud Build API, 123

Cloud Filestore API, 123
Cloud Identity and Access Management (Cloud IAM), 114-118
Cloud ML (Cloud Machine Learning), 16
Cloud Resource Manager API, 123
Cloud Shell, 131
Cloudera, 5, 172
clouds
    about, 37
    deployment and, 5
    GPUs, 23
    images, 82
    workloads in the, 81
cluster parameter, 90
ClusterRbacConfig object, 266
clusters
    adding to context file, 92
    AKS, 179-182
    Amazon EKS, 157, 161
    Kubernetes, 217-219
    on-premise, 246
    utilization of, 73
Coldline Storage, 111
collection, 248
command-line
    common operations for, 104
    Kubernetes operations from, 89-96
command-line interface (CLI)
    Azure Cloud Platform, 177
    deploying Kubeflow using, 131-141
    installing AWS, 147
    running machine learning jobs on Kubeflow using, 44
composability, of cloud vendors, 7
Compute Engine API, 123
compute services, 145
compute time, 199
Compute Unified Device Architecture (CUDA), 77
computer vision, 2, 21-23, 199
concept drift, 200, 212
CONFIG environment variable, 137, 184
configuration variables, 137
configuring
    AWS CLI, 148
    Credentials tab, 128-131
    kfctl, 159, 183
confusion matrix, 35, 45
container

about, 9
    Azure Cloud Platform, 176
    submitting to Kubernetes, 251
    TensorFlow, 96
container image, 8
container management
    about, 83
    artifact repositories and, 103
container orchestration platform, 5
containerized process, 11
context
    adding clusters to file, 92
    getting current, 91
    switching, 92
control plane
    about, 68, 244-245
    Istio, 259
    securing, 246
Controller Manager (AWS CloudWatch), 163
controllers, custom, 252
convolutional neural networks (CNNs), 77
CPUs, model serving and, 199
Credentials tab, configuring, 128-131
credentials, Azure Cloud Platform, 182
CronJobs, 252
custom images, GPUs and, 60
custom resource definitions (CRDs), 66, 253

D

DaemonSets, 252
data engineering, 18
data engineers, skillsets of, 72
data lake, 4
Data Lake Storage (Azure), 169, 171
data patterns, 75
data plane, 260
data science, 18
data scientist, 70, 72
datacenter, 81
Dean, Jeff
    "Numbers Everyone Should Know", 74
Debian, installing Azure CLI, 177
dedicated data patterns, 75
deep learning
    cloud running with, 82
    defined, 2
    transformers, 210
Deep Learning (Patterson and Gibson), 2
default endpoint, 204, 211

dependencies
    best practices, 57-60
    managing, 57-60
    pre-built model servers and versions of, 212
Deployment Manager API, 123
deployments
    authorizing network access to, 189
    blue-green, 207
    custom transformers, 228-230
    customizing, 161
    InferenceService, 224
    Istio policies, 267
    Kubeflow and application, 68
    Kubeflow configuration and, 159-161
    Kubeflow using command-line interface,
        131-141
    models to production for application inte-
        gration, 23
    of models on KFServing, 220
    process of, 158-164
    troubleshooting, 164
destination rules, in Istio, 261
DevOps, 18, 72
Dex, 46, 70, 241-243
directed acyclic graph (DAG), 34
Disk storage (Azure), 169, 169
distributed-worker job, 27
Docker
    about, 5, 8
    basic commands, 96
    building custom notebook, 58
    using, 95
    using to build TensorFlow containers, 96
Docker Hub, 83, 95, 96, 103
Docker Swarm, 9
Dockerfile, 58, 60, 96, 103
Domain Name Service (DNS), 267
downloading
    Google Cloud SDK, 121
    kfctl, 159, 183
dynamic scaling, 9, 86

E

eksctl
    deploying Amazon EKS clusters with, 158
    installing CLI for Amazon EKS, 151
enabling APIs for projects, 123-125
end-user authentication, with JWT, 240
endpoints, 204, 207, 211, 249

ensembling, 220
enterprise infrastructure, running, 4-6
enterprise security integration, 65
environment variables
    CONFIG, 137, 184
    creating required, 133
    PROJECT, 136
    setting Kubeflow deployment, 137, 184
    setting up for frctl, 135
    setting up for kfctl, 184
    ZONE, 135
Envoy, 259, 260
eventing, as a core component of Knative, 84
execution, 62
experiments, 62
Explain API method, 205
explainer, 208

F

fabric controller (FC), 175
Fairing library, 30
field-programmable gate array (FPGA), 8
File storage (Azure), 169
first party services access, 239
Flashable, 102
flowers-2 model, 222
forecasting, 84
frameworks
    machine learning, 30
    supported by Kubeflow components, 201
free-tier account, 120, 146

G

gateways
    host access to Kubernetes cluster, 99
    in Istio, 261
gcloud
    about, 120, 133
    setting configuration variables, 137
GCP Console application, 118
geography (Azure), 167
Gibson, Adam
    Deep Learning, 2
GitHub, 61, 70, 103
Google BigQuery, 120
Google Cloud, 81
Google Cloud Identity-Aware Proxy (Cloud
    IAP)
    about, 45, 238

Google Cloud, 112-118
  Google Cloud Platform and, 239
Google Cloud Load Balancer (GCLB), 45
Google Cloud Platform (GCP), 109-142
  about, 16, 37, 109
  creating projects in console, 122
  Identity-Aware Proxy (IAP), 112-118, 239
  installing Kubeflow on, 121-125
  major services offered with, 110
  portal, 126
  pricing for, 112
  projects for application deployments, 118
  security and, 114-118
  service accounts, 119
  setting up OAuth for, 125-131
  signing up for, 120
  storage, 111
Google Cloud SDK
  downloading, 121
  installing, 120, 121
Google Cloud Storage, 120, 214, 222
Google Compute Engine, 120
Google Container Registry, 83, 95, 103
Google Kubernetes Engine (GKE)
  about, 6, 38
  creating a managed cluster, 123
Google Next, 16
GPU (graphics processing unit)
  about, 8
  anti-use cases, 77
  best practices, 60-62
  cloud, 23
  model accuracy and, 20
  model serving and, 199
  models benefiting from, 77-79
  multiple, 62, 76
  planning for, 75-79
  running notebooks on, 18-20
  use cases, 76
graph support, 202
gsutil tool, 120
GUI, deploying Kubeflow with a, 131

H
hardware drivers, 10
HDInsight, 172
helm 3, 217
"Hidden Technical Debt in Machine Learning"
    (Sculley), 14

HTTP API, 208
HTTP method, 196
HTTPS, 238
hybrid deployment, 5
hyperparameters
  defined, 32
  tuning, 31

I
ID Tokens, 242
identification proxy, 45
Identity and Access Management (IAM)
    API, 123
  Authenticator, installing AWS, 151
identity model, Istio, 264
identity providers, 237
impersonation, 50
inference-per-second (IPS), 197-199
InferenceService, 204-206, 214, 220, 224
infrastructure
  about, 233
  Active Directory (AD), 237
  authentication, 234
  authorization, 234
  cloud, 81
  control plane, 244-245
  Dev, 241-243
  end-user authentication with JWT, 240
  identity providers, 237
  Identity-Aware Proxy (IAP), 238
  Kerberos, 235
  Kubernetes considerations, 79
  lightweight directory access protocol
      (LDAP), 235
  OAuth, 240
  on-premise, 80
  OpenID Connect (OIDC), 240
  placement, 82
  planning, 79-83
  public key, 233
  resilient, as a primary benefit of Kubernetes,
      11
  service accounts, 244
  Simple and Protected GSS_API Negotiation
      Mechanism (SPNEGO), 241
  transport layer security (TLS), 236
  treating models as, 207
  webhook, 236
  X.509 certificates, 236

Infrastructure as a Service (IaaS)), 111
ingress, 246, 256, 260-262
ingress controller, 67
installations
    about, 65
    choosing components for, 67
    container management, 83
    data patterns, 75
    GPU planning, 75-79
    infrastructure planning, 79-83
    security planning, 65-70
    serverless container operations with Kna-
        tive, 83
    sizing and growing, 84-87
    users, 70-73
    workloads, 73-75
installing
    AWS CLI, 147
    AWS IAM Authenticator, 151
    Azure CLI, 177
    eksctl CLI for Amazon EKS, 151
    Google Cloud SDK, 120, 121
    JFrog Artifactory OSS, 103
    jq, 151
    kfctl, 183
    KFServing on Kubernetes cluster, 217-219
    kubectl, 90-93, 151
    Kubeflow, 105, 182-188
    Kubeflow on Azure Kubernetes, 177-188
    Kubeflow on Google Cloud Platform,
        121-125
    Kubeflow on-premise, 89-107, 97
    Metadata SDK, 62
instances, leaving running, 120
integration
    of Kerberos, 100
    of storage, 100-102
Internet Engineering Task Force (IETF), 236
IPython, 29
isolation
    multitenancy and, 48
    multiuser, 52
Istio
    about, 28, 42, 244
    architecture, 258-260
    authorization, 265-268
    Control Plane, 259
    core features of, 257
    KFServing and, 46

operations in Kubeflow, 45-47
security architecture, 262-264
service mesh management with, 255-268
versions of, 257
Istio Gateway, 46
Istio ingress gateway, 189
Istio RBAC Authorization Policy, 51

J
JFrog Artifactory OSS, 103
jobs
    isolation, as a primary benefit of Kuber-
        netes, 11
    managing dependencies, 57-60
jq, installing, 151
JSON Web Token (JWT), 45, 113, 240
Julia, 29
Jupyter Notebook App
    about, 12
    integrating with Kubeflow, 30
    using, 29
Jupyter Web App, 53-56
JupyterHub, 53, 69

K
K80, 82
Katib, 32
Keras, 27-28
Kerberos
    about, 235
    Dex and, 243
    integration of, 100
$KF_DIR environment variable, 137
$KF_NAME environment variable, 137
kfctl
    about, 104-107
    configuring, 159, 183
    downloading, 159, 183
    installing, 183
    Kubeflow deployment with, 138
    setting up, 134
    setting up environment variables for, 135,
        184
KFServing
    about, 35, 201-203
    advantages of using, 203
    core concepts in, 204-212
    deploying models on, 220
    installing on Kubernetes cluster, 217-219

managing models with, 217-231
security model, 216
transformers, 210
KFServing Inference Services, 204
kfserving-samples, 222
KFServingClient, 206
kind field, 248, 252
Knative, serverless container operations with, 83
kube-proxy, 249
kubeadm-dind, 89
kubectl
    about, 104
    commands, 68
    installing, 90-93, 151
    path, 49
    plug-in, 100
    using, 93-95
Kubeflow
    about, 12-14
    accessing, 104
    accessing UI post-installation, 141
    architecture of, 43
    authentication and, 234
    basic install process, 97-104
    best practices, 57-63
    common access storage patterns, 101
    common use cases, 18-24
    compared with Kubernetes, 28
    components of, 24-35
    confirming deployment, 138-141
    deployed applications and, 68
    deploying using command-line interface, 131-141
    deployment with kfctl tool, 138
    installing, 105, 182-188
    installing on Azure Kubernetes, 177-188
    installing on Google Cloud Platform, 121-125
    installing on-premise, 89-107, 97
    integrating Jupyter Notebook with, 30
    interacting with, 104
    Istio operations in, 45-47
    job bandwidth, 101
    JupyterHub and, 53
    major usage patterns of, 67
    multitenancy architecture, 48-52
    on Amazon Web Services, 150
    origins of, 16

profiles, 50
relationship with TensorFlow, 15
running jobs on, 44
running on Amazon Web Services, 143-165
running on Azure, 167-189
running on Google Cloud, 109-142
setting deployment environment variables, 137
user-access routes for clusters, 49
users of, 17
versions of, 55, 257
website, 1
Kubeflow Dashboard UI, 104
Kubeflow distributed microservice architecture, 28, 42, 256
Kubeflow Governance Proposal, 16
Kubeflow job, 101
Kubeflow notebook platform, 18
Kubeflow Pipelines
    about, 13
    architecture of, 56
    basic concepts of, 34-35
    running machine learning jobs on Kubeflow using, 44
    using, 32
Kubeflow UI, 28
kubelet, 249
Kubernetes
    architecture of, 43
    compared with Kubeflow, 28
    components running on, 66
    considerations for building clusters, 97
    core concepts, 247-253
    endpoints, 249
    for production application deployment, 8-12
    gateway host access to clusters, 99
    glossary, 98
    ingress APIs, 262
    machine learning on, 1-18
    managed on EKS, 146
    objects, 251
    operations from command line, 89-96
    pod, 249
    primary benefits of, 11
    resource model, 252
    service accounts and, 244
    spec, 250
    status, 250

submitting containers to, 251
Kubernetes API, components extending, 66
Kubernetes Dashboard, 68
Kubernetes Engine API, 123
Kubernetes Horizontal Pod Autoscaler, 9
Kubernetes Pod, 27, 101, 259
Kubernetes RBAC Rolebinding, 51
Kubernetes-native, 1
Kubernetes: Up and Running, 12

L

Lewi, Jeremy, 16
lightweight directory access protocol (LDAP), 70, 235
line of business, as a team, 18
LinkedIn, 70
load balancer, 45, 67, 116
local container filesystem, 214
local image environment, 58
local machine, 39
logging, 163
loud, 145

M

mac OSX
    Google Cloud SDK and, 121
    installing Azure CLI, 177
    installing kubectl on, 90
machine learning (ML)
    defined, 2, 31
    evolution of, 2-4
    frameworks for, 30
    hidden technical debt in, 14
    model inference, 192
    model inference serving with KFServing, 35
    model training, 192
    on Kubernetes, 1-18
    shared multitenant environment, 21
    tools as components of Kubeflow, 26-27
Machine Learning Metadata Service, 44, 62
managed Kubernetes, 38, 152-158
mAP score, 23
Mesos, 9
metadata component, in Kubeflow, 31
Metadata SDK
    basic usage of, 63
    installing, 62
metadata.name field, 252
metadata.namespace field, 252

Microsoft, 70
Microsoft Azure, 81
Minikube, 39, 89, 217
MinIO, 35, 45
Mixer component, 259
model inference
    about, 74
    defined, 36
    scaling, 197-199
    serving with KFServing, 35
model integration
    building intuitions for, 194-196
    KFServing, 201-216
    managing models with KFServing, 217-231
    model management, 191-201
model serving
    CPU versus GPU, 199
    KFServing, 201-216
    managing models with KFServing, 217-231
    model management, 191-201
    pre-built servers, 212-216
models
    benefiting from GPUs, 77-79
    deploying to production for application
        integration, 23
    GPUs and accuracy of, 20
    managing, 191-201
    managing traffic with canarying, 226-228
    managing with KFServing, 217-231
    removing deployed, 231
    revision tracking, 231
    rolling back deployed, 230
    treating as infrastructure, 207
MPI, 26, 66
multi-armed bandits, 220
Multi-Regional Storage, 111
multitenancy architecture, 48-52
multiuser architecture, 49
multiuser authorization flow, 49
multiuser isolation, 52
MXNet, 26
MySQL, 35, 45

N

namespace parameter, 90
namespaces, referencing in Kubeflow, 50
Nearline Storage, 111
NetApp A800, 102
network access, authorizing to deployment, 189

next-generation infrastructure (NGI), 6-7
notebook controller, 55
notebook server launcher, 53-56
notebooks
    advantages of, 19
    architecture of, 53-56
    common usage patterns of, 19
    multiple, 62
    programming languages and, 29
    running machine learning jobs on Kubeflow
        using, 44
    running on GPUs, 18-20
    using GPUs with, 60
    validating code using the GPU, 61
    versions of, 55
"Numbers Everyone Should Know" (Dean), 74
Nvidia DGX-1, 80
Nvidia TensorRT Inference Server, 212
Nvidia Titan X, 74
Nvidia Triton Inference Server, 35, 201
Nvidia's NVLink, 77, 80

O

OAuth, 125-131, 173, 240
OAuth Proxy, 68
objects
    Kubernetes, 251
    storage of, block storage versus, 112
observability, as a core feature of Istio, 257
OIDC connectors, 69, 245
on-premise, 38, 80, 89-107
on-premise Artifactory installs, 95
on-premise clusters, 246
on-premise deployment, 5
on-premise multitenant environment, 21
ONNX, 201
OpenID Connect (OIDC), 45, 240, 241
OpenID provider, 237
operation teams, 70
operations
    common command-line, 104, 131
    Google storage upload, 112
    Istio, 45-47, 255-268
    Kubernetes, from command line, 89-96
    machine learning, 191
    serverless container, 83
    transactional, 74
operators, custom, 252
origin authentication, 264

outlier detection, 211
overmarketed, 3, 87

P

P100, 82
P4, 82
parameters, 32
password-only authentication, 126
passwords, 245
Patterson, Josh
    Deep Learning, 2
pencil icon, 129
persistent volume claims (PVCs), 101, 102, 214
PersistentVolumes (PV), 35, 45, 102
Pilot component, 259
pip, installing AWS CLI using, 147
pipeline, 21-23
Pipeline Service, 56
Pipelines Persistence Agent, 57
placement, of infrastructure, 82
planning
    for GPUs, 75
    infrastructure, 79-83
plan_gpu, 79
platforms, 37
plug-ins, custom, 51
pod, 8, 249
policies, Istio, 263, 267
portability, of cloud vendors, 7
POST method, 196
pre-built model servers, 212-216
Predict API method, 205
predictions, scaling, 210
predictor API, 208, 222
premium SSD, 170
preprocess, 210
profiles, Kubeflow, 50
profiling users, 70
programming languages, notebooks and, 29
PROJECT environment variable, 136
project ID, 128
Prometheus, 28, 42
public clouds, 37
public key encryption, 233
public key infrastructure (PKI), 233
Python
    about, 29
    container repositories and, 96
    TensorFlow model, 220

updating, 121, 147
PyTorch, 17, 26, 201, 212, 221
PyTorch Serving, 28, 214

Q

quota, resource, 125

R

R, 29
R-CNN, 74
receiver operating characteristics (ROC) curve,
    35, 45
redirect URI, 129
Regional Storage, 111
regions
    in Amazon Web Services (AWS), 143
    in Google Cloud Platform (GCP), 110
replication factor, 85
resource groups, 174, 179
resource mode, Kubernetes, 252
resource quota, 51, 125
resource type, 248
resources
    Azure Cloud Platform, 174
    custom, 252
REST APIs, 195
revision tracking, 231
role-based access control (RBAC), 42
    about, 28, 244
    authorization and, 234
    Istio and, 265-268
rolling back deployed models, 230
run, 62
running
    Kubeflow on Amazon Web Services,
        143-165
    Kubeflow on Azure, 167-189
    Kubeflow on Google Cloud, 109-142

S

SAML identity provider, 70, 237
scalability, of cloud vendors, 7
scaling
    about, 86
    model inference throughput, 197-199
    multiple GPUs and, 76
    predictions, 210
Scheduler (AWS CloudWatch), 163

scikit-learn, 201
Sculley, D.
    "Hidden Technical Debt in Machine Learn-
        ing", 14
secret-key cryptography, 100
security
    Amazon Cloud, 145
    as a core feature of Istio, 257
    Azure Cloud Platform, 172-174
    Istio architecture, 262-264
    KFServing, 216
security planning
    about, 65
    background of, 67
    components extending Kubernetes API, 66
    components running on Kubernetes, 66
    integration of, 69
    Kubeflow and deployed applications, 68
    motivation for, 67
Seldon Core, 209, 211
Seldon Core Serving, 35
serverless container operations, with Knative,
    83
service accounts
    Azure Cloud Platform, 174
    in Google Cloud Platform (GCP), 119
    Kubernetes and, 244
service mesh
    API Gateways versus, 260
    with Istio, 255-268
ServiceRole, 266
ServiceRoleBinding, 266, 268
serving, as a core component of Knative, 84
set-cluster command, 92
set-context command, 92
set-credentials command, 92
SETI@Home model, 77
shared multitenant environment, for machine
    learning, 21
sidecar, 55, 259-261
signing up
    for Amazon Web Service (AWS), 146
    for Google Cloud Platform (GCP), 120
Simple and Protected GSS_API Negotiation
    Mechanism (SPNEGO), 241
single sign-on (SSO), 45, 173, 241, 243
single-cluster, 11
single-process job, 27
single-worker job, 27

skillsets, varying, 72
Sklearn, 212-216, 221
Spark, 3, 5
Spartakus, 28
spec, 250
standard HDD/SSD, 170
StatefulSets, 55, 249, 252
status, 250
storage
    about, 85
    Amazon Web Service (AWS), 144
    Azure Cloud Platform, 169-172
    in Google Cloud Platform (GCP), 111
    integration of, 100-102
    object versus block, 112
subcomponents, 37, 53
SubjectAccessReview API, 50

T

T4, 82
team alignment, 21
tensor processing units (TPUs), 8
TensorFlow
    about, 12, 81, 201, 208
    relationship with Kubeflow, 15
    using, 26
    using Docker to build containers, 96
TensorFlow Batch Prediction, 36
TensorFlow Serving, 35
TensorRT, 212, 221
tf-operator, 26, 30, 66
TFJob, 27, 30, 66
third-party services access, 239
tokens, 245
tracing, 257
traffic management
    as a core feature of Istio, 257
    for models with canarying, 226-228
    in Istio, 260-262
transactional workloads, 74
transfer learning, 21-23
transformers, 209, 228-230
transient data patterns, 75
transport authentication, 264
transport layer security (TLS), 161, 236

U

Ubuntu, installing Azure CLI, 177
UI post-installation, accessing Kubeflow, 141

Ultra SSD, 170
unified management, as a primary benefit of
    Kubernetes, 11
updating Python, 121, 147
usage patterns, of notebooks, 19
use case, 18-24, 76, 79, 143, 169-172, 196, 208,
    233, 262
user credentials, 132
user parameter, 90
usernames, 245
users
    about, 70
    Active Directory integration and managing,
        99
    profiling, 70
    varying skillsets, 72

V

V100, 82
versions
    Istio, 257
    Kubeflow, 257
virtual machines (VMs), 175
virtual services, in Istio, 261

W

wall clock, 199
Web APIs, 207
web-user interfaces, 118, 120
webhook, 236, 245
Windows, installing Azure CLI, 177
workloads, 73
workspace, 62

X

X.509 certificates, 69, 236
XGBoost, 201

Y

YAML, 27, 56, 81, 94, 104, 137, 155, 159, 184,
    205, 212-216, 220-223, 226, 251, 265, 267
YARN, 5

Z

zero trust, 238
ZONE environment variable, 135
zone identifier, 135

About the Authors

Josh Patterson is CEO of Patterson Consulting, a solution integrator at the intersection of big data and applied machine learning. In this role, he brings his unique perspective blending a decade of big data experience and wide-ranging deep learning experience to Fortune 500 projects. At the Tennessee Valley Authority (TVA), Josh drove the integration of Apache Hadoop for large-scale data storage and processing of smart grid phasor measurement unit (PMU) data. Post-TVA, Josh was a principal solutions architect for a young Hadoop startup named Cloudera (CLDR), as employee 34. After leaving Cloudera, Josh cofounded the Deeplearning4j project and coauthored *Deep Learning: A Practitioner's Approach* (O'Reilly).

Michael Katzenellenbogen is an independent consultant with a deep and wide technological background and experience. He had the good fortune of getting involved with technology at a young age, and has been witness to the birth of the internet and its various transformations and stages. Having grown up with and alongside the internet has allowed him to become adept in cutting-edge technologies. Michael has a deep background in data management, software architecture, and leveraging new and emerging technologies in creative and novel ways. His roles included managing data for the *New York Times*, leveraging big data platforms, such as Hadoop, early on, as well as in the role of principal solutions architect at Cloudera, helping F100 enterprises architect and implement very large data and compute clusters. Michael's current focus is in helping enterprises lower the barrier to entry for machine learning, leveraging technologies such as Kubernetes and Kubeflow.

Austin Harris is a distributed systems engineer based in Chattanooga, Tennessee. Austin is a specialist in Apache Kafka and distributed systems architecture. He has applied his knowledge via consulting with companies to architect data pipelines in order to handle and analyze big data in real-time. He has worked in fields including smart city infrastructure, wearable technologies, and signal processing. Austin received a master's degree in computer science from the University of Tennessee at Chattanooga. While attending the University of Tennessee Austin published research on machine learning activity recognition techniques, HIPAA-compliant architectures, and real-time dynamic routing algorithms.

Colophon

The animal on the cover of *Kubeflow Operations Guide* is the common greenshank (*Tringa nebularia*). This tall wading bird breeds across northern Europe and Asia, then migrates south to winter in southern Africa and Asia as well as Australia.

The common greenshank averages about 12 inches long, and has long greenish legs, a brownish-grey back and tail, and white undersides. They feed on small prey such as frogs and fish, as well as invertebrates.

They nest in freshwater marshes and wet meadows, laying four eggs which are cryptically colored to hide them from predators. The parent birds generally share incubation duties.

The common greenshank is listed on the IUCN list as being of Least Concern. Because this bird is very visible and has been fairly ubiquitous across its range, population studies only began to be undertaken in the late twentieth century. Many of the animals on O'Reilly covers are endangered; all of them are important to the world.

The color illustration on the cover is by Karen Montgomery, based on a black-and-white engraving from *British Birds*. The cover fonts are Gilroy Semibold and Guardian Sans. The text font is Adobe Minion Pro; the heading font is Adobe Myriad Condensed; and the code font is Dalton Maag's Ubuntu Mono.

O'REILLY®

There's much more where this came from.

Experience books, videos, live online training courses, and more from O'Reilly and our 200+ partners—all in one place.

Learn more at oreilly.com/online-learning